Bridging the Gap

Innovation Brokerage in China

ASIA-PACIFIC BUSINESS SERIES

(ISSN: 1793-3137)

Series Editor
Léo-Paul Dana
Professor
ICD Business School, Paris, France & Dalhousie University, Canada

---

Published

Vol. 16 *Bridging the Gap: Innovation Brokerage in China*
edited by Antonio Crupi, Dominique Lepore & Francesca Spigarelli

Vol. 15 *Emerging and Evolving Business and Management Issues in Vietnam: Research and Practice*
edited by Hoai Trong Nguyen, Thanh Dinh Su, Toan Luu Duc Huynh & Angelina Nhat-Hanh Le

Vol. 14 *Women Entrepreneurs in the Middle East: Context, Ecosystems, and Future Perspectives for the Region*
edited by Dina Modestus Nziku, Léo-Paul Dana, Helene Balslev Clausen & Aidin Salamzadeh

Vol. 13 *Indian SMEs and Start-Ups: Growth through Innovation and Leadership*
edited by Léo-Paul Dana, Omvir Gautam, Ashish Gupta & Naman Sharma

Vol. 12 *Cooperatives as a Catalyst for Sustainability: Lessons Learned from Asian Models*
edited by Léo-Paul Dana, Naman Sharma, Sneha Kumari, K K Tripathy, B P Pillai & R Jayalakshmi

Vol. 11 *Organising Entrepreneurship and MSMEs Across India*
edited by Léo-Paul Dana, Naman Sharma & Satya Ranjan Acharya

Vol. 10 *Guanxi and Business (Third Edition)*
by Yadong Luo

Vol. 9 *Asian Models of Entrepreneurship: From the Indian Union and Nepal to the Japanese Archipelago: Context, Policy and Practice (Second Edition)*
by Léo-Paul Dana

Vol. 8 *Catalyst for Change: Chinese Business in Asia*
edited by Thomas Menkhoff, Hans-Dieter Evers, Chay Yue Wah & Hoon Chang Yau

Vol. 7 *From Adam Smith to Michael Porter: Evolution of Competitiveness Theory (Extended Edition)*
by Dong-Sung Cho & Hwy-Chang Moon

The complete list of the published volumes in the series can also be found at
http://www.worldscientific.com/series/apbs

Asia-Pacific Business Series – Vol. 16

Bridging the Gap

Innovation Brokerage in China

Edited by
Antonio Crupi
University of Messina, Italy
Dominique Lepore
Universitas Mercatorum, Italy
Francesca Spigarelli
University of Macerata, Italy

World Scientific
NEW JERSEY • LONDON • SINGAPORE • BEIJING • SHANGHAI • TAIPEI • CHENNAI

Published by

World Scientific Publishing Co. Pte. Ltd.
5 Toh Tuck Link, Singapore 596224
USA office: 27 Warren Street, Suite 401-402, Hackensack, NJ 07601
UK office: 57 Shelton Street, Covent Garden, London WC2H 9HE

Library of Congress Control Number: 2025006453

British Library Cataloguing-in-Publication Data
A catalogue record for this book is available from the British Library.

Asia-Pacific Business Series — Vol. 16
BRIDGING THE GAP
Innovation Brokerage in China

ISBN 978-981-98-0760-4 (hardcover)
ISBN 978-981-98-0761-1 (ebook for institutions)
ISBN 978-981-98-0762-8 (ebook for individuals)

For any available supplementary material, please visit
https://www.worldscientific.com/worldscibooks/10.1142/14168#t=suppl

Desk Editors: Murali Appadurai/Venkatesh Sandhya

Typeset by Stallion Press
Email: enquiries@stallionpress.com

https://doi.org/10.1142/9789819807611_fmatter

About the Editors

Antonio Crupi is an Associate Professor at the University of Messina, Italy. He is also a Research Affiliate with the Institute of Management of Sant'Anna School of Advanced Studies, Italy, and with the Strategic and Technology Innovation Management (STIM) at the Institute of Manufacturing of the University of Cambridge, UK. His research concerns open innovation, digital transformation, and intellectual property. His current research focuses on intellectual property rights systems, strategic use of intellectual property, entrepreneurial dynamics, and university–industry interactions. His works have been published in high-quality peer-reviewed journals and presented at international conferences.

Dominique Lepore is a tenure-track Assistant Professor in applied economics at Universitas Mercatorum, Italy. She received her industrial PhD with a thesis on the collaborative approaches of Industry 4.0. Her research fields are related to innovation ecosystems, digital transformation of SMEs, and innovation intermediaries. She is a member of the National Centre for Applied Economics Studies (c.MET05) and of the Italian Society of Economics and Industrial Policies (SIEPI). She has been a visiting researcher in Poland, Spain, and Israel and presented her work both at national and international conferences. She has also been involved in interdisciplinary research projects focused on innovation and funded by the Horizon 2020 and Horizon Europe framework.

Francesca Spigarelli is a Full Professor of Applied Economics at the Department of Law at the University of Macerata. She is a member of the Steering Board of c.MET05, the National University Centre for Applied Economic Studies in Italy and she is a Member of the Executive Board of the Chinese Globalization Association cancell what in red and add She has been directing the China Center at University of Macerata since 2013. She also serves as an Italian representative for the Shadow Strategic Programme Committee of the European Commission — sub group Widening Participation and Strengthening the European Research Area, Horizon Europe. Her main research fields are multinational enterprises from emerging countries, the Chinese economy and growth, as well as internationalization strategies of enterprises.

https://doi.org/10.1142/9789819807611_fmatter

About the Contributors

Marco Begani has been the Regional Manager (China) for the International Affairs Dept. of PoliTO since 2016. Within the International Affairs Dept., he currently serves as a Manager of the Center in coordination with the academic and administrative staff involved in the activities with China, mainly working on project planning, budgeting, and implementation; strategy design; daily relations and communication with partners; setting up cooperation frameworks and negotiating/preparing agreements and contracts; organising and participating in PoliTO promotional initiatives in China.

Marco Bonaglia is a PhD candidate at the School of Business Administration and Economics of Chongqing University, with a research topic on tourism management. Previously, he worked in Milan for non-profit organizations dealing with Chinese investments in Italy and Sino–Italian relations. His latest publication is the scientific paper titled "Digital transformation and digital dynamic capabilities improvement in low-medium technology sector: evidence from Thai family firms" for the journal "Asian Business & Management". He regularly publishes articles on China economic development, China innovation, and China tourism on the Galileo Galilei Italian Institute website.

Michele Bonino, an architect, is a Full Professor of Architecture and Urban Design at the Politecnico di Torino, where he is Head of Department of Architecture and Design and the Rector's Delegate for Relations with China and Asian Countries. He was a Visiting Professor at Tsinghua University in

Beijing and a Visiting Scholar at the Massachusetts Institute of Technology (MIT) in Boston. Along with Sun Yimin, he was the Academic Curator of the Shenzhen 2019 Architecture/Urbanism Biennale. For the Politecnico, he coordinated the architectural design of the Visitor Center for the XXIV Winter Olympic Games (Beijing 2022, Shougang site) and curated the "China Goes Urban" exhibition at the Oriental Art Museum of Turin (with F. Governa and S. Pellecchia, 2020–2021). He participated in the Venice Biennale of 2004, 2010 (Italy Pavilion) and 2021 (China Pavilion).

Baolian Chen is a PhD candidate at the School of Economics and Management, Beijing Jiaotong University, where her research focuses on platform strategy and innovation management. Her articles have been published in *Humanities and Social Sciences Communications*.

Tiago Branco Coelho is currently the Market Research and Business Development Manager at Takenaka Corporation, one of Japan's largest and most prestigious design and construction firms. Based in Singapore, he belongs to Takenaka's Asia Regional Headquarters from where he covers Southeast Asia and India. In the exercise of his professional role, he is responsible for conducting market research to identify new areas of growth and future construction projects and expand Takenaka's network of business and institutional contacts, and for the company's commercial strategy for the data center market and non-Japanese capital projects. Before joining Takenaka Corporation, he conducted on-the-ground market research on macroeconomic and public policy developments in different countries, including Angola, Argentina, and Myanmar. Alongside experiences in the private sector, Tiago has also worked in the public sector as a member of the political and economic section of the Embassy of Portugal in Madrid, Spain. Tiago holds two MA degrees: one in International Political Economy from the S. Rajaratnam School of International Studies (RSIS), Nanyang Technological University of Singapore, and another in International Politics from the School of Oriental and African Studies (SOAS), University of London. He has published op-ed articles on international affairs in the Portuguese newspaper *Observador*.

Jacopo Cricchio is a Postdoctoral Researcher in Innovation Management at the Sant'Anna School of Advanced Studies in Pisa. His PhD focused on the evolution of the Chinese Artificial Intelligence innovation ecosystem, with a particular emphasis on the role of open innovation, knowledge brokers, and regional differences. During his previous studies, he visited

Copenhagen Business School, Zhejiang University, and the University of International Business and Economics in Beijing. His research interests include open innovation, innovation policy, STI policy for biodiversity, innovation ecosystems, and intellectual property management.

Lei Cui is a DBA candidate at Emlyon Business School. He is the CEO and Board Member of Shende Green Medical Era, the first MRgPHIFU technology innovation platform in China. Cui, as a professional manager of technology incubators, has rich operational management experience in private, listing, and multinational corporations in different industries, such as coal, energy, transportation, and medical.

Anna Facchinetti is the China Research and Project Coordinator at the University of Bergamo, where she develops and manages research and innovation partnerships with leading Chinese research institutions. She is the former Country Coordinator of EURAXESS China, a role under the European Commission's Directorate-General for Research and Innovation. In this capacity, she coordinated the network of European and Chinese researchers, conducted analysis and monitoring of Sino-European science and technology affairs, managed public relations, and organized events. Previously, she served as the Executive Director, and earlier as a Program Manager, of the Galileo Galilei Italian Institute in Chongqing from 2015 to 2020, overseeing academic and intersectoral collaborations between China and Italy in different fields.

Antonio Frisoli is a Full Professor of Engineering Mechanics and Robotics at Scuola Superiore Sant'Anna, where he leads the Human-Robot Interaction (HRI) area (http://humanrobotinteraction.santannapisa.it/) at PERCRO laboratory. He is currently responsible for the Scuola Sant'Anna macronode of the Artes 4.0 competence center on collaborative robotics. He is an IEEE Senior Member and Associate Editor for IEEE Robotics Automation Magazine and covers several scientific and editorial roles in scientific societies (Eurohaptics, ICORR), international conferences, and journals. His research interests are in the areas of collaborative robotics, rehabilitation robotics, wearable robotics and exoskeletons, multimodal interaction and haptics, wearable devices, and virtual reality. He is very active in technology transfer and open innovation and has been the co-founder of two spin-offs: Wearable Robotics Srl, a leading company in the area of exoskeletons, and Next Generation Robotics Srl, which is commercializing UV disinfection and collaborative robots.

Lorenzo Gonzo, is distinguished fellow at Fondazione Bruno Kessler – FBK (Trento) and Chief Advisor for International Cooperation at the International Technology Transfer Network – ITTN (HongKong). From 2012 to 2022 he has been serving for the Italian Ministry of Foreign Affairs and International Cooperation first, as Expert on science and technology and, successively, as science Attachè at the Consulate General of Italy in Chongqing (China). From 1988 to 2011, he has been working as scientist in the field of microelectronics at FBK. Mr. Gonzo, holds a degree and a PhD in Physics from University of Trento and the Technical University of Munich (DE), respectively.

Maria Gottardo teaches Chinese language at the University of Bergamo. She is the author of essays on the modern Chinese language, on translation and, in the literary field, she has dealt in particular with the writer Zhang Ailing and her non-fiction production. Along with Monica Morzenti, she has translated from Chinese about 20 narrative works by modern and contemporary authors, including Lao She, Zhang Ailing, Zhang Jie, Zhu Wen, Su Tong, and Bi Feiyu.

James Hoadley is the Associate Director of the Georgia Tech Center for International Business Education and Research and a regular lecturer on International Business. Prior to joining the Georgia Tech CIBER, he lived and worked in Asia and is a published author on numerous Asian business and economic topics.

Xinhua Jiang is a PhD candidate in the Institutes of Science and Development, Chinese Academy of Sciences, and University of Chinese Academy of Sciences. Her research interests include innovation management and technology transfer.

Giuseppe Lanfranchi, a 31-year-old business economics graduate with a specialization in marketing and management, has a rich tapestry of professional experiences that have shaped his journey. Over the years, Giuseppe has delved deep into various roles, from steering digital marketing campaigns in the sports sector to pioneering innovative business development strategies. His passion for continuous learning and growth led him to the University of Messina, where he is currently pursuing a doctorate. Here, Giuseppe is channeling his focus on research, innovation management, digital technologies, and sustainability, aiming to bridge the gap between academic insights and real-world applications. With a keen eye on the future, Giuseppe is committed to driving change and fostering sustainable practices in the business landscape.

John R. McIntyre, PhD, is a Professor of strategy and innovation at the Scheller College of Business and also a Professor of international relations at the Sam Nunn School of International Affairs, Georgia Institute of Technology, Atlanta, Georgia, USA. He is the founding Director of the Georgia Tech Center for International Business Education and Research, a national center of excellence, created in 1993. He is author of eighteen books and 170 articles and chapters. He is also a recipient of the National Order of Merit of France (Knight).

Alberto Di Minin is a Full Professor of Management at Sant'Anna School of Advanced Studies of Pisa and a Research Fellow with the Berkeley Round Table on the International Economy (BRIE), University of California, Berkeley. He teaches innovation management and innovation policy and serves as the Italian Delegate with the OECD — Working Party on Innovation and Technology Policy. Additionally, he holds the position of Co-Editor-in-Chief of the *R&D Management* journal and is a member of the International Advisory Board of the California Management Review. His research focuses on open innovation, the appropriation of innovation, and science and technology policy. He also works on technology transfer, intellectual property, and R&D management. As a freelancer with *Il Sole 24 Ore*, Italy's leading financial daily newspaper, he analyzes and writes about the Italian and European innovation ecosystem.

Federico Pasini brings nearly 20 years of experience in strengthening international cooperation with expertise in sustainable development, environmental protection, and energy efficiency. He worked for more than a decade in China, first as a technology and policy cooperation supervisor at an EU–China Centre on clean energies based at Tsinghua University and second as the Head of the Program Management Office at the Sino-Italian Cooperation Program for Environmental Protection. After working as a consultant for the International Renewable Energy Agency (IRENA) in 2021 and 2022, since 2023, he is the Chief Operating Officer at Italy China Council Foundation. Federico holds a PhD in International Law and published two books and several articles in both EU and Chinese journals.

Yanming Ren is a climate change and sustainability expert with 18 years of experience in international cooperation. She served as project manager and policy consultant for several bilateral and multilateral cooperation programs focused on tackling the climate crisis, led by the Chinese Ministry of Ecology and Environment, the British Embassy in China, and the Task Force of the Italian Environment Ministry in Beijing. Through such a professional path, Yanming developed an in-depth knowledge of how the international and European policies have influenced the elaboration of Chinese agenda on climate change and sustainable development.

Guofeng Shen is a Professor and PhD supervisor at Shanghai Jiaotong University, Visiting Associate Professor at Harvard Medical School, and Chairman of Shende Green Medical Era. He received his post-PhD from the School of Biomedical Engineering at Shanghai Jiaotong University. Shen is a member of the Procedural Committee of the International Society of Therapeutic Ultrasound (ISTU) and the Chairman of the 13th ISTU Conference. He is a leading researcher on the Magnetic Resonance–Guided High-Intensity Focused Ultrasound (MRgHIFU) in China. He has published over 100 academic papers. He has been awarded 13 invention patents and 3 software copyrights.

Nan Wang is a Professor at the Business School of Beijing Technology and Business University. Her research focuses on innovation management, knowledge management, and internet user behavior. She has published in *Technological Forecasting and Social Change*, *Journal of Business Research*, *Technology in Society*, and so on.

Liya Wang is a PhD candidate at the School of Economics and Management, Beijing Jiaotong University, where her research focuses on enterprise digital transformation. Her articles have been published in *Technological Forecasting and Social Change.*

Chuanjuan Wu has been a Senior Manager of global supply chain at several multinational corporations for more than twenty years. Wu received her Doctor of Business Administration from Emlyon Business School.

Ya-Feng Zhang is an Assistant Professor at the Faculty of Business, City University of Macau. He studied at the Institutes of Science and

Development, Chinese Academy of Sciences and received his PhD in management from the University of Chinese Academy of Sciences (UCAS). He has been a visiting PhD at Scuola Superiore Sant'Anna (Pisa, Italy). He used to work at UCAS as a researcher. His main research areas include the following: management of intellectual property and innovation, and commercialization of technology and patents. His research has been funded by the National Natural Science Foundation of China (NSFC) and several other organizations. His articles have been published in journals including *R&D Management*, *Economics of Innovation and New Technology*, *International Review of Law and Economics*, and *Asian Journal of Technology Innovation*.

https://doi.org/10.1142/9789819807611_fmatter

Contents

About the Editors v

About the Contributors vii

Introduction xvii

Chapter 1 Collaborative Efforts for Boosting Innovation: The Complex Role of Innovation Intermediaries in China 1
Antonio Crupi, Dominique Lepore, and Francesca Spigarelli

Chapter 2 Role and Significance of Public Innovation Intermediaries in China: The Case Study of China Society of Technical Economics (CSTE) 13
Yanming Ren and Federico Pasini

Chapter 3 The Role of the Chinese Government as an Innovation Broker in the Chinese Commercial Aircraft Industry 31
John R. McIntyre and James R. Hoadley

Chapter 4 The Role of Innovation Intermediaries in Low-Medium-Technology Sectors in China: Evidence from Chinese Construction Industry 55
Giuseppe Lanfranchi, Tiago Branco Coelho, and Antonio Crupi

Chapter 5 Preparing Lab Technologies for the Market: Proof-of-Concept Centers in China 83
Xinhua Jiang and Ya-Feng Zhang

Chapter 6 Navigating Transnational Innovation: Best Practices in Academic Cooperation between Italy and China 107
Marco Begani, Marco Bonaglia, Michele Bonino, Anna Facchinetti, Antonio Frisoli, Lorenzo Gonzo, and Maria Gottardo

Chapter 7 How to Improve Open Innovation in China's SMEs? The Role of Open Innovation Networks and Platforms 135
Nan Wang and Liya Wang

Chapter 8 Building an AI Open Innovation Ecosystem: The Case of Baidu 151
Jacopo Cricchio, Alberto Di Minin, and Dominique Lepore

Chapter 9 Sustainable Supply Chain Management as the Innovation Intermediary: Analysis on Frugal Innovation in Small and Medium-Sized Manufacturing Enterprises in China 163
Nan Wang and Baolian Chen

Chapter 10 The Engagement Ecosystem as an Innovation Broker: A Case from China 191
Chuanjuan Wu, Lei Cui, and Guofeng Shen

Index 209

https://doi.org/10.1142/9789819807611_fmatter

Introduction

This book is a comprehensive exploration of the role and functions played by innovation intermediaries in China's rapidly evolving innovation and technological context.

A series of in-depth case studies and analyses examine how different types of intermediaries — from government agencies to academic institutions and private enterprises — contribute to China's innovation framework.

As China transitions to an innovation-driven economy, such intermediaries act as bridges between various stakeholders, including governments, universities, research centers, firms, and citizens. Within the innovation ecosystem, they are in charge of facilitating knowledge transfer, collaboration, and technological advancement across diverse sectors and countries, from a global perspective.

By investigating specific examples such as the China Society of Technical Economics, Proof of Concept Centers, and tech giants like Baidu, this book explores the nature of innovation brokerage in the Chinese context. It suggests future lines of research as well as relevant policy and managerial implications.

Throughout its chapters, the volume focuses on several key themes crucial to understanding China's innovation dynamics.

The book's first chapter reviews how collaboration can benefit innovation, and focuses on the the rise of open innovation in China. Then, the role of innovation intermediaries in China is presented considering key policies and exemplary cases outlining these structures' complex and multivariate role.

The following chapters discuss the case of public innovation intermediaries, exemplified by the case study of the China Society of Technical Economics (CSTE) (Chapter 2), and the government involvement in innovation, particularly in strategic sectors like the commercial aircraft industry (Chapter 3).

This book also addresses the critical intersection of innovation and sustainability, focusing on China's construction sector (Chapter 4), and investigates the commercialization of research through Proof of Concept Centers (Chapter 5).

International collaboration in innovation is another significant theme, highlighted by a study on academic cooperation between Italy and China (Chapter 6).

Then, the role of open innovation networks and platforms is discussed by reviewing the literature on open innovation in the case of Small and Medium-sized Enterprises (Chapter 7). In particular, the emergence of private enterprises as innovation brokers is examined through Baidu's AI open innovation ecosystem (Chapter 8).

The last two chapters consider, from a broader perspective, supply chain management (Chapter 9) and engagement ecosystems (Chapter 10) as innovation intermediaries. This latter type of ecosystem is introduced as a novel form of innovation brokerage in China.

Each chapter offers complementary valuable insights into how innovation intermediaries deal with China's unique institutional environment, support international cooperation, and drive sustainable innovation practices. They also highlight the complex interplay between government policies, market forces, and technological advancements that shape the Chinese innovation landscape, which is quite unique and relevant from a global perspective.

By bringing together contributions from both Chinese and international scholars, this book provides an understanding of the challenges and opportunities in China's innovation system, exploring how intermediaries adapt to the country's rapidly changing economic and technological context and contribute to its ambition of becoming a global innovation leader.

https://doi.org/10.1142/9789819807611_0001

Chapter 1

Collaborative Efforts for Boosting Innovation: The Complex Role of Innovation Intermediaries in China

Antonio Crupi[*,¶], Dominique Lepore[†,§], and Francesca Spigarelli[‡,||]

[*]*Department of Economics, University of Messina, Italy*

[†]*Department of Economics, Statistics and Business, Universitas Mercatorum, Italy*

[‡]*Department of Law, University of Macerata, Italy*

[§]*dominique.lepore@unimercatorum.it*

[¶]*crupi.antonio@unime.it*

[||]*francesca.spigarelli@unimc.it*

Abstract

In China's rapidly evolving innovation landscape, collaborative efforts among diverse stakeholders drive the development of groundbreaking solutions. This imperative is fostered by recent governmental policies that emphasize the need for cohesive collaboration among government, industries, and academia.

However, effective knowledge and resource exchange among these stakeholders poses significant challenges due to the differing objectives and interests.

To navigate these complexities, China must adapt its institutional environment to foster collaborative relationships among key innovation actors. In addressing these challenges, innovation intermediaries emerge as facilitators, bridging gaps between diverse actors and facilitating knowledge exchange and integration. The landscape of innovation intermediaries in China is diverse, ranging from government-initiated entities to private-sector agents, each with varying degrees of effectiveness and alignment with broader innovation goals.

Keywords: Collaboration, China, innovation intermediaries, triple helix, open innovation.

1. Introduction

In China, the innovation ecosystem is evolving rapidly. According to the Global Innovation Index (GII) of 2023, China is an innovation leader ranked at the 12th position among the 132 economies studied. This position is a remarkable improvement considering the country's 29th position back in 2015. Moreover, the GII shows that the country is positioned as the 1st among the upper-middle-income group economies. In terms of gross domestic expenditure on R&D, China is the second absolute spender after the United States. Moreover, China's R&D as percentage of Gross Domestic Product (GDP) has risen from 1.71% in 2010 to 2.45% in 2021. The business sector accounts for the largest expenditure on R&D increasing from 60% to 76.6% in 2020. The government is instead the second-largest R&D performer accounting for 15,7% of GERD in 2020. Additionally, China recorded 2.28 million researchers in 2020, which is the largest number in the world (OECD, 2023).

To continue boosting innovation, collaboration among different actors, including government, industries, and academia is imperative. In these regards, the Chinese government has issued a set of policies where relations among key stakeholders are becoming relevant, including the Chinese 14th Five-Year Plan (2021–2025) and the Long-Range Objectives to 2035 (Yao *et al.*, 2021).

However, when considering collaborative approaches to innovation, ensuring an effective exchange of knowledge and resources among different stakeholders can be challenging due to different objectives and interests (Lepore, 2023). Furthermore, China has to adjust some elements of its institutional environment to facilitate the relations between key innovation actors and develop its own collaborative models (Cai, 2014).

Thereby, innovation intermediaries are necessary to foster and adjust collaborative approaches to innovation (Howells, 2006).

This chapter aims to introduce why innovation intermediaries are needed for boosting innovation as well as their multivariate nature within the Chinese innovation ecosystem.

After reviewing how collaboration can benefit innovation, a focus is dedicated to the rise of open innovation in China. Then, the role of innovation intermediaries in China is presented. Lastly, some conclusive remarks are outlined.

2. Collaborative Efforts for Boosting Innovation

Collaboration among many different stakeholders is necessary for supporting the development of innovative products and processes. Indeed, innovative solutions are often driven by exchanges of knowledge, skills, and resources among government, industry, and academia in the form of a Triple Helix model (Etzkowitz, 2008). The Triple Helix indicates not only the relationship between university, industry, and government but also the internal transformation within each of these spheres. In particular, the university has been transformed from a teaching institution into one which combines teaching with research and plays an active role in technology and knowledge transfer. The Triple Helix model has also evolved into a Quadruple Helix model. This model adds as the fourth helix the "public", more precisely defined as the "media-based and culture-based public" (Etzkowitz and Leydesdorff, 2000).

In the era of Industry 4.0, collaboration between academia, government, firms, and users is crucial. Industry 4.0 based on technologies such as the Internet of Things (IoT), Artificial Intelligence (AI), and blockchain, connects products, machines, and people with the environment and combines production, information technology, and the internet (Kagermann *et al.*, 2013). In this complex scenario, the exchange of knowledge and resources can support firms adopt and develop innovative solutions. This is especially true for Small and Medium-Sized Enterprises (SMEs) facing financial and organizational constraints that obstacle their innovative performance (Lepore *et al.*, 2023).

Collaboration among stakeholders becomes even more crucial as we transition from Industry 4.0 to Industry 5.0. This paradigm places more emphasis on human progress and well-being, overcoming the lack of attention of Industry 4.0 for the climate crisis, planetary emergency, and social tensions (Breque *et al.*, 2021).

Concerning collaborative efforts for boosting innovation, the Chinese government has issued a set of relevant policies and regulations. These policies were introduced to facilitate the development of national scientific and technological innovation. Among these, the Chinese 14th Five-Year Plan (2021–2025) and the Long-Range Objectives to 2035 signal that China will optimize the resource allocation and knowledge sharing from scientific research institutes, universities, and enterprises, to enhance the efficiency of the innovation chain (Yao *et al.*, 2021).

Focusing on academic collaborations in China, Zhou and Wang (2023) suggest that the government and universities should jointly launch R&D institutions to advance business incubation and regional industrial and economic development. The authors specify that within this type of partnership, universities, and scientific research institutions should be the source of technology and entrepreneurs while the government should act as financial support and technology buyer. Similarly, when focusing on academic collaborations, Kafouros *et al.* (2015) argue that institutions in China greatly impact their effectiveness.

In a more general perspective, Jensen and Schøtt (2014) note that even if networking and innovation are as extensive in China as abroad, and networking has a positive effect on innovation, the benefits in China are less than in the rest of the world. The authors suggest that this lesser efficiency is due to the guanxi tradition, referring to relationships that are long-term and supportive but that probably do not promote innovation.

The Triple Helix model has been used to investigate the relationships between the three helices in China. Li *et al.* (2020) by using this analytical framework found that interactions within the three helices have a positive impact on regional entrepreneurship by impacting the local entrepreneurial environment and advancing entrepreneurship activities. Furthermore, their study recognizes the significance of networking connections in facilitating the exchange of high-quality information, enhancing trust among collaborators, and fostering sustained collaboration and shared growth among academic institutions, the business sector, and government bodies. However, Cai (2014), acknowledging that the Triple Helix concept has been developed in advanced economies, suggests that China has to develop its own collaborative model. In particular, to optimise its innovation policies, China needs to adjust some elements of its institutional environment to facilitate the relations between key innovation actors (Cai, 2014).

The rise of open innovation in China further illustrates the shift toward more inclusive and externally engaged innovation practices, as the following paragraph addresses.

2.1 *The rise of open innovation*

The Open innovation paradigm is defined as "the use of purposive inflows and outflows of knowledge to accelerate internal innovation and expand the markets for external use of innovation" (Chesbrough, 2006, p. 1). This paradigm suggests that ideas can come from inside and outside the company and can go to market from inside or outside the company. Three core processes can be differentiated in open innovation. The outside-in process is based on integrating external knowledge sources, the inside-out process focuses on transferring ideas outside, for instance, by licensing intellectual property, and the coupled is grounded on co-creation with partners (Enkel *et al.*, 2009).

China, alongside South Korea, emerged as a leading Asian country in open innovation research. China's prominent position can be attributed to its strong commitment to fostering an innovative economy on a global scale. This commitment is evident in the strategies adopted by Chinese companies to enhance their innovation capabilities, including technology licensing (Le *et al.*, 2019). Indeed, Chinese firms have employed a variety of open innovation models since the reforms of the science and technology system in the mid-1980s. Policies introduced by the Chinese government for acquiring foreign technology, industry-university collaboration, and the "go global" strategy have encouraged Chinese firms to open innovation modes (Fu and Xiong, 2011).

Empirical studies indicate that Chinese companies operating in high-tech sectors widely adopt open innovation strategies to enhance their innovation capabilities. Specifically, these firms leverage technology licensing agreements to acquire new technologies, forge long-term partnerships with foreign counterparts to access cutting-edge innovations, collaborate with domestic universities and research institutes to extend their technological strength, and engage with local industries to further develop their technological expertise (Wang *et al.*, 2012).

Other studies highlight the barriers to the adoption of open innovation by Chinese firms explaining that these might be largely related to the comparatively weak domestic research expertise and limited organisational absorptive capabilities, with this most particularly evident for SMEs. At the same time, it is also confirmed that external knowledge sources from inter-firm networking are more important in creating the benefits of open innovation for Chinese SMEs than their larger peers (Huang *et al.*, 2015).

3. Bridging the Gap: The Nature of Innovation Intermediaries in China

Collaboration itself is not straightforward. The variety of actors, spanning government, academia, industries, and recently also citizens share different objectives and interests. What makes it more complex is that they often speak different languages (Lepore, 2023). Moreover, as previously discussed, China has to facilitate relationships among innovation key actors, developing its own collaborative models (Cai, 2014).

This is why it becomes significant to consider the role of innovation intermediaries. Innovation intermediaries are structures that connect two or more parties in innovation processes (Howells, 2006). These entities by focusing on transferring and integrating external knowledge are also identified as boundary spanners, gatekeepers, and knowledge brokers (Haas, 2015). More specifically, innovation intermediaries can drive the sharing of technology-related knowledge, offer knowledge-based services, and provide policy advice. Through their multiple functions, intermediaries can support firms, especially SMEs, in introducing and developing innovative products or processes (Crupi *et al.*, 2020).

China is aware of the importance of implementing policies for innovation intermediaries. The first policies of this kind refer to the 1980s when the reform of the science and technology (S&T) regime began (Wang and Wang, 2017). Among these policies, the Torch Programme was introduced in 1988 to support the commercialization of Chinese R&D. This Programme includes elements of decentralized institutional and policy experimentation such as an enterprise-dominated financing scheme and incubator activities (Heilmann *et al.*, 2013).

The literature reveals a broad range of innovation intermediaries in China. In these regards, Xiaoyuan and Yanning (2011) distinguish three levels based on their involvement in the R&D activities of an enterprise. The core layer includes structures such as research centers offering advanced engineering and technological services including technology testing and design. The supporting layer is represented by organizations, such as technology consulting firms, providing advisory services for various types of innovation challenges. Lastly, the corresponding layer features organizations like business incubators, science parks, high-tech development zones, and venture capital organizations which provide training, equipment, and financial support for innovation activities.

Dalziel and Yao (2010) analyzed six main types of innovation intermediaries in China, including government research institutes, property-based enablers such as science parks and business incubators, technology transfer offices, economic development organizations, industry associations, and business financing and support programs. The author noticed that most of these innovation intermediaries are initiated, financed, and operated by the government and may be poorly suited to support innovation that crosses industrial or disciplinary boundaries.

Indeed, there are studies such as that of Yao *et al.* (2022) focusing on Chinese industrial associations as institutional intermediaries providing both information and legitimacy. Such institutional linkages can, on the one hand, strengthen firm innovation by facilitating access to necessary government support and, on the other hand, impede it because they create regulatory institutional pressures (Yao *et al.*, 2022). In a more general perspective, the Chinese government itself has been also recognized as a broker in facilitating technology transfer and lowering costs and risks (Wang, 2010). In opposition, some studies focused their attention on private technology service agents in China, especially within industrial clusters. Their role as technology gatekeepers and spanners, technical problem solvers, and innovation resource integrators can drive technological development and business growth (Guo and Guo, 2013).

Going more in-depth some remarkable functions can be found. This is the case of science parks which can connect domestic and international triple helices by linking academia, governments, and firms through partnerships and networking activities (Compagnucci *et al.*, 2021). International connections are also identified as a key function of business incubators. In particular, Gao *et al.* (2021) show that these structures can act as international knowledge intermediaries and facilitate the international growth of startups originating from emerging markets and ultimately create international linkages between the networks of knowledge creation and knowledge application.

University satellite institutes are another type of innovation intermediary analyzed in China. These institutes can help overcome local barriers to university-industry interaction, interregional technology transfer, and innovation. They can do so by brokering relevant knowledge to local industry and by gathering resources to create a critical mass for attracting external resources (Conlé *et al.*, 2023).

When considering innovation intermediaries, scholars have also addressed specific sectors that deserve attention in the Chinese context. Referring to agricultural innovation, Li *et al.* (2022) recognize that little emphasis has been given to the role of innovation intermediaries in supporting the coevolution process of innovation at the community level in rural China. The authors offer a case study of the Science and Technology Backyard (STB) as a novel type of innovation support intervention designed to promote technical change at the community level. The authors note the evolution of this farming service from knowledge brokers to systemic innovation intermediaries has enabled the coevolution process of innovation inside villages. Instead, by focusing on the smart grid industry, OI intermediaries are developing in the web-based technology marketplace as in the cases analyzed by Chen *et al.* (2016). These intermediaries in particular help Chinese firms to address energy development and conservation issues providing great opportunities for collaborations.

Interestingly, individuals, especially as teams, can cover boundary-spanning activities. These individuals possess abilities suited to crossing organization boundaries as in the case of international joint ventures (Jiang *et al.*, 2023). In these regards, Bai *et al.* (2021) show that top-level interpersonal ties have positive effects on both exploratory and exploitative innovation and operating-level interpersonal ties have a greater positive effect on exploitative innovation than on exploratory innovation.

Moreover, Kaiji *et al.* (2022) emphasize the critical role of team boundary-spanners in Chinese companies as innovation triggers. Managers who conduct boundary-spanning activities, including connecting with external resources, negotiating project scopes, and managing external interactions, are focal in enhancing team performance and driving innovation. These activities also improve organizational learning and job performance by facilitating knowledge flows and collaboration, especially in technology transfer contexts.

4. Conclusions

In the rapidly evolving innovation ecosystem of China, collaboration among different innovation actors plays a critical role. Collaborative efforts are central to China's innovation strategy as outlined in recent policies and scholarly contributions. The rise of open innovation in China further illustrates the shift toward more inclusive and externally engaged innovation practices.

The chapter also addresses the challenges of collaborative innovation, including the adjustment of institutional environments and the development of China's own collaborative models. Innovation intermediaries emerge as critical facilitators, bridging gaps between diverse actors and fostering effective knowledge exchange and collaboration.

These intermediaries, ranging from research centers and consulting firms to incubators and science parks, play a multivariate role in supporting China's innovation ecosystem.

There is thus a need to focus on specific cases of innovation intermediaries to understand and compare their nature and role. This investigation is the aim of the following chapters, which explores the dynamics and strategic importance of these entities within China's innovation ecosystem.

References

Bai, X., Wang, Q., Sheng, S., and Li, J. J. (2021). Cross-level interpersonal ties and IJV innovation: Evidence from China. *Journal of Business Research*, 134, 618–630. https://doi.org/10.1016/j.jbusres.2021.05.047.

Breque, M., Nul, L. D., and Petridis, A. (2021). Industry 5.0: Towards a sustainable, human-centric and resilient European industry. *European Commission, Directorate-General for Research and Innovation.* https://doi.org/10.2777/308407.

Cai, Y. (2014). Implementing the Triple Helix model in a non-Western context: An institutional logics perspective. *Triple Helix*, 1(1), 1. https://doi.org/10.1186/s40604-014-0001-2.

Chen, H. H., Chen, S., and Lan, Y. (2016). Attaining a sustainable competitive advantage in the smart grid industry of China using suitable open innovation intermediaries. *Renewable and Sustainable Energy Reviews*, 62, 1083–1091. https://doi.org/10.1016/j.rser.2016.03.008.

Chesbrough, H. W. (2006). Open innovation: A new paradigm for understanding industrial innovation. In *Open Innovation: Researching a New Paradigm*, edited by H. Chesbrough, W. Vanhaverbeke, and J. West. Oxford: *Oxford University Press.*

Compagnucci, L., Lepore, D., and Spigarelli, F. (2021). Exploring the foreign exposure of Chinese science parks in a triple helix model. *Forum for Social Economics*, 50(3), 330–354. https://doi.org/10.1080/07360932.2020.1759440.

Conlé, M., Ten Brink, T., and Zhao, W. (2023). Innovation platforms as a tool for anchoring non-local knowledge: Smart specialisation strategies in Guangdong, China. *Industry and Innovation*, 30(6), 694–718. https://doi.org/10.1080/13662716.2022.2132919.

Crupi, A., Del Sarto, N., Di Minin, A., Gregori, G. L., Lepore, D., Marinelli, L., and Spigarelli, F. (2020). The digital transformation of SMEs — a new knowledge broker called the digital innovation hub. *Journal of Knowledge Management*, 24(6), 1263–1288. https://doi.org/10.1108/JKM-11-2019-0623.

Dalziel, M. and Yao, W. (2010). Innovation intermediaries in China. *SSRN Electronic Journal*, pp. 1–28. https://doi.org/10.2139/ssrn.2630739.

Enkel, E., Gassmann, O., and Chesbrough, H. (2009). Open R&D and open innovation: Exploring the phenomenon. *R&D Management*, 39(4), 311–316. https://doi.org/10.1111/j.1467-9310.2009.00570.x.

Etzkowitz, H. (2008). *The Triple Helix* (ed.). New York: Routledge. https://doi.org/10.4324/9780203929605.

Etzkowitz, H. and Leydesdorff, L. (2000). The dynamics of innovation: From national systems and "Mode 2" to a triple helix of university–industry–government relations. *Research Policy*, 29(2), 109–123. https://doi.org/10.1016/S0048-7333(99)00055-4.

Fu, X. and Xiong, H. (2011). Open innovation in China: Policies and practices. *Journal of Science and Technology Policy in China*, 2(3), 196–218.

Gao, Q., Cui, L., Lew, Y. K., Li, Z., and Khan, Z. (2021). Business incubators as international knowledge intermediaries: Exploring their role in the internationalization of start-ups from an emerging market. *Journal of International Management*, 27(4), 100861. https://doi.org/10.1016/j.intman.2021.100861.

Guo, J. and Guo, B. (2013). How do innovation intermediaries facilitate knowledge spillovers within industrial clusters? A knowledge-processing perspective. *Asian Journal of Technology Innovation*, 21(sup2), 31–49. https://doi.org/10.1080/19761597.2013.819245.

Haas, A. (2015). Crowding at the frontier: Boundary spanners, gatekeepers and knowledge brokers. *Journal of Knowledge Management*, 19(5), 1029–1047. https://doi.org/10.1108/JKM-01-2015-0036.

Heilmann, S., Shih, L., and Hofem, A. (2013). National planning and local technology zones: Experimental governance in China's torch programme. *The China Quarterly*, 216, 896–919. https://doi.org/10.1017/S0305741013001057.

Howells, J. (2006). Intermediation and the role of intermediaries in innovation. *Research Policy*, 35(5), 715–728. https://doi.org/10.1016/j.respol.2006.03.005.

Huang, F., Rice, J., and Martin, N. (2015). Does open innovation apply to China? Exploring the contingent role of external knowledge sources and internal absorptive capacity in Chinese large firms and SMEs. *Journal of Management & Organization*, 21(5), 594–613.

Jensen, K. W. and Schøtt, T. (2014). Firms' innovation embedded in their networks of collaboration: China compared to the world. *Journal of Chinese Economic and Business Studies*, 12(3), 273–292. https://doi.org/10.1080/14765284.2014.931427.

Jiang, F., Liu, L. X., and Li, J. (2023). From horizontal knowledge sharing to vertical knowledge transfer: The role of boundary-spanning commitment in international joint ventures. *Journal of International Business Studies*, 54(1), 182–202. https://doi.org/10.1057/s41267-022-00507-9.

Kafouros, M., Wang, C., Piperopoulos, P., and Zhang, M. (2015). Academic collaborations and firm innovation performance in China: The role of region-specific institutions. *Research Policy*, 44(3), 803–817. https://doi.org/10.1016/j.respol.2014.11.002.

Kagermann, H., Wahlster, W., and Helbig, J. (2013). *Recommendations for implementing the strategic initiative Industrie 4.0: Securing the future of German manufacturing industry*. Final report of the Industrie 4.0 Working Group. Frankfurt: Acatech.

Kaiji, X., Crupi, A., Di Minin, A., and Cesaroni, F. (2022). Team boundary-spanning activities and performance of technology transfer organizations: Evidence from China. *The Journal of Technology Transfer*, 47, 33–62. https://doi.org/10.1007/s10961-021-09843-8.

Le, H. T. T., Dao, Q. T. M., Pham, V. C., Tran, D. T., and Del Giudice, M. (2019). Global trend of open innovation research: A bibliometric analysis. *Cogent Business & Management*, 6(1). https://doi.org/10.1080/23311975.2019.1633808.

Lepore, D. (2023). Intermediaries in innovation systems: Match or mismatch? *Journal of the Knowledge Economy*. https://doi.org/10.1007/s13132-023-01566-5.

Lepore, D., Vecciolini, C., Micozzi, A., and Spigarelli, F. (2023). Developing technological capabilities for Industry 4.0 adoption: An analysis of the role of inbound open innovation in small and medium-sized enterprises. *Creativity and Innovation Management*, 32(2), 249–265. https://doi.org/10.1111/caim.12551.

Li, J., Leeuwis, C., Heerink, N., and Zhang, W. (2022). The science and technology backyard as a local level innovation intermediary in rural China. *Frontiers of Agricultural Science and Engineering*, 9(4), 558. https://doi.org/10.15302/J-FASE-2022465.

Li, M., He, L., and Zhao, Y. (2020). The triple helix system and regional entrepreneurship in China. *Entrepreneurship & Regional Development*, 32(7–8), 508–530. https://doi.org/10.1080/08985626.2019.1666168.

OECD. (2023). *OECD science, technology and innovation outlook 2023: Enabling transitions in times of disruption*. OECD. https://doi.org/10.1787/0b55736e-en.

Wang, B. (2010). Can CDM bring technology transfer to China? — An empirical study of technology transfer in China's CDM projects. *Energy Policy*, 38(5), 2572–2585. https://doi.org/10.1016/j.enpol.2009.12.052.

Wang, C. (Chengwei), and Wang, L. (2017). Unfolding policies for innovation intermediaries in China: A discourse network analysis. *Science and Public Policy*, 44(3), 354–368, scw068. https://doi.org/10.1093/scipol/scw068.

Wang, Y., Roijakkers, N., Vanhaverbeke, W., and Chen, J. (2012). How Chinese firms employ open innovation to strengthen their innovative performance. *International Journal of Technology Management*, 59(3/4), 235. https://doi.org/10.1504/IJTM.2012.047245.

Xiaoyuan, Z. and Yanning, Z. (2011). Development of Chinese science and technology intermediaries and their integration into the open innovation paradigm. *Technology Analysis & Strategic Management*, 23(1), 25–48. https://doi.org/10.1080/09537325.2011.537103.

Yao, N., Guo, Q., and Tsinopoulos, C. (2022). The bright and dark sides of institutional intermediaries: Industry associations and small-firm innovation. *Research Policy*, 51(1), 104370. https://doi.org/10.1016/j.respol.2021.104370.

Yao, X., Hu, Y., Gong, H., and Chen, D. (2021). Characteristics and evolution of China's industry–university–research collaboration to promote the sustainable development: Based on policy text analysis. *Sustainability*, 13(23), 13105. https://doi.org/10.3390/su132313105.

Zhou, J. and Wang, M. (2023). The role of government-industry-academia partnership in business incubation: Evidence from new R&D institutions in China. *Technology in Society*, 72, 102194. https://doi.org/10.1016/j.techsoc.2022.102194.

https://doi.org/10.1142/9789819807611_0002

Chapter 2

Role and Significance of Public Innovation Intermediaries in China: The Case Study of China Society of Technical Economics (CSTE)

Yanming Ren[*,§] **and Federico Pasini**[†,‡]

[*]*COSCO Shipping Lines, Genoa, Italy*

[†]*Italy China Council Foundation, Milan, Italy*

[‡]*federico.pasini@gmail.com*

[§]*renyanming2010@gmail.com*

Abstract

Over the past decade, China's innovation intermediaries have played an increasingly important role in helping companies showcase their technologies, expand their business network, access external resources, and unveil market opportunities. Yet, despite their growing relevance, little in-depth analysis exists on the specific role of publicly supported innovation intermediaries.

This case study examines a unique public innovation intermediary named China Society of Technical Economics (CSTE) — namely, a member organization of the China Association for Science and Technology — whose mission is to study the optimal allocation of resources, explore methods for transforming science into productivity, and promote the integration of technology and economy.

In this respect, CSTE aims to stimulate innovation in China by applying technical and economic methodologies, such as value engineering to enterprise management, and directly participating in the management modernization process of China's enterprises.

Incorporating evidence from implemented activities and services, CSTE-related reports and literature as well as interviews with the organization leaders, this case study discusses the specificities and added value of CSTE. As a result, it is argued that this innovation intermediary plays a crucial role in supporting companies in the different phases toward China's high-quality development.

Keywords: Public innovation intermediaries, China's technological development, China Society of Technical Economics (CSTE), interorganisational networking, cooperation and training, technological competitiveness.

1. Introduction

Innovation intermediaries, whether public or private entities, foster both individual firm-level innovation and broader systemic advancements. They facilitate this through diverse means, including establishing knowledge networks among organizations, disseminating information on specific technologies, and offering knowledge-driven services as well as guidance to policymakers (Caloffi *et al.*, 2022, p. 3).

In this respect, China's innovation intermediaries' scenario is no exception. Also in China, intermediaries play an increasingly important role in helping companies to showcase their technologies, expand their business network, access external resources, and unveil market opportunities. Yet, despite their growing relevance, little in-depth analysis exists on the specific role of publicly supported intermediaries and addressing this research gap is key to better understand their contribution to innovation (Jeon *et al.*, 2018).

This chapter aims to shed light on one of the earliest public innovation intermediaries in China, namely the China Society of Technical Economics (CSTE), to understand what are the key strengths that allowed this organisation to support China's modernisation process and companies over the past four decades. To do so, we first introduce the core challenges that companies encounter to stay competitive in the evolving business landscape. Then, we analyze CSTE's features and patterns, to deepen its role and significance. Hence, this chapter is structured as follows. In Section 2, we review the key characteristics and roles of public innovation intermediaries and display the applied methodology. Section 3 introduces our case study: after providing background information about CSTE together with its overall objective, we describe the organization's key features to help companies face the complexities of China's fast-growing technological environment. In Section 4, we identify and deepen CSTE's three main patterns (and related activities), namely provide knowledge-intensive services, promote interorganizational networking, cooperation, and training, and foster reform and high-quality development. Finally, Section 5 outlines the strengths of the organization: incorporating evidence from CSTE's implemented activities and services, related reports and literature, as well as extensive interviews with its leaders, this case study discusses the specificities of CSTE and ultimately derives its added value.

In sum, it is argued that this public innovation intermediary plays a crucial role in supporting companies in the different phases of China's economic development.

2. Public Innovation Intermediaries and Technological Revolution

Over the last decade, technological advancements such as artificial intelligence (AI), blockchain, and the internet of things have profoundly influenced and transformed production processes and their associated value chains (Caloffi *et al.*, 2022, p. 5). While these technological developments offer significant opportunities for progress — in terms of access to new markets, creation of innovative products and services, and greater efficiency — companies face challenges in leveraging them due to a lack of understanding and skills (Lepore *et al.*, 2020).

Indeed, the successful integration of new technologies into business processes constitutes a profound change that demands, on one hand, specific resources and competencies and, on the other, structural flexibility and a readiness for change. The challenges associated with adapting to this new technological paradigm can be diverse: smaller businesses suffer more from resource constraints, while larger companies face more often flexibility issues. That said, all companies need to demonstrate adaptability and a willingness to embrace the transformative shift. Recognizing and addressing these challenges is crucial for firms seeking to stay competitive in the evolving business landscape (Rossi *et al.*, 2020, p. 2). In this context, innovation intermediaries have become more and more fundamental and, as of today, they play a key role in sharing technology-related knowledge, providing knowledge-based services, linking organizations, and connecting national businesses to the global context (Lepore *et al.*, 2020, p. 497).

Innovation intermediaries are instrumental in facilitating the adoption and smooth integration of new technological and organizational systems and processes. Beyond this, they actively promote collaborations among small and medium-sized enterprises (SMEs) and enable partnerships between SMEs and larger companies. Additionally, they contribute significantly to disclose valuable market opportunities (Rossi *et al.*, 2020, p. 2). Indeed, public innovation intermediaries play diverse roles and engage in a wide array of activities, contingent upon their policy mandates. When operating in non-market environments, they intervene where market mechanisms or innovation systems fall short, or where public interests are paramount. Nonetheless, many public innovation intermediaries actively participate in market-driven transactions as well (Rossi *et al.*, 2020, p. 7).

The primary value proposition of public innovation intermediaries lies in assisting firms in innovating and enhancing their capacities. They achieve this by providing information, access to innovation infrastructures, and other knowledge-intensive services to individual organizations, particularly SMEs, which form their key counterparts and beneficiaries. Organizational activities typically include conducting company visits to grasp the specific needs of client firms, performing knowledge and technology audits, organizing information-sharing events (e.g., workshops on emerging technologies or available public funding schemes), and identifying potential business or innovation partners. To effectively address the cognitive and managerial shortcomings of SMEs and start-ups and enhance their absorptive capacity, public innovation intermediaries must possess deep familiarity with the industrial, technological, and local contexts in which these entities operate (Rossi *et al.*, 2020, p. 10).

Moreover, public innovation intermediaries facilitate the transfer of knowledge and technology between research organizations and businesses, primarily targeting these segments. Offering support in patenting and licensing constitutes a pivotal aspect of their services. They facilitate the alignment between research and industry by assessing the competencies and knowledge of both sectors and creating opportunities for collaboration, such as through publicly funded applied research initiatives or personnel exchanges. Given that public funding of such intermediaries aims to mitigate industry interaction deficiencies, public intermediaries

Table 1. Interviews conducted in 2023 and 2024.

Month and Year of Interview	Position	Relationship to CSTE	Location of the Interview
September 2023	Director	CSTE Employee	Beijing
September 2023	Deputy Director	CSTE Employee	Beijing
November 2023	Expert	Expert of CSTE	From remote
January 2024	Expert	Expert of CSTE	From remote

must be proficient in communicating effectively with both basic and applied research spheres. Therefore, they typically possess a blend of research and industrial development expertise, often tailored to their specific sectors of focus, along with a deep understanding of the local context. Also, specialized skills in negotiation, contract development, and intellectual property management are essential for managing research projects involving diverse stakeholders from both public and private realms (Rossi *et al.*, 2020, p. 10).

Reviewing the existing literature in combination with analyzing the features of arguably the first innovation intermediary in China, namely the China Society of Technical Economics (CSTE), allows us to investigate the possible links between the key patterns generally embraced by public innovation intermediaries and CSTE's activities, as well as added values. This case study integrates insights from theoretical frameworks and research on public innovation intermediaries. It was conducted by employing a combination of in-depth interviews with CSTE experts and employees (listed in Table 1) carried out in 2023 and 2024, and secondary sources. The secondary sources encompassed existing literature, annual and activity reports, internal communication documents, meeting minutes, and other information gathered from relevant websites.

3. The China Society of Technical Economics: A Public Intermediary

The China Society of Technical Economics (CSTE) (former "China Technology and Economic Research Society") was established with the approval of the State Council of China in November 1978, one month before the Third Plenary Session of the Eleventh Central

Committee — which marked the beginning of the "Reform and Opening Up" policy of China.[1]

Since the 1980s, CSTE's overall objective has been to support the reform of the overall economic structure of China in its different stages of development. As stated by one of the organization's leaders: "the mission of CSTE has always been, and still is, to explore the ways and methods for transforming science and technology into productivity, promote the integration of technology and economy, study the optimal allocation of resources, and promote the reform and high-quality development. Today, CSTE is an academic and non-profit organization member of the China Association for Science and Technology. Over the past 40 years since its establishment, CSTE has accumulated more than one hundred thousand members and currently has 34 branches, including 17 professional committees. It covers all the major areas of China's economy, such as transportation, coal, petrochemical, telecommunication, energy, environment, as well as intellectual property rights and finance, namely the key topics for accelerating the transition from technology to productivity".[2]

In the light of the information we have gathered, there are at least four CSTE's features — interconnected with its *public* nature and funding — which over time have allowed this organization to play a key role in helping companies face the complexities of China's fast-growing technological environment.

First, CSTE has the rightfulness to act as an intermediary since it has been authorized to do so by a public authority, i.e., the China Association for Science and Technology. Given this endorsement, which comes with public funding for carrying out its activities, CSTE is recognized as a credible and unbiased organization able to guarantee the interests of all its members. In this respect, the CSTE contributes to strengthen the technological competitiveness of different provinces in China by analyzing and

---

[1] China's 'Reform and Opening Up' policy was launched in 1978 under the leadership of Deng Xiaoping, with the objective to achieve economic growth through the active introduction of foreign capital and technology while maintaining its commitment to socialism. Foreign investments, new technologies, and the management of know-how eventually allowed China to trigger a rapid economic development and a progressive rise in national incomes. (Fang, 2018, pp. 1–10).

[2] A director of CSTE interviewed by the authors, Beijing, September 2023a.

drawing the possible paths each technology should follow to ensure its resilience and future development.[3]

Second, through its operations in the past four decades, CSTE has been able to build a pool of reliable professionals and specialists, on whom the organization can rely on for effectively carrying out its intermediation tasks. In other words, the CSTE has developed an in-depth knowledge of the technical and economic competencies needed in China's different provinces and sectors, to be able to mobilize key experts for responding to the specific needs of each sector or province. In this way, CSTE also acts as a national coordinator that allows fostering cooperation opportunities among the different parts of the country.

Third, public funding has guaranteed the survival of the CSTE for a long time. This has enabled it to reinforce its reputation and trust throughout the years. Indeed, CSTE's capacity to carry out activities and projects supported companies to identify both innovation and business opportunities as well as to promote their know-how and technical solutions all over the country.

Finally, over the years, CSTE has undergone a process of constant development and adaptation that pushed the organization to adjust its services for responding as efficiently as possible to the needs of its members and stakeholders.[4]

Since the initiation of the "Reform and Opening Up" policy, CSTE has primarily directed its services toward state-owned enterprises, recognizing their significant role in the economy. However, as the landscape has evolved with the growth of the private economy, it has expanded its support to a diverse range of stakeholders, including SMEs and large private enterprises, as well as state-owned companies.

As a result, the organization's focus areas have adapted in response to the pace of China's economic and technological development. For instance, the 2023 annual conference of CSTE prominently addressed the realm of AI. During this event, a workshop dedicated to the discussion of AI innovation and its applications in supporting company development was organized. This workshop engaged research institutions, companies

[3] CSTE (2017), 中国技术经济学会简介 [Introduction to the China Society of Technical Economics]. https://www.cste.org.cn/site/content/2.html; A director of CSTE interviewed by the authors, Beijing, September 2023.

[4] *Ibid.*

actively involved in AI research, and those who have successfully implemented AI in their business and production processes.[5]

In sum, being a public innovation intermediary has proved to be CSTE's *conditio sine qua non* as well as added value for successfully carrying out its activities over the past four decades.

4. Key Patterns and Activities of CSTE

It is possible to argue that CSTE undertakings follow three main patterns: (1) provide knowledge-intensive services, (2) promote interorganizational networking, cooperation, and training, and (3) foster reform and high-quality development. A closer look at each of these patterns results in a deeper understanding of CSTE's mission and activities.

(1) Knowledge Intensive Services

Broadly speaking, intermediaries leverage their know-how to deliver knowledge-intensive services to companies. These services encompass a wide spectrum and include the following: sharing specialized knowledge and skills; conducting assessments and trials of emerging technologies; tailoring existing technologies to meet specific needs; assisting in the identification and selection of suitable technological solutions; collaborating on strategies to foster business and innovation; advising on the management and protection of intellectual property; anticipating future technological trends and diagnosing current technological landscapes; assisting in the accreditation and validation of technologies, while navigating regulatory frameworks; providing support in bringing innovations to the market; assessing the outcomes and impact of innovation initiatives. These diversified services highlight the multifaceted role that intermediaries play in supporting companies, across various stages of their innovation processes (Rossi *et al.*, 2020, p. 3).

Since the launch of Deng Xiaoping's 'Reform and Opening Up' policy in China, CSTE has been elaborating and applying technical and economic theories and methodologies (e.g. *value engineering*) to enterprise management, thus directly participating in the modernization process of

---

[5]CSTE (2023), 中国技术经济学会第三十届学术年会,在深圳成功举办 [The 30th Annual Academic Conference of the China Society of Technical Economics in Shenzhen]. https://www.cste.org.cn/site/content/1786.html.

the country's state-owned enterprises. Indeed, the promotion of value engineering by CSTE has been robustly implemented across numerous industries, such as spanning machinery, electronics, textiles, light industry, petrochemicals, coal, mining and metallurgy, construction, transportation, electric power, national defense, agriculture, commerce, materials, and finance. The impact of these efforts is exemplified by the endorsement and successful application of value engineering principles in the aforementioned sectors. For instance, the former Chairman and General Manager of Shougang Group,[6] Mr. Luo Bingsheng, highlighted the significant impact of the extensive collaboration between the CSTE and Shougang Group. He emphasized that this collaborative effort played a crucial role in the reform and development of Shougang, leading to the creation of the renowned 'Shougang Experience'.[7]

This successful partnership model extends beyond Shougang, with other notable state-owned enterprises also benefiting from the application of technical and economic theories and methods under the support of CSTE. Examples include China Aerospace Science and Industry Corporation, China National Offshore Oil Corporation, China First Heavy Industries, YTO, ZTE, Guangxi LiuGong Machinery Company, TCL, and Weichai Group. These instances underline the broader positive influence and effectiveness of CSTE's contributions to various sectors, fostering innovation, development, and success within and among China's state-owned enterprises.

Moreover, the CSTE provides companies with access to the expertise present in CSTE's broad network (i.e., stakeholders from government, research institutes and universities, and private sector) and explores ways to transform science and technology into productivity. For instance, on May 5, 2023, CSTE took a significant step by launching a new initiative named 'Science and Technology Service Workstation'. The term 'workstation' refers to platforms established by CSTE in collaboration with enterprises, institutions, civil society, and other entities, to offer a range of

---

[6]Established in 1919 and headquartered in Beijing, the Shougang Group has played a pivotal role in shaping China's iron and steel sector. The company's diversification into mining, machinery, as well as other sectors shows its constant effort to becoming a versatile entity within China's industrial landscape. https://www.shougang.com.cn/en/ehtml/index.html.

[7]For more information about the so-called "Shougang Experience", see https://www.sohu.com/a/745904245_121040153.

services, including member development, scientific research, technical consultation, experimental demonstrations, exchange, and training. To ensure the effective operation of this new workstation system, CSTE has formulated a specific document titled 'China Society of Technology and Economics Science and Technology Service Workstation Management Measures (Trial)'.[8] The initiative aims to provide a broader spectrum of companies with access to services that support the integration of science and technology with the economy. It seeks to enhance collaborative interactions among various innovative resources, guide science and technology and innovation elements to grassroots levels, establish a bridge for cooperation among all science and technology workers, and bolster their capabilities in science and technology services and innovation. This initiative, CSTE's leaders argue, reflects the organization's commitment to fostering a conducive environment for collaboration, knowledge-sharing, and innovation across diverse sectors.[9]

CSTE has further expanded its reach by establishing the 'Science and Technology China Wuhou Yuehu Science and Technology Service Workstation' in Chengdu city, in collaboration with the Chengdu Wuhou District Science and Technology Association. This specific workstation in Chengdu is strategically focused on the development of a robust industrial circle and chain within the city. The primary objectives of the Chengdu workstation include transforming the intellectual resources of national academic talents into industrial innovation advantages, facilitating the transfer and transformation of high-end scientific research results, and creating a hub to attract high-end talents and intellectual resources. The overarching goal is to stimulate innovation and creativity among talents and drive the deep integration of science and technology with the local economy. To achieve these goals, the workstation will organize members in the Chengdu area to participate in various activities, such as science and technology information consultation, resource sharing, and docking services. As highlighted by a CSTE Director we interviewed, this initiative reflects the organization's commitment to fostering regional innovation ecosystems and leveraging intellectual resources to drive economic development in Chengdu.[10]

---

[8]CSTE (2017), 中国技术经济学会简介 [Introduction to the China Society of Technical Economics] https://www.cste.org.cn/site/content/2.html.

[9]A director and a deputy-director of CSTE interviewed by the authors, Beijing, September 2023.

[10]A director of CSTE interviewed by the authors, Beijing, September 2023.

(2) Interorganizational Networking, Cooperation, and Training

Interorganizational networking stands out as a pivotal function of intermediaries. This task involves the creation and sustenance of networks through the establishment of linkages with external knowledge providers, facilitating knowledge flows, and supporting collaborative efforts. Intermediaries play a crucial role in providing information and advice, diffusing valuable information and best practices across their networks, and actively scanning and identifying new sources of knowledge. Put another way, on one hand, these networking activities are crucial for intermediaries to act as effective conduits, facilitating the exchange of knowledge, promoting collaboration, and staying up to date with emerging sources of information and innovation. On the other hand, such active engagement in interorganizational networks improves the intermediary's capacity to play a critical role in promoting innovation and knowledge dissemination within and across different sectors.

The interorganizational network serves as a catalyst for cooperation opportunities, bringing together essential elements like policy, finance, expertise, and knowledge necessary for technology innovation and transfer. A compelling example of this is the Industrial Science and Technology Service Group for Tianfu Avenue Science and Technology Innovation Corridor in Sichuan Province, established through collaboration between CSTE and various partners including the Sichuan University Industry Group, Business School, and Industrial Technology Research Institute; National Southwest Center for Technology Transfer; Institute of Quantitative Economics and Technical Economics of the Chinese Academy of Social Sciences; School of Economics and Management of the University of Electronic Science and Technology of China.[11] This initiative is focused on industrial innovation within the Chengdu-Chongqing twin city circle. Several CSTE experts we interviewed argued that the diversified participation in the service group illustrates how CSTE's vast network is capable of mobilizing and integrating cross-disciplinary and cross-regional professionals and resources from government, industry, academia, and finance — based on specific needs. Among the activities of this service group, there are the so-called 'Science and Technology Innovation China Technology Roadshows', organized in local

[11] Innovation China (2023), "科创中国"天府大道科创走廊产业科技服务团 ["Science and Innovation in China", Tianfu Avenue Science and Innovation Corridor, Industrial Technology Service Team].

cities. These roadshows have established a platform for exchanges and cooperation, expediting the implementation and transformation of scientific research results, and contributing to the construction of local industrial ecosystems and innovation ecological chains.[12]

Besides fostering interorganizational networking, CSTE has also trained talents from all the provinces of China who possess a deep understanding of science and technology, proficiency in technological applications, knowledge of economics and management, and competence in both natural and social sciences. In this respect, the experts and scholars of CSTE are instrumental in cultivating talents for business management and innovation across China and play a key role in China's economic development, contributing to the nurturing of a considerable number of world-class enterprises. A CSTE Director we interviewed stated the following: "by imparting diverse skills and knowledge to the talents CSTE trains, the organisation has been instrumental in shaping a workforce capable of driving innovation and managerial excellence, furthering China's economic development on both national and global scale".[13]

Given its public nature, CSTE benefits from increased access to public resources for organizing training activities. Indeed, in 2023, CSTE has been entrusted by the Ministry of Human Resources and Social Security to organize an advanced training course on 'Professional Technology Transfer and Transformation Capacity Improvement in New Materials Direction'. The primary goal of this initiative is to promote technology transfer and enhance the professional and technical capabilities of technical managers in the field. CSTE received dedicated funding and support from the government to organize and conduct this specialized training. Indeed, leveraging its extensive network, the CSTE engaged experts from universities, legal professionals, and private companies to contribute their expertise. Hence, the training encompassed knowledge sharing on the latest technology trends, experiences in successful transitions, and insights on the different routes for obtaining financial support. As a result, over 80 professionals specializing in the field of new materials participated in the training program. This example, a CSTE expert argued, showcases how CSTE utilizes its public standing and network to create impactful training opportunities, fostering knowledge exchange and skill enhancement in critical areas of technology transfer and professional development.[14]

---

[12]CSTE's expert interviewed by the authors, Beijing, November 2023.

[13]A director of CSTE interviewed by the authors, Beijing, September 2023.

[14]CSTE's expert interviewed by the authors, Beijing, November 2023.

(3) Reform and High-Quality Development

Given its government background, CSTE operates in close alignment with the main economic fields and major national needs identified by the government. It aims to serve innovation-driven development and support the scientific decision-making processes of the government at both national and local levels.

In particular, the CSTE actively participates in the drafting and discussion process of documents and provides reference opinions for major decisions of the Party Central Committee and the State Council. Moreover, CSTE is engaged in the drafting and revision of laws and regulations and in the preparation of key national plans, including those related to economic and social development, major science and technology initiatives, industry plans, and regional development strategies.

Also, the organization provides science-based consulting opinions for decision-making and the demonstration of major national engineering, construction, and scientific research projects. The know-how of CSTE's experts has been instrumental in the assessment and demonstration of the major projects of national significance and impact, such as the Three Gorges Project, West-to-East Gas Transmission, West-to-East Electricity Transmission, South-to-North Water Diversion, Conversion of Farmland to Forests, Olympic Stadiums, Million-Ton Ethylene and Ton-level Oil Refining, Million-kilowatt Ultra-supercritical Power Station, Beijing-Shanghai High-speed Railway, Qinghai-Tibet Railway, and Lunar Exploration Project.

Since the 2006 release of the 'National Medium and Long-term Science and Technology Development Plan (2006–2020)', which, for the first time, introduced the concept of 'building an innovative country as a major strategic choice for the future', CSTE has consistently been at the forefront of exploring innovation theory and conducting policy research in China. Hence, CSTE has actively contributed to shaping the theoretical frameworks and policies that underpin China's approach to innovation, not least deepening on the concept of 'technological economy', namely the science that delves into the optimal allocation of resources, particularly focusing on innovation.[15]

---

[15] *Ibid.*

5. The Added Value of CSTE

Besides the analysis of the patterns and activities described above, a set of interviews with CSTE leaders and experts conducted at the end of 2023 and the beginning of 2024 helped further deepen the strengths of the organization and ultimately derive its added value.

One critical feature CSTE possesses in providing support to Chinese companies is its agnostic nature with respect to different technologies. Indeed, CSTE does not aim to exclusively promote a specific technology or product. Instead, it provides a range of technological offerings for solving given needs. Through this approach, companies seeking technological solutions are provided with a greater variety of potential options. Besides, by not being confined to a predefined set of solutions, CSTE keeps many doors of technological innovation open. Such flexibility supports the development and implementation of a dynamic and adaptable environment for innovation.

As a matter of fact, some private intermediaries, such as consulting companies, could also offer customized solutions to clients without being tied to certain specific technologies. However, in practice, these firms often aim to maximize profits by commoditizing technological offerings as much as possible. Instead, as argued by a CSTE expert during our interview, CSTE adopts a distinctive approach by actively facilitating the diffusion of different technologies to a broad spectrum of adopters, especially in the early stages of technological development when commoditized solutions are often limited (Rosenberg, 1997; Rossi *et al.*, 2020).

Another distinctive feature of CSTE is that by its very nature, it has the mandate and expertise to support a broad variety of public and private entities. This distinguishes the CSTE from the private intermediaries which usually attempt to target a specific region or sector. As a result, CSTE has enriched its ability and experience to deal with these actors over time. Put another way, the independence of CSTE from specific technological solutions and its ability to collaborate with a vast range of actors can benefit companies — being them SMEs or large companies — in looking for cost-effective solutions. By working with CSTE, SMEs that are financially unable to have access to the services of private intermediaries can reach out to potential technological solution providers or get more opportunities to present their technologies. Similarly, large companies — particularly those which are in the early phase of development — can benefit from the variety of technological solutions CSTE may put forward.[16]

Moreover, differently from other intermediaries, CSTE facilitates the integration of resources in developing projects with a public interest. The training activities entrusted by the government, and mentioned above in point 2 of paragraph 4, are a clear example of such an added value. CSTE's involvement in and contribution to China's regional development, through a broad range of national- and provincial-level projects embracing cohesive perspectives for enhancing the development of regions, unarguably contributes to building solid regional industrial ecosystems and innovation chains.[17]

Finally, CSTE is particularly helpful in coordinating the activities and resources to address the systematic problems companies are facing, in order to enable technology transfer. An illustrative case is the 'Industrial Digital Financial Technology Application Laboratory', established jointly by CSTE, the Small and Medium Enterprises Development Promotion Center of the Ministry of Industry and Information Technology, the Internet Industry Research Institute of Tsinghua University, and Juliang Group. The Laboratory intends to apply big data, cloud computing, and other latest technologies to develop a tool which can assist SMEs in applying for loans and investments from financial investment institutions. With this tool, the company's broad assets are evaluated, analyzed, and priced, providing an effective tool for financial institutions to offer economic support to SMEs.[18]

6. Conclusions

While technological advancements offer momentous opportunities for progress, companies face challenges in leveraging them due to a lack of understanding and skills. Recognizing and addressing these challenges is crucial to staying competitive and innovation intermediaries — such as

[16] CSTE's expert interviewed by the authors, Beijing, January 2024.

[17] See, for instance, CSTE's launching of the 'Science and Technology Service Workgroup', discussed in paragraph 4.

[18] CSTE's expert interviewed by the authors, Beijing, January 2024.

the China Society of Technical Economics (CSTE) — play a key role in supporting companies to do so.

The review of the existing literature combined with the analysis of arguably the first innovation intermediary in China, namely CSTE, allowed us to draw a direct relation between the key patterns generally embraced by innovation intermediaries and CSTE's activities as well as added values.

Our analysis has shown that thanks to its public nature and funding, CSTE has been able to provide — over four decades — adjustable innovation intermediary services in response to the pace of China's development. Today, CSTE provides Chinese companies with knowledge-intensive support and promotes interorganizational networking, cooperation, and training. Moreover, in light of its government background, it informs the decision-making processes related to innovation, both at national and local levels.

Besides analyzing the background as well as the most recent and relevant activities of CSTE, the interviews with its experts, carried out in 2023 and 2024, helped further deepen the strengths of the organization. CSTE's added value rests on its agnostic approach vis-à-vis technologies, support to both public and private entities, contribution to industrial ecosystems and innovation chains, and tools to enable technology transfer.

This case study addressed a notable gap in the existing research landscape, which lacks comprehensive analysis regarding the specific contributions of publicly supported innovation intermediaries. Despite their pivotal role in enhancing the technological competitiveness of private entities in response to the swiftly evolving economic landscape, there remains a dearth of in-depth examination on this subject. By delving into the role of CSTE, this chapter aims to contribute to filling this gap.

As a result, we argue that CSTE stems as an example of public innovation intermediaries that evolved along with China's economic and technological development, and (still) plays a critical role in pursuing innovation toward the country's high-quality development.

References

Caloffi, A., Colovic, A., Rossi, F., and Russo, M. (2022). New business models for public innovation intermediaries supporting emerging innovation systems: the case of the Internet of Things. *Technological Forecasting and Social Change*, 175, 1–38.

Fang, C. (2018). Perceiving truth and ceasing doubts: What can we learn from 40 Years of China's reform and opening up. *China & World Economy*, 26(2), 1–22.

Jeon, B. K. and Phelps, N. A. (2018). From ugly ducklings to beautiful swans? The role of local public intermediaries in the revival of the Daegu textile industry. *Geoforum*, 90, 100–107.

Lepore, D. and Spigarelli, F. (2020). Integrating industry 4.0 plans into regional innovation strategies. *Local Economy,* 35(5), 496–510.

Rosenberg, N. In *The Mosaic of Economic Growth*, Eds. R. Landau, T. Taylor, and G. Wright, "Uncertainty and Technological Change" (Stanford University Press, Stanford, 1997), pp. 91–110.

Rossi, F., Caloffi, A., Colovic, A., and Russo, M. (2020). Public innovation intermediaries and digital co-creation. Research contribution to the OECD TIP Co-creation project, *OECD*, 1–16.

https://doi.org/10.1142/9789819807611_0003

Chapter 3

The Role of the Chinese Government as an Innovation Broker in the Chinese Commercial Aircraft Industry

John R. McIntyre and James R. Hoadley

Center for International Business Education and Research
Georgia Institute of Technology, Atlanta, Georgia

ciber@scheller.gatech.edu

Abstract

The commercial aviation industry in China is on the brink of replicating its success in high-speed rail, aiming to become a global leader in commercial aviation. This transition is heavily influenced by the Chinese government's multifaceted involvement as a key facilitator of innovation within the nation's commercial aircraft industry. Acting in roles as diverse as client, regulator, and administrator, the government not only shapes the trajectory of innovation but also significantly impacts the development and competitiveness of the sector. Through strategic initiatives such as joint ventures, advanced manufacturing technologies, and the fostering of industrial clustering and technological advancements, the government has catalyzed the sector's growth.

The aim of this chapter is to demonstrate that innovation brokering in China's commercial aviation sector is unique due to the government's heavy involvement at all stages of the innovation process. This government engagement is critical for technological advancement, industry growth, and achieving a competitive advantage in the global commercial aircraft sector. While there is debate regarding the balance between government intervention and market dynamics, the evidence suggests that the government's proactive approach is vital for fostering a conducive environment for innovation and technological advancement. Through an analysis of the government's role as an innovation broker, this chapter contributes to the understanding of China's strategic approach to becoming a significant player in the global aviation industry, offering insights into the complex interplay between government policy and market-driven innovation.

Keywords: China, commercial aviation, government innovation brokering, technological advancement, market dynamics, global competitiveness.

1. Introduction

China is poised to repeat in commercial aviation what it has done in high-speed rail to become a major global leader (McIntyre and Hoadley, 2021). The Chinese government is a key facilitator of innovation within the nation's commercial aircraft industry, serving in multifaceted roles as a client, regulator, and administrator. These roles collectively influence and shape the trajectory of innovation in the sector, as highlighted by Gong *et al.* (2013). The government's efforts in promoting knowledge transfer and the development of advanced manufacturing capabilities, through mechanisms like joint ventures and the adoption of cutting-edge production technologies, are pivotal, according to Lai (2022). Wang (2023) further underscores the government's proactive stance in encouraging industrial clustering and technological advancements. The effectiveness of innovation in the high-technology domain is significantly boosted by government grants and support for private R&D initiatives, a point emphasized by Hong *et al.* (2015). The contribution of Chinese returnee entrepreneurs and professionals in propelling technological innovation and industrial growth is notable, as observed by Zhou and Hsu (2010). Li and Reimers (2015) point out the strategic role of the government in driving innovation through the establishment of industrial value chains and indigenous technological standards, which in turn supports the commercial aircraft sector's expansion. Local manufacturing policies are strategically designed to complement the central government's innovation agenda, aiming to break through existing barriers and enhance manufacturing sophistication (Nahm, 2017). However, the role of market forces in stimulating innovation and industrial progress is a topic of debate, with some viewing government intervention as a limiting factor on market dynamics (Wuttke, 2017). Overall, the Chinese government's involvement is crucial for technological advancement, industry growth, and achieving a competitive advantage in the commercial aircraft sector (So and Wang, 2022).

In the commercial aviation industry, government innovation brokers play an essential role in mediating between various stakeholders, fostering collaboration, and facilitating knowledge sharing. This industry is globally recognized for its contribution to economic growth (Valdés *et al.*, 2019). Sergeeva and Liu (2019) describe these brokers as key to encouraging partnerships and information exchange across different socio-economic entities. Their collaboration with companies, government entities, and associations is crucial for the sector's expansion and maintaining its global standing (Fleming, 2021). The significant impact of government innovation brokers on the dynamics of government-industry relationships within the aviation sector is documented by Lee (1984). Zhao (2017) highlights their contribution to leadership, support for innovation, and enhancing the sector's competitiveness. They are instrumental in commercializing intellectual property and developing advanced technological products (Zinnurov, 2021). Their role includes providing financial support and incentives for industrial growth (Eceral and Köroğlu, 2015). During emergencies, such as the COVID-19 pandemic, the importance of government support and financial assistance becomes even more critical for the industry to overcome challenges and adapt to changing conditions (So and Wang, 2022). Government innovation brokers are thus key drivers of innovation and growth in the commercial aviation industry (Lin, 2018).

This chapter seeks to highlight the distinct nature of innovation brokering within China's commercial aviation industry, underscored by the substantial involvement of the government at every phase of the innovation cycle. The involvement of the government is deemed essential for fostering technological progress, industry expansion, and securing a competitive edge in the international commercial aviation market. There exists a discussion around the equilibrium between state intervention and the forces of the market, yet it is evident that the government's forward-looking stance plays a crucial role in creating an environment conducive to innovation and technological growth. By examining the government's participation as an innovation broker, this section aims to enhance comprehension of China's methodical strategy to carve out a prominent position in the worldwide aviation sector, providing an in-depth look at the sophisticated relationship between state policies and the incentives of market-driven innovation.

The structure of this chapter is a thorough review of existing literature, leading to a case study of the development of two commercial aircraft in China in the current era, the ARJ21 and the C919, followed by analysis and conclusions.

2. The Role of the Government as an Innovation Broker

The Chinese science and technology intermediary system has evolved since the 1980s, with distinct levels of intermediaries providing services ranging from technical advice to market development. The Chinese government has implemented various support policies to aid the growth of these intermediaries, with a focus on technology transfer and evolution, while showing less emphasis on enterprise development and open innovation. Surveys conducted with IT enterprises in Beijing and Jiangsu provinces reveal that enterprises seek services primarily for market development, financial aid, and industrial competition intelligence, with concerns about the quality and efficiency of services provided by intermediaries. Large-scale enterprises and SMEs exhibit differing priorities in utilizing intermediary services, with SMEs showing more active engagement in open innovation practices (Xiaoyuan and Yanning, 2011).

The role of government as an innovation broker is a multifaceted and crucial aspect in fostering innovation within economies. Government intervention in innovation processes has evolved from a traditional "hands-off" approach to a more proactive "assisted linear" model, where governments act as facilitators and brokers in innovation networks (Etzkowitz and Zhou, 2017). This shift recognizes the significant impact that government programs can have on innovation at both national and local levels. Governments are increasingly seen as key players in innovation ecosystems, working alongside industry and society to promote responsible innovation through various dimensions such as anticipation, reflectiveness, inclusiveness, and responsiveness (Zheng *et al.*, 2020).

Holland *et al.* (2023) explore the evolving roles of innovation intermediaries in facilitating the scaling of engineering biology processes through advanced AI technologies, highlighting their shift from traditional roles like funding and technology transfer support to more dynamic functions like knowledge brokering and collaboration facilitation. It also identifies a growing emphasis on addressing governance issues and sustainability, driven by various stakeholders including public funders and venture capitalists, though such roles are less prevalent than the traditional and network-oriented functions.

In the context of China, despite a centralized political system, the government has been observed to play dual roles in innovation adoption — as an active facilitator and an involved backer rather than solely relying on coercion (Huang and Wiebrecht, 2021). This highlights the dynamic nature of government involvement in innovation processes, where governments can act as enablers and supporters rather than imposing strict regulations. Moreover, government support has been found to have a positive effect on firms' innovation capabilities, as seen in examples like Chinese automakers benefiting from government-led negotiations with foreign firms for technology transfer (Wang *et al.*, 2019).

The intermediary role of the state in governing innovation processes is also emphasized in the literature, where governments are seen as crucial intermediaries in facilitating innovation interactions between different parties (Todeva, 2013). This intermediary function involves not only providing resources and incentives for innovation but also creating conducive policy environments that support innovation, such as through subsidies, intellectual property legislation, and innovation vouchers (Xu *et al.*, 2022; Tian *et al.*, 2021). Additionally, the ability of public policy to influence open innovation dynamics, education, intellectual property, and cooperation is essential in shaping the innovation landscape (Yun *et al.*, 2019).

Overall, the synthesis of these references underscores the pivotal role of government as an innovation broker, showcasing how governments can act as facilitators, enablers, and intermediaries in driving innovation within economies. By understanding and leveraging the multifaceted roles of governments in innovation processes, societies can harness the full potential of innovation for economic growth and societal development.

3. Bridging the Gap in the Commercial Aviation Sector

Yin *et al.* (2022) investigated the impact of science-technology intermediaries (STIs) on regional innovation in China across 31 provinces from 2000 to 2019, finding a robust positive effect of STIs on innovation. They highlight three mechanisms through which STIs enhance innovation: reducing transaction costs to stimulate collaboration, facilitating optimal redistribution of innovation-related resources, and strengthening capacity to absorb knowledge spillovers from neighboring provinces and foreign countries. This is relevant to commercial aviation innovation in the following ways:

STIs improve regional innovation performance, which applies to commercial aviation. In complicated sectors like aircraft manufacturing, where technical advances are quick and vital for competitive advantage, STIs can stimulate innovation by supporting research and development settings. STIs influence innovation through transaction cost reduction, resource reallocation, and knowledge spillover absorption, providing a strategic framework for commercial aircraft development innovation. STIs can help aircraft manufacturers and research institutes, or foreign technology partners collaborate, cutting transaction costs and facilitating the flow of information and resources needed to create breakthrough aviation technologies. The policy proposals for emerging economies emphasize the necessity of establishing innovative settings beyond acquiring resources. China's commercial aviation sector needs not just technological and human capital expenditures but also an environment that promotes their optimal use. STI-friendly policies can improve innovation tactics, which are necessary for competitive aircraft production. Market methods to optimize innovation-related resources emphasize the need for a balance between government involvement and market-driven innovation. This implies that while government assistance is important for China's commercial aviation, building a market environment that organically stimulates innovation via competition, trade, and investment may help accelerate progress. The Chinese commercial aviation sector has similar problems to the study of STIs loosening barriers to foster innovation. A more linked STI network can help enterprises access the resources and information they need to innovate by overcoming market flaws. The dynamic effect of STIs on innovation and the emphasis on knowledge spillover imply that long-term involvement with STIs can boost innovation. Continuous participation with STIs can improve commercial aircraft development's capacity to absorb and deploy sophisticated technology, sustaining innovation.

The aviation sector has witnessed significant advancements in recent decades, partly attributed to the presence of innovation brokers who serve as intermediaries (Winch, 2007). These brokers are commonly established as public–private collaborations with the explicit purpose of validating novel concepts and facilitating the spread of innovation (Winch, 2007).

The facilitation of innovation in the aviation industry is contingent upon the active collaboration among a wide range of stakeholders. Collaborative endeavors among airlines, manufacturers, suppliers, universities, and governments have resulted in the emergence of novel goods, services, business models, and operational processes (Pereira 2021; Lüke 2018; Schneider 2013). Pereira (2021) highlights that a collaborative effort has been undertaken by prominent entities such as International Airlines Group, Emirates, Singapore Airlines, Boeing, and JetBlue. The objective of this collaboration is to foster advancements that enhance operational efficiency, elevate the quality of customer experience, facilitate market expansion, and advocate for sustainable practices.

The utilization of Big Data has become a significant internal approach for facilitating innovation within the aviation industry (Lüke, 2018). The substantial surge in data derived from many sources such as operations, maintenance, customer interactions, and other areas presents both prospects for enhancements driven by analytics and difficulties in effectively managing and harnessing these extensive quantities of information (Lüke, 2018). The establishment of reference architectures and frameworks aimed at the acquisition, integration, and analysis of aviation data has the potential to enable organizations to leverage the advantages offered by Big Data (Lüke, 2018).

According to Schneider (2013), the implementation of business model innovation has facilitated the ability of aviation companies to effectively respond and adjust to shifts within the industry. In response to several factors such as the rise in air traffic, globalization, technological advancements, and growing environmental concerns, there has been a notable emergence of new value propositions, value-generating mechanisms, and customer benefit-oriented offers (Schneider, 2013). Schneider (2013) highlights that maintenance, repair, and overhaul (MRO) companies have adapted their business models in response to changes occurring within the aircraft manufacturing and airline sectors.

Policy and regulation play a significant role in influencing the trajectory of innovation within the aviation industry. According to Andrew (2012), the facilitation of innovation might be enhanced by governmental backing of transnational collaboration and the engagement of the private sector in infrastructure and air traffic management. Governments encounter challenges in their efforts to ensure the effectiveness of infrastructure and service delivery, indicating that the adoption of commercial ideas could potentially be beneficial (Andrew, 2012).

In conclusion, the aviation industry is being propelled forward in terms of innovation by key factors such as collaboration, data utilization, business model innovation, and policy changes. The facilitation of ongoing innovation could be achieved through the establishment of partnerships among various stakeholders, the development of novel frameworks for the management of aviation data, the adjustment of business models to align with industry trends, and the provision of governmental support for transnational collaboration and private sector engagement.

Government agencies have played a crucial role in the growth of China's commercial aircraft manufacturing industry. The industry has benefitted significantly from governmental regulations and initiatives. Li (2018) highlights the importance of technological advancements in China's high-end equipment manufacturing, particularly in aircraft production. Strategies such as forming partnerships and adopting advanced production technologies have been key to enhancing China's manufacturing capabilities (Lai, 2022). Qin and Mkhitaryan (2018) note the positive impact of regulations that encourage collaboration between universities and the industry, enhancing innovation within the sector. Additionally, initiatives like the "Made in China 2025" program have been designed to reorganize and advance the industrial sector, with a focus on aerospace (Qi, 2018). These efforts aim to boost China's standing in the global aircraft manufacturing market (Goldstein, 2006), with indirect influences from the government proving especially effective (Qin and Mkhitaryan, 2018).

The "Made in China 2025" initiative aims to position China as a leader in global manufacturing by boosting competitiveness in areas such as advanced IT, robotics, aviation, and new energy vehicles (Liu, 2018; Yu, 2018). It embraces global trends like Industry 4.0, promoting lean and intelligent manufacturing (Wang *et al.*, 2016; Shaffer and Gao, 2020). Collaboration across government, industry, and academia is vital to the initiative's success, fostering innovation and technological progress

(Kenderdine, 2017; Zamorin, 2023). It also integrates the military-industrial complex, indicating a holistic approach to national development (Zamorin, 2023). The initiative's broad impact includes enhancing sectors such as construction through technologies like Building Information Modeling (BIM) (Li and Yang, 2017) and fostering green innovation (Xu, 2022).

"Made in China 2025" has significant global implications, particularly in the context of international trade and the economic rivalry between China and the United States. It signals China's transition toward high-quality, innovation-driven manufacturing, emphasizing core technologies and essential components (Liu, 2018; Rashidin *et al.*, 2020; Shi and Iqbal, 2021). This strategic shift aims not just to redefine China's role in the global manufacturing landscape but also to position the country at the forefront of future technological innovations.

The development of China's commercial aircraft industry is of significant importance from a political and economic perspective, heavily influenced by government support and involvement. This aligns with China's strategic goal to become a global leader in aerospace manufacturing and technology (Goldstein, 2005; Niosi and Zhao, 2013).

Li (2018a) highlights the critical role of China's commercial aviation sector in driving the country's economic transformation and progress. Further, research by Zhang *et al.* (2021) confirms the sector's essential contribution to economic growth, job creation, and technological advancement. The industry's expansion has a positive ripple effect on related sectors such as aviation services, tourism, and logistics, enhancing the overall economic landscape. Additionally, the growth of China's aviation industry has been instrumental in the development and expansion of domestic airlines, significantly boosting the nation's economic development (Zhang *et al.*, 2021). This comprehensive growth underscores the commercial aviation industry's pivotal role in China's broader economic strategy and development.

4. The Brokerage Role of the Chinese Government in the Commercial Aircraft Industry

The aircraft manufacturing industry in China has been characterized by significant government interference, which encompasses state ownership and the implementation of supportive regulations (Goldstein, 2005).

State-owned firms have exerted significant influence by promoting technological progress and adapting ownership arrangements to meet the specific needs of the industry (Goldstein, 2005; Schneider *et al.*, 2013). According to Goldstein (2005), the government has established a range of measures aimed at promoting research and development, investment, and collaboration within the sector. The interventions implemented have the objective of augmenting China's competitiveness within the global aviation market and promoting the expansion of indigenous manufacturing capabilities (Huang, 2016).

The commercial aviation sector in China is considered a crucial industry for the country's progress in terms of economic and technological development (Li, 2018). According to Li (2018), the industrial sector plays a crucial role in fostering innovation and advancing the growth of advanced manufacturing, hence facilitating China's objective of shifting from a labor-intensive economic model to a technology-driven one. Furthermore, the utilization of carbon nanotubes and fiber composites in the manufacturing of aircraft has been facilitated by this development, resulting in the production of aircraft that are both lower in weight and more fuel-efficient (Singla and Chawla, 2010).

Lai (2022) states that the emergence and growth of the commercial aircraft sector in China have come to represent not only a symbol of national unity but also a testament to the country's resilience and resistance. The Chinese populace has derived a sense of pride and achievement from the industry, which signifies their resolute endeavor to establish a self-reliant and globally competitive manufacturing domain (Niosi and Zhao, 2013; Lai, 2022). The significance of Chinese manufacturing employees in the acquisition of skills and information from international counterparts, leading to the advancement of the sector, is underscored by historical study (Lai, 2022).

The expansion of the Chinese commercial aviation sector does not solely influence economic considerations but also encompasses noteworthy geopolitical ramifications. China seeks to decrease its dependence on foreign aircraft manufacturers, with a special focus on those based in the United States and Europe. China's objective of bolstering its domestic aircraft manufacturing capabilities is driven by the desire to augment its strategic autonomy, mitigate vulnerabilities, and extend its global aviation influence (Ohlandt, 2023).

The Chinese commercial aircraft industry has been progressively enhancing its competitive viability in comparison with industry leaders

Airbus and Boeing. According to Xu (2022), the rise of the industry may be attributed to the support provided by the government and the implementation of a comprehensive development strategy. The market leadership of Airbus and Boeing, which has historically been dominant, is currently being challenged by the emergence of smaller commercial aircraft businesses (Ellis, 2013). Nevertheless, the Dreamliner manufactured by Boeing, including a composite airframe, is a noteworthy accomplishment and a very energy-efficient aircraft within the company's historical context (Sosa *et al.*, 2015). Airbus and Boeing have encountered subsidy issues in the World Trade Organization, which exemplify the competitive nature of the aviation industry (Carbaugh and Olienyk, 2004). According to Ohlandt (2023), the involvement of Chinese investors in the U.S. aviation sector and the wider aerospace industry has played a role in enhancing the competitive edge of China's commercial aircraft manufacturing sector. The Chinese commercial aviation industry has made significant progress and has become a formidable contender against established players, such as Airbus and Boeing (Beaugency *et al.*, 2015).

The role of the Chinese government as an innovation broker in complex industries is multifaceted and influential. Research by Vrande *et al.* (2009) highlights the differential management of open innovation by large, established companies and small start-ups, reflecting their distinct positions within the innovation system (Gong *et al.*, 2013). further suggest the establishment of a not-for-profit organization to act as an intermediary innovation broker, driving technology progress within complex systems industries like construction. Moreover, Chesbrough *et al.* (2020) clarify the role of the government as an orchestrator of open innovation and developing dynamic capabilities through the content analysis of presidential speeches and exploratory case studies of high-speed rail and semiconductor industries in China. This underscores the government's pivotal role in shaping innovation dynamics within complex industries.

The Chinese government's role as an innovation broker is also evident in its influence on the allocation of resources and its impact on enterprise technological innovation, as indicated by (Ma *et al.*, 2022). Additionally, the government's support and its "entrepreneurial role" in high-tech sectors, such as the high-speed railway system, raise questions about the extent to which government support influences the innovation effectiveness of Chinese firms (Petti *et al.*, 2017). Furthermore, the government's support and its influence on the innovation efficiency of wind power industries in China have been widely studied, emphasizing the complex relationship between government grants, private R&D funding, and innovation efficiency in transition economies (Jiang *et al.*, 2015). These studies collectively underscore the significant and complex role of the Chinese government as an innovation broker in shaping the innovation landscape within complex industries.

A new report by the Australian Strategic Policy Institute highlights that China is outpacing the United States and other Western countries in developing advanced technologies and retaining talent, leading in 37 of 44 critical and emerging technology fields such as electric batteries and 5G/6G communications. The report emphasizes China's potential to establish a monopoly in several areas, underlining the importance of long-term policy planning and the significant gap between China and the US in high-impact scientific research output.

5. The Case of the COMAC ARJ21 and C919

The ARJ21 (Advanced Regional Jet 21) commercial aircraft has a significant development history. Initially, the program focused on creating a passenger version capable of carrying 85–90 passengers with a range of 2000 nautical miles (Smith and Zhang, 2014). The aircraft was designed using the Framework for Advanced Supersonic Transport (FASST) developed at the Aerospace Systems Design Laboratory at the Georgia Institute of Technology (ASDL GT), a parametric and simulation methodology, but primarily concentrating on subsonic commercial aircraft (Zhang *et al.*, 2023). The ARJ21 program involved the development of the ARJ21-700 feeder liner, which underwent flight characteristics airworthiness compliance verification in China through handling qualities rating method (HQRM) (Fan *et al.*, 2015).

In terms of safety considerations, research has been conducted on the wake evolution and risk control of the ARJ21 aircraft during takeoff and landing phases (Pan *et al.*, 2022). Additionally, studies have analyzed the impact response and sensitivity of steel-plate concrete containment structures against large commercial aircraft, emphasizing the importance of material and geometric parameters on impact resistance (Li *et al.*, 2021). Furthermore, refined damage evolution analyses have been carried out for scenarios involving large commercial aircraft crashing into nuclear power plants, highlighting the need for comprehensive safety assessments (Zou *et al.*, 2019). These assessments are vital both for the ARJ21 aircraft itself, as well as building a framework of safety testing for use on later projects like the C919.

The development of the ARJ21 also aligns with the broader context of the aviation industry. Commercial aircraft design has evolved to meet operational, economic, and performance demands, necessitating a multi-disciplinary optimization approach to enhance efficiency and reduce costs (Peoples and Willcox, 2006). Moreover, the adoption of fly-by-wire flight control technology in the ARJ21 reflects advancements in aircraft systems and airworthiness verification processes (Zhang *et al.*, 2012).

The development of the COMAC (Commercial Aircraft Corporation of China, Ltd.) C919 commercial aircraft has been a significant endeavor marked by various technological advancements and strategic decisions. Initiated in 2008, the C919 program required substantial parts from 3D printing, showcasing the technological demands it presented (Bai *et al.*, 2021). The Chinese government played a crucial role in supporting COMAC through intelligence efforts to obtain necessary technologies for the C919, reflecting China's ambition within its national strategic plan of "Made in China 2025" (Li and Farrell, 2020; Thuy and Yan, 2023). Additionally, the huge domestic aviation market in China, government financing, and policies mandating technology sharing with local partners contributed to COMAC's progress in developing the C919 (Contractor, 2013).

The development of the C919 involved collaborations with global suppliers for components like LEAP engines, which are utilized in various commercial aircraft, including the C919 (Mayer *et al.*, 2017; Maier *et al.*, 2019). Furthermore, the use of advanced materials like Al-Li alloy 2060 in the fuselage and 3D woven carbon fiber reinforced composites in components like fan blades showcased the adoption of innovative manufacturing technologies in the C919 program (Bai *et al.*, 2018; Maier *et al.*, 2019). The application of ORT architecture in manufacturing components for the C919, A320neoneo, and 737-MAX highlighted the technological advancements incorporated in these aircraft (Saleh and Soutis, 2017).

Moreover, the C919 program was part of a broader research plan in China focusing on the crash-worthy design of civil airplanes, emphasizing safety considerations in the development process (Yang *et al.*, 2020). The architectural innovation in the C919, particularly in its airframe design, indicated COMAC's potential to drive advancements in the aerospace industry (Tyroler-Cooper and Peet, 2011). The selection of the Integrated Modular Avionics (IMA) architecture for the C919 aligned with the trend observed in the design of modern civil and military aircraft, emphasizing reliability and advanced avionics systems (Zhao *et al.*, 2018).

The Chinese Government plays a role as an innovation broker in the Chinese commercial aircraft industry by supporting and funding projects like the C919 developed by the Commercial Aircraft Corporation of China (COMAC). However, despite being touted as a homegrown success, the C919 relies heavily on foreign suppliers for its components, with approximately 90% of its main suppliers coming from North America and Europe (Toh, 2023) (Kennedy, 2020). This reliance on foreign technology has led experts to view the C919 more as a non-Chinese airplane with "Chinese paint on it" (Toh, 2023). The government's ambition is for COMAC to eventually compete against established manufacturers like Airbus and Boeing, but analysts believe this goal may be challenging to achieve in the near future (Toh, 2023). The most expensive and complex component of any aircraft are the engines, and as mentioned above, the C919 currently uses a version of the CFM LEAP, which also powers the Airbus 320neo series and Boeing 737-MAX. However, there is a government-supported attempt by Shanghai-based Aero Engine Corporation of China to develop its CJ-1000 high-bypass turbofan engine to be used on the C919 instead (Lee, 2024). Despite receiving massive state funding and attention, COMAC is not yet considered on par with leading commercial aircraft manufacturers like Boeing and Airbus (Kennedy, 2020).

Despite these efforts, challenges remain, such as delays in certification for aircraft like the C919, continued reliance on imported parts, and skepticism about the commercial success of projects like the C919 and ARJ-21 (Agarwal, 2022). The effectiveness of China's industrial policies in commercial aviation manufacturing is still a subject of evaluation, with experts suggesting a reevaluation of investments and policies in this industry for better outcomes (Crane, 2014) (Agarwal, 2022).

6. Analysis

The Chinese government's role as an innovation broker in the commercial aircraft industry is multifaceted and profoundly influential, integrating functions as a client, regulator, and administrator to shape the trajectory of innovation within this high-technology sector. Through concerted efforts in fostering knowledge transfer and advanced manufacturing capabilities, the government has catalyzed the development of a competitive commercial aircraft industry. Initiatives such as joint ventures and the adoption of cutting-edge production technologies, as highlighted by Lai (2022), along with the encouragement of industrial clustering and technological advancements underscored by Wang (2023), exemplify the government's proactive approach to innovation.

Government grants and support for private R&D initiatives further enhance the effectiveness of innovation, demonstrating a commitment to fostering a conducive environment for technological advancement. The strategic establishment of industrial value chains and indigenous technological standards, as noted by Li and Reimers (2015), plays a critical role in driving the sector's growth. Moreover, the government's encouragement of the return of Chinese entrepreneurs and professionals to contribute to technological and industrial development further amplifies its role as an innovation broker.

However, the interaction between government intervention and market forces raises debates on the balance between fostering innovation and allowing market dynamics to stimulate industrial progress. While the government's involvement is crucial for technological advancement and achieving a competitive advantage in the global arena, as argued by So and Wang (2022), the extent to which this intervention may impede or facilitate market-driven innovation remains a subject of discussion. Overall, the Chinese government's active engagement as an innovation broker is pivotal in shaping the commercial aircraft sector's landscape, facilitating its growth, and setting the stage for China to become a significant player in the global aviation industry.

The case studies of the COMAC ARJ21 and C919 aircraft elucidate the critical role of the Chinese government as an innovation broker within the ambit of commercial aviation, underscoring its strategic foray into this sector. The insights derived from these developments accentuate several pivotal themes:

Strategic government intervention and innovation management: The genesis and evolution of the ARJ21 and C919 programs are emblematic of a strategic, government-led innovation ecosystem, primarily orchestrated under the scope of the "Made in China 2025" national strategy. This government intervention has not only provided the requisite financial and policy scaffolding but has also engendered pivotal international technological collaborations, showcasing a sophisticated model of state-led innovation brokerage.

Government-facilitated technological advancement and safety initiatives: The government's imperative in steering research and development toward safety and technological enhancements is evident. Initiatives have supported the ARJ21's development with comprehensive safety studies and propelled the C919's integration of avant-garde technologies and materials. This includes the embracement of 3D printing technologies, the utilization of Al-Li alloys, carbon fiber composites, and the adoption of Integrated Modular Avionics architecture.

Navigating international dependencies through strategic government mediation: The state's mediation in international collaborations, especially in the context of the C919's dependency on critical components from global suppliers, illustrates the government's strategic diplomacy in balancing technological dependencies with aspirations for autonomy.

Governmental oversight in addressing project challenges: The developmental trajectories of the ARJ21 and C919 highlight a series of challenges, from certification delays to technological dependences. The government's ongoing support and strategic recalibrations are crucial in navigating these impediments, aiming to affirm China's position within the global aviation industry, vis-à-vis established entities, such as Airbus and Boeing.

Prospects for future development under government scrutiny: Anticipated future developments suggest a sustained governmental commitment toward strategic reassessment and support for COMAC's endeavors. This could entail policy and investment strategy adjustments to surmount existing hurdles and secure the long-term ascendancy and competitiveness of China's indigenous commercial aircraft on the international stage.

7. Conclusions

The Chinese government's strategic role as an innovation broker in the commercial aviation sector demonstrates a holistic strategy to promoting technical progress and economic development. The government has influenced the direction of innovation by fulfilling roles as a client, regulator, and administrator. This has been achieved through strategies including joint ventures, sophisticated manufacturing capabilities, and backing private research and development. The sector has been positioned for global competitiveness through these initiatives, along with the deliberate construction of industrial value chains and indigenous technology standards. The interplay between government intervention and market forces is a complex component of this situation, prompting more discussion on the best approach to encourage innovation and economic advancement. Although there may be critiques about market dynamics, the Chinese government's engagement is unquestionably vital for the sector's progress. The government's collaborative, supporting, and strategic responsibilities aid in the expansion of the commercial aircraft sector and also contribute greatly to China's objective of becoming a major force in global aviation. This strategic intervention showcases a state-led innovation approach that might provide useful insights for other industries and nations dealing with the interaction between government policy and market-driven innovation.

References

Agarwal, A. (2022, April 22). Evolution, progress and status of commercial aviation manufacturing industry in China. *China Focus*. https://chinafocus.ucsd.edu/2022/04/22/evolution-progress-status-of-commercial-aviation-manufacturing-industry-in-china/.

Bai, W., Fang, H., Wang, Y., Zeng, Q., Hu, G., Bao, G., … and Wan, Y. (2021). Academic insights and perspectives in 3D printing: A bibliometric review. *Applied Sciences*, 11(18), 8298. https://doi.org/10.3390/app11188298.

Bai, X., Li, H., Zeng, Y., Wang, M., Lyu, F., and Meng, Q. (2018). Experimental investigation on creep forming of a new Al-Li-Cu-Mg alloy plate. *MATEC Web of Conferences*, 190, 12007. https://doi.org/10.1051/matecconf/201819012007.

Beaugency, A., Sakinç, M., and Talbot, D. (2015). Outsourcing of strategic resources and capabilities: Opposing choices in the commercial aircraft manufacturing. *Journal of Knowledge Management*, 19(5), 912–931. https://doi.org/10.1108/jkm-01-2015-0040.

Bloomberg News. (2020). China's Boeing wannabe could land in U.S. government crosshairs. *Bloomberg.com*. https://www.bloomberg.com/news/features/2020-10-12/china-aerospace-firm-avic-raises-us-alarm-over-ties-to-ge-airbus.

Carbaugh, R. and Olienyk, J. (2004). Boeing-Airbus subsidy dispute: A sequel. *Global Economy Journal*, 4(2), 1850024. https://doi.org/10.2202/1524-5861.1047.

Chesbrough, H., Heaton, S., and Mei, L. (2020). Open innovation with Chinese characteristics: A dynamic capabilities perspective. *R* and *D Management*, 51(3), 247–259. https://doi.org/10.1111/radm.12438.

Chu, B., Zhang, H., and Jin, F. (2010). Identification and comparison of aircraft industry clusters in China and United States. *Chinese Geographical Science*, 20(5), 471–480. https://doi.org/10.1007/s11769-010-0421-5.

Contractor, F. (2013). Punching above their weight. *International Journal of Emerging Markets*, 8(4), 304–328. https://doi.org/10.1108/ijoem-06-2013-0102.

Crane, K. (2014). The effectiveness of China's industrial policies in commercial aviation manufacturing. *RAND Corporation*. https://www.rand.org/content/dam/rand/pubs/testimonies/CT400/CT465/RAND_CT465.pdf.

Eceral, T. and Köroğlu, B. (2015). Incentive mechanisms in industrial development: An evaluation through defense and aviation industry of Ankara. *Procedia — Social and Behavioral Sciences*, 195, 1563–1572. https://doi.org/10.1016/j.sbspro.2015.06.192.

Ellis, D. (2013). Business intelligence enhances strategic, long-range planning in the commercial aerospace industry. *International Journal of Business Intelligence Research*, 112–124. https://doi.org/10.4018/978-1-4666-2650-8.ch008.

Etzkowitz, H. and Zhou, C. (2017). Innovation incommensurability and the science park. *R*and *D Management*, 48(1), 73–87. https://doi.org/10.1111/radm.12266.

Fan, L., Wang, L., and Tan, X. (2015). Digital virtual flight testing and evaluation method for flight characteristics airworthiness compliance of civil aircraft based on HQRM. *Chinese Journal of Aeronautics*, 28(1), 112–120. https://doi.org/10.1016/j.cja.2014.12.013.

Fleming, G. (2021). Commercial aviation, a new era: Summary of the 2017 TQA workshop. *Inter Noise*, 263(3), 3896–3899. https://doi.org/10.3397/in-2021-2551.

Francisco, W., Ferreira, F., Ferreira, E., Cividanes, L., Coutinho, A., and Thim, G. (2015). Functionalization of multi-walled carbon nanotube and mechanical property of epoxy-based nanocomposite. *Journal of Aerospace Technology and Management*, 7(3), 289–293. https://doi.org/10.5028/jatm.v7i3.485.

Goldstein, A. (2006). The political economy of industrial policy in China: The case of aircraft manufacturing. *Journal of Chinese Economic and Business Studies*, 4(3), 259–273. https://doi.org/10.1080/14765280600991628.

Gong, L., Shen, X., Jiang, S., and Carr, C. (2013). Technology progress in the Chinese construction industry under the iron-fist of government. *Technology Analysis & Strategic Management*, 25(4), 387–402. https://doi.org/10.1080/09537325.2013.774343.

Holland, C., McCarthy, A., Ferri, P., and Shapira, P. (2024). Innovation intermediaries at the convergence of digital technologies, sustainability, and governance: A case study of AI-enabled engineering biology. *Technovation*, 129, 102875. https://doi.org/10.1016/j.technovation.2023.102875.

Huang, B. and Wiebrecht, F. (2021). The dynamic role of governments in adopting policy innovations in China. *Policy & Politics*, 49(4), 633–651. https://doi.org/10.1332/030557321x16292224745415.

Huang, Y. (2016). The prospect of engaging China in the ICAO global MBM scheme. *Climate Policy*, 17(4), 476–484. https://doi.org/10.1080/14693062.2016.1164656.

Hurst, D. (2023, March 2). China leading US in technology race in all but a few fields, thinktank finds. *The Guardian*. https://www.theguardian.com/world/2023/mar/02/china-leading-us-in-technology-race-in-all-but-a-few-fields-thinktank-finds.

Jiang, H., Hong, S., Wang, L., Xu, Y., and Zhao, D. (2015). Government grants, private R&D funding and innovation efficiency in transition economy. *Technology Analysis and Strategic Management*, 27(9), 1068–1096. https://doi.org/10.1080/09537325.2015.1060310.

Kawase, K. (2023). China's Comac soars, helped by state-backed funding. *Nikkei Asia*. https://asia.nikkei.com/Business/Aerospace-Defense-Industries/China-s-COMAC-soars-helped-by-state-backed-funding.

Kenderdine, T. (2017). China's industrial policy, strategic emerging industries, and space law. *Asia & the Pacific Policy Studies*, 4(2), 325–342. https://doi.org/10.1002/app5.177.

Kennedy, S. (2020). China's COMAC: An aerospace minor leaguer. *CSIS*. https://www.csis.org/blogs/trustee-china-hand/chinas-comac-aerospace-minor-leaguer.

Kumar, K., Nair, C., and Ninan, K. (2007). Silica fiber-polybenzoxazine-syntactic foams: Processing and properties. *Journal of Applied Polymer Science*, 107(2), 1091–1099. https://doi.org/10.1002/app.27165.

Lai, J. (2022). Research on the relationship between national war, establishment, and development from the perspective of work pressure: Taking Hangzhou Central Aircraft Factory as an example. *The International Journal of Neuropsychopharmacology*, 25(Supplement_1), A65–A66. https://doi.org/10.1093/ijnp/pyac032.090.

Lee, A. (2024). How monumental is China's challenge to build its own jet engine for the C919? *South China Morning Post*. https://www.scmp.com/economy/china-economy/article/3251482/how-monumental-chinas-challenge-build-its-own-jet-engine-c919-it-seeks-aviation-self-reliance.

Lee, D. (1984). Herbert Hoover and the development of commercial aviation, 1921–1926. *Business History Review*, 58(1), 78–102. https://doi.org/10.2307/3114529.

Li, J. and Yang, H. (2017). A research on development of construction industrialization based on BIM technology under the background of Industry 4.0. *MATEC Web of Conferences*, 100, 02046. https://doi.org/10.1051/matecconf/201710002046.

Li, J., Lin, G., Pan, R., and Li, L. (2021). Influence of different sites on impact response of steel-plate concrete containment against a large commercial aircraft. *Energies*, 14(16), 4957. https://doi.org/10.3390/en14164957.

Li, M. and Reimers, K. (2015). Innovation in China's information and communications technology industry. *Chinese Management Studies*, 9(1), 27–37. https://doi.org/10.1108/cms-01-2015-0017.

Li, S. and Farrell, M. (2020). The emergence of China, inc.: Behind and beyond the trade war. *International Journal of Emerging Markets*, 16(4), 745–764. https://doi.org/10.1108/ijoem-12-2019-1103.

Li, Y. (2018). Supply chain management of aircraft industry. https://doi.org/10.2991/meici-18.2018.42.

Li, W. (2018). Research on dilemma and countermeasures of core technology breakthroughs in China's high-end equipment manufacturing industry. https://doi.org/10.2991/iceemr-18.2018.182.

Lin, S. (2018). The structural characteristics of innovation ecosystem: A fashion case. *European Journal of Innovation Management*, 21(4), 620–635. https://doi.org/10.1108/ejim-09-2017-0115.

Lin, W., Lu, J., Zhu, J., and Xu, L. (2022). Research on the sustainable development and dynamic capabilities of China's aircraft leasing industry based on system dynamics theory. *Sustainability*, 14(3), 1806. https://doi.org/10.3390/su14031806.

Liu, K. (2018). Chinese manufacturing in the shadow of the China-US trade war. *Economic Affairs*, 38(3), 307–324. https://doi.org/10.1111/ecaf.12308.

Ma, E., Hu, Q., and Wei, X. (2022). Effect of China's land resource allocation method on enterprise technological innovation: Promoting or inhibiting. *Frontiers in Environmental Science*, 10. https://doi.org/10.3389/fenvs.2022.766246.

Maier, R., Vintila, I., Mihalache, R., Vilag, V., Sima, M., and Dragan, V. (2019). Decreasing the mass of turbomachinery subassemblies using advanced polymer composites. *Materiale Plastice*, 56(4), 687–692. https://doi.org/10.37358/mp.19.4.5254.

Mayer, S., Erdely, P., Fischer, F., Holec, D., Kastenhuber, M., Klein, T., … and Clemens, H. (2017). Intermetallic β-solidifying γ-TiAl based alloys: From fundamental research to application. *Advanced Engineering Materials*, 19(4). https://doi.org/10.1002/adem.201600735.

McIntyre, J. R. and Hoadley, J. R. (2021). Chinese commercial aircraft manufacturing policy: The view from the commanding heights. In F. Spigarelli & J. R. McIntyre (Eds.), *The new Chinese dream: Palgrave studies of*

internationalization in emerging markets. Palgrave Macmillan, Cham. https://doi.org/10.1007/978-3-030-69812-6_7.
Nahm, J. (2017). Exploiting the implementation gap: Policy divergence and industrial upgrading in China's wind and solar sectors. *The China Quarterly*, 231, 705–727. https://doi.org/10.1017/s030574101700090x.
Niosi, J. and Zhao, J. (2013). China's catching up in aerospace. *International Journal of Technology and Globalisation*, 7(1/2), 80. https://doi.org/10.1504/ijtg.2013.052032.
Ohlandt, C. (2023). U.S.-China aviation competition: Military, commercial, and general aviation are different. https://doi.org/10.7249/cta2692-1.
Pan, W., Wang, J., Xu, Y., Jiang, Q., and Luo, Y. (2022). Approach and landing aircraft wake encounter risk based on reynolds-averaged navier-stokes numerical simulation. *International Journal of Aerospace Engineering*, 2022, 1–24. https://doi.org/10.1155/2022/9126755.
Peoples, R. and Willcox, K. (2006). Value-based multidisciplinary optimization for commercial aircraft design and business risk assessment. *Journal of Aircraft*, 43(4), 913–921. https://doi.org/10.2514/1.14147.
Pereira, B., Lohmann, G., and Houghton, L. (2021). The role of collaboration in innovation and value creation in the aviation industry. *Journal of Creating Value*, 7(1), 44–59. https://doi.org/10.1177/23949643211010588.
Petti, C., Rubini, L., and Podetti, S. (2017). Government support and R&D investment effectiveness in Chinese SMEs: A complex relationship. *Asian Economic Papers*, 16(1), 201–226. https://doi.org/10.1162/asep_a_00504.
Qi, Y. (2018). Research on the position and influencing factors of Chinese manufacturing industry in the evolution of global value chain. https://doi.org/10.2991/icmcs-18.2018.79.
Qin, Y. and Mkhitaryan, D. (2018). The influence of government policies on university-industry collaboration in China. https://doi.org/10.2991/msmi-18.2018.36.
Rains, T. (2023). China's first-ever large homegrown airliner has finally made its inaugural flight — meet the Comac C919. *Business Insider*. https://www.businessinsider.com/comac-c919-chinese-commercial-jet-built-rival-boeing-and-airbus-2022-2.
Rashidin, M., China, E., and Javed, S. (2020). "Made in China 2025" strategy and trade hostility: The United States vs China. *Asian Journal of Business Research*, 10(3). https://doi.org/10.14707/ajbr.200088.
Saleh, M. and Soutis, C. (2017). Recent advancements in mechanical characterisation of 3D woven composites. *Mechanics of Advanced Materials and Modern Processes*, 3(1). https://doi.org/10.1186/s40759-017-0027-z.
Schneider, M., Kremmer, K., Weidmann, S., and Fürbeth, W. (2013). Interplay between parameter variation and oxide structure of a modified PAA process.

Surface and Interface Analysis, 45(10), 1503–1509. https://doi.org/10.1002/sia.5248.

Sergeeva, N. and Liu, N. (2019). Social construction of innovation and the role of innovation brokers in the construction sector. *Construction Innovation*, 20(2), 247–259. https://doi.org/10.1108/ci-02-2019-0016.

Shaffer, G. and Gao, H. (2020). A new Chinese economic order? *Journal of International Economic Law*, 23(3), 607–635. https://doi.org/10.1093/jiel/jgaa013.

Shi, H. and Iqbal, Q. (2021). Chinese SMEs in Industry 4.0, 1968–1977. https://doi.org/10.4018/978-1-7998-8548-1.ch099.

Singla, M., and Chawla, V. (2010). Mechanical properties of epoxy resin — fly ash composite. *Journal of Minerals and Materials Characterization and Engineering*, 3(9), 199–210. https://doi.org/10.4236/jmmce.2010.93017.

Smith, D. and Zhang, M. (2014). Linking, leveraging and learning: Sectoral systems of innovation and technological catch-up in China's commercial aerospace industry. *Global Business and Economics Review*, 16(4), 349. https://doi.org/10.1504/gber.2014.065361.

So, S. and Wang, R. (2022). China's aviation industry during the Covid-19 pandemic. *Journal 5051*, 7(1), 25–40. https://doi.org/10.55493/5051.v7i1.4576.

Sosa, E., Darlington, T., Hanos, B., and O'Rourke, M. (2015). Microwave-assisted healing of thermally mendable composites. *Smart Materials Research*, 2015, 1–8. https://doi.org/10.1155/2015/248490.

Thuy, D. and Yan, B. (2023). Divergences between the European Union and China on reducing international aviation emissions. *Asia Europe Journal*. https://doi.org/10.1007/s10308-023-00657-x.

Tian, D., Xiao-han, G., and Wang, P. (2021). Innovation vouchers and the sustainable growth of high-tech SMEs: Evidence from China. *Sustainability*, 13(20), 11176. https://doi.org/10.3390/su132011176.

Todeva, E. (2013). Governance of innovation and intermediation in triple helix interactions. *Industry and Higher Education*, 27(4), 263–278. https://doi.org/10.5367/ihe.2013.0161.

Toh, M. (2023). China's answer to Boeing and Airbus isn't as 'homegrown'. *CNN Business*. https://www.cnn.com/2023/06/02/tech/comac-c919-china-aircraft-intl-hnk/index.html.

Tyroler-Cooper, S. and Peet, A. (2011). The Chinese aviation industry: Techno-hybrid patterns of development in the C919 program. *Journal of Strategic Studies*, 34(3), 383–404. https://doi.org/10.1080/01402390.2011.574981.

Valdés, R., Burmaoglu, S., Tucci, V., Campos, L., Mattera, L., and Comendador, V. (2019). Flight Path 2050 and ACARE goals for maintaining and extending industrial leadership in aviation: A map of the aviation technology space. *Sustainability*, 11(7), 2065. https://doi.org/10.3390/su11072065.

van de Vrande, V., de Jong, J., Vanhaverbeke, W., and de Rochemont, M. (2009). Open innovation in SMEs: Trends, motives and management challenges. *Technovation*, 29(6-7), 423–437. https://doi.org/10.1016/j.technovation.2008.10.001.

Wang, B., Zhao, J., Wan, Z., Ma, J., Li, H., and Ma, J. (2016). Lean intelligent production system and value stream practice. *DTEM ICEM*. https://doi.org/10.12783/dtem/icem2016/4106.

Wang, J. (2023). Does environmental regulation promote eco-innovation performance of manufacturing firms? Empirical evidence from China. *Energies*, 16(6), 2899. https://doi.org/10.3390/en16062899.

Wang, L., Jin, J., and Banister, D. (2019). Resources, state ownership and innovation capability: Evidence from Chinese automakers. *Creativity and Innovation Management*, 28(2), 203–217. https://doi.org/10.1111/caim.12305.

Winch, G. M. and Courtney, R. (2007). The organization of innovation brokers: An international review. *Technology Analysis & Strategic Management*, 19(6), 747–763. https://doi.org/10.1080/09537320701711223.

Wuttke, J. (2017). The dark side of China's economic rise. *Global Policy*, 8, 62–70. https://doi.org/10.1111/1758-5899.12439

Xiaoyuan, Z. and Yanning, Z. (2011). Development of Chinese science and technology intermediaries and their integration into the open innovation paradigm. *Technology Analysis & Strategic Management*, 23(1), 25–48. https://doi.org/10.1080/09537325.2011.537103.

Xu, L. (2022). Towards green innovation by China's industrial policy: Evidence from Made in China 2025. *Frontiers in Environmental Science*, 10. https://doi.org/10.3389/fenvs.2022.924250.

Xu, X., Chen, X., Xu, Y., Wang, T., and Zhang, Y. (2022). Improving the innovative performance of renewable energy enterprises in China: Effects of subsidy policy and intellectual property legislation. *Sustainability*, 14(13), 8169. https://doi.org/10.3390/su14138169.

Yang, X., Ma, J., Wen, D., and Yang, J. (2020). Crashworthy design and energy absorption mechanisms for helicopter structures: A systematic literature review. *Progress in Aerospace Sciences*, 114, 100618. https://doi.org/10.1016/j.paerosci.2020.100618.

Yin, H.-T., Wen, J., and Chang, C.-P. (2022). Science-technology intermediary and innovation in China: Evidence from State Administration for Market Regulation, 2000–2019. *Technology in Society*, 68, 1–13. https://doi.org/10.1016/j.techsoc.2022.101864

Yu, Y. (2018). A trade war that is unwarranted. *China & World Economy*, 26(5), 38–61. https://doi.org/10.1111/cwe.12255.

Yun, J., Park, K., Hahm, S., and Kim, D. (2019). Basic income with high open innovation dynamics: The way to the entrepreneurial state. *Journal of Open*

Innovation: Technology, Market, and Complexity, 5(3), 41. https://doi.org/10.3390/joitmc5030041.

Zamorin, V. (2023). Participation of the Chinese military-industrial complex in the implementation of the state plan "Made in China — 2025". *Problemy Dalnego Vostoka*, 2, 105. https://doi.org/10.31857/s013128120025262-9.

Zhang, J., Wuebbles, D., Pfaender, H., Kinnison, D., and Davis, N. (2023). Potential impacts on ozone and climate from a proposed fleet of supersonic aircraft. *Earth's Future*, 11(4). https://doi.org/10.1029/2022ef003409.

Zhang, Y., Cao, K., and Dong, W. (2021). Research on improvement and optimisation of modelling method of China's civil aircraft market demand forecast model. *The Aeronautical Journal*, 125(1289), 1157–1191. https://doi.org/10.1017/aer.2021.16.

Zhang, Y., Li, Y., and Gao, Y. (2012). Commercial transport aircraft flight simulator flying qualities airworthiness verification. *Applied Mechanics and Materials*, 235, 170–175. https://doi.org/10.4028/www.scientific.net/amm.235.170.

Zhao, C., Wang, P., and Yan, F. (2018). Reliability analysis of the reconfigurable integrated modular avionics using the continuous-time Markov chains. *International Journal of Aerospace Engineering*, 2018, 1–8. https://doi.org/10.1155/2018/5213249.

Zhao, S. (2017). Problems and countermeasures of aviation industry development in Henan Province. *MATEC Web of Conferences*, 100, 01008. https://doi.org/10.1051/matecconf/201710001008.

Zheng, L., Ma, L., Huang, T., and Tang, H. (2020). Collaborative governance for responsible innovation in the context of sharing economy: Studies on the shared bicycle sector in China. *Journal of Open Innovation: Technology, Market and Complexity*, 6(2), 35. https://doi.org/10.3390/joitmc6020035.

Zhou, Y. and Hsu, J. (2010). Divergent engagements: Roles and strategies of Taiwanese and mainland Chinese returnee entrepreneurs in the IT industry. *Global Networks*, 11(3), 398–419. https://doi.org/10.1111/j.1471-0374.2010.00302.x.

Zinnurov, V. (2021). Market mechanisms of the strategy of innovative development of the Russian aviation industry: Problems and indicators of the economy of intellectual property. *Intellectual Property Law*, 1, 19–25. https://doi.org/10.18572/2072-4322-2021-1-19-25.

https://doi.org/10.1142/9789819807611_0004

Chapter 4

The Role of Innovation Intermediaries in Low-Medium-Technology Sectors in China: Evidence from Chinese Construction Industry

Giuseppe Lanfranchi[*,‡], Tiago Branco Coelho[†,§], and Antonio Crupi[*,¶]

[*]*Departments of Economics, University of Messina, Italy*

[†]*Research and Development Department, Singapore*

[‡]*Giuseppe.lanfranchi@unime.it*
[§]*tiago.branco.coelho@gmail.com*
[¶]*crupi.antonio@unime.it*

Abstract

In the vanguard of transitioning toward Society 5.0, China's construction industry stands at the forefront, epitomizing not just economic heft but also a beacon of societal metamorphosis and techno-physical synthesis. Amidst China's economic transformation and pivot to a model of state capitalism, innovation intermediaries have emerged as central players in augmenting sustainability and technological progression within this sector. This chapter critically analyzes the innovation intermediaries' transformative role, from fueling competition post-economic liberalization to navigating the complexities of high-tech and low-to-medium-tech interactions, particularly within the construction domain. It highlights the innovation chasm within urban precincts and proffers strategic intermediary deployment as a remedy, especially pertinent as China forges ahead toward Society 5.0 — a confluence of digital and corporeal spheres. Yet, the conundrum persists: while the Communist Party's oversight has catalyzed R&D resource allocation, recent authoritarian inclinations, especially under Xi Jinping's aegis, could thwart such dynamism. The narrative juxtaposes China's technology adoption strides in construction against the benchmarks set by regional forerunners like Japan and Singapore, dissecting the incumbent challenges — low productivity, decarbonization, safety, cost surges, schedule slippages, and fragmented industry structure impeding technological embracement. It culminates by envisioning the road ahead, contemplating the role of innovation intermediaries in China grappling with stringent governance and geopolitical friction with the United States.

Keywords: Society 5.0, R&D, construction, China.

1. Introduction

We are currently witnessing a period of rapid and profound change, characterized by the digitalization of our society and the advent of emerging digital technologies that are substantially transforming the very nature of entrepreneurship and the paradigms linked to all aspects of doing business (Crupi *et al.*, 2022). This digital transformation is reshaping various aspects of corporate structures, including labor, marketing, sales, and technology, indicating that these modifications are both widespread and crucial to the ongoing evolution of modern business practices (Almeida *et al.*, 2020). At the same time, this technological advancement is accelerating the obsolescence of products, a trend that has become apparent across multiple industries. As technological innovations continue to progress at an accelerated pace, the cycle of product renewal becomes faster, leading to products becoming outdated more quickly than ever before (Xie *et al.*, 2020). This rapid obsolescence necessitates continuous innovation and adaptation strategies within industries to sustain competitiveness and relevance in a swiftly changing market environment. In this evolving landscape, innovation intermediaries, defined as agents or brokers who facilitate linkages and communication among previously disconnected parties in any aspect of a firm's innovation process (Howells, 2006), are increasingly acknowledged as a critical external factor in promoting technology transfer across diverse groups (Crupi *et al.*, 2021; Lindkvist *et al.*, 2019). Innovation intermediaries often occupy a critical junction, situated between the creators and users of knowledge (Smedlund, 2006). These entities extend beyond mere facilitation of knowledge transfer; they enhance the ability of firms to acquire and assimilate new knowledge, effectively boosting their absorptive capacities (Kokshagina *et al.*, 2017). Furthermore, intermediaries serve as vital sources of knowledge through mechanisms such as technical consultations, engineering education, and workshops aimed at introducing cutting-edge technologies (Fukugawa, 2017). Their involvement is especially crucial in the formation and administration of knowledge ecosystems, which are intricate networks comprised of individuals, institutions, organizations, and technologies. These ecosystems are responsible for the creation, interpretation, dissemination, and application of knowledge (Marozzo *et al.*, 2023). To explore this phenomenon further, we focus on a Japanese construction multinational company which operates globally but has a strong presence in the Asian market, especially in China. Our ambition is to explore how they successfully implement and cooperate with the Chinese construction market. To examine their behavior, we relied on a qualitative research design, typical of emerging topic areas (Eisenhardt, 1989), collecting both primary and secondary data from different sources. As for primary data, we conducted interviews in which we asked the business development manager of the company to explain their innovation intermediaries' strategy and processes, what actions they put in place to compete for construction bids in China, and how they build up the projects. We then complemented this information with data gathered from secondary sources, such as official data, press releases, and firms' websites; information retrieved on firms' websites was particularly useful to better understand how the company interacts with the innovation intermediaries in China. Based on theoretical sampling criteria, according to which cases are selected because they are particularly suitable for illuminating a phenomenon and for extending relationships and logic among variables (Eisenhardt,1989; De Massis and Kotlar, 2014), we selected this construction company as an empirical basis to conveniently examine our phenomenon of interest (Siggelkow, 2007). Within this framework, the connections facilitated by innovation intermediaries occur within spaces known as triple helix environments, which involve academia, industry, and government collaboration (Duan and Jin, 2021). These interactions may evolve into a quadruple helix model by incorporating the interests of local authorities, businesses, academic institutions, and the broader society.

In such settings, intermediaries also play a crucial role in interpreting information, particularly when the knowledge interests of involved parties diverge significantly. Moreover, in contexts marked by high complexity and uncertainty, these entities require enhanced resources and authority to effectively draw participants for productive cooperation. As the complexity and novelty of the challenges increase, the roles and functions of innovation intermediaries must adapt to meet these evolving demands (Iturrioz *et al.*, 2015). Particularly relevant is their role in the Chinese socio-economic landscape, where the evolution and role of innovation intermediaries have been crucial in promoting technology transfer and corporate innovation. These intermediaries, including government research institutes, science parks, business incubators, technology transfer offices, economic development organizations, industry associations, and business financing and support programs, have played a significant role in enabling the innovativeness of firms (Dalziel and Yao, 2010). Moreover, innovation intermediaries have positively contributed to regional innovation, especially in high-tech industries, highlighting their essential role in enhancing regional innovative capacities (Wu and Xu, 2013). Government support for these innovation intermediaries in China has manifested through policies aimed at promoting technology transfer. However, policy analysis has revealed significant challenges such as functional fragmentation and uneven regional development, suggesting the need for improvements in the functional positioning of intermediaries and the strengthening of mechanisms for the introduction and training of talents (Li and Cheng, 2017). The impact of intermediaries on corporate innovation in China has been further examined, showing that ties with intermediaries contribute to innovation by expanding the breadth of external innovation searches and reducing search costs. This chapter aims to dissect how innovation intermediaries are aiding enterprises in maneuvering through the complexities of China's rapidly changing technological environment (Kaiji *et al.*, 2022). Specifically, it will examine the role of innovation intermediaries in supporting the Chinese construction sector. Indeed, the globalized construction market is leading to a network of internationally interconnected projects and the rise of new competitors (Liu *et al.*, 2016). To remain competitive in such an environment, contractors are compelled to embrace innovations in products, services, and business models, as these three innovation types are essential for value creation in construction firms (Pan and Li, 2016).

2. Low-Medium-Technology Sectors

In the past decade, the innovation literature has mainly targeted high-tech (HT) sectors celebrated for their high return on investment and pivotal role in shaping new societies and economies. In general terms, innovation in LMT sectors is pivotal yet often overshadowed by high-tech industries. However, this emphasis on high-tech sectors has relegated to a somewhat secondary position the study of Low and Medium Technology (LMT) industries, which are equally critical to ensure long-term economic growth in both developed and emerging economies (Chong and Liu, 2023; Rotaba and Beaudry, 2012). While HT sectors are the primary producers of General Purpose Technologies (GPT), LMT sectors are their main users, integrating these technologies into their processes, organizations, and marketing strategies (Robertson *et al.*, 2009; Freddi, 2009). As underscored by Kirner *et al.* (2009), LMT sectors, despite their lower investment in traditional R&D, continue to contribute significantly to economic growth and technological advancement. For instance, Sandven *et al.* (2005) reveal that LMT sectors accounted for a higher percentage of manufacturing growth than high-tech sectors in OECD countries between 1981 and 1998. LMT firms innovate by integrating high-tech components into their existing products and processes, often acting as major consumers of high-tech innovations (Robertson *et al.*, 2003). This interaction promotes a balanced technological advancement across various sectors, crucial for comprehensive economic development. Moreover, the innovation process in LMT sectors often involves adapting new technologies to fit traditional frameworks, a strategy that requires subtlety and ingenuity, particularly as these firms frequently operate with legacy technologies (Patel and Pavitt, 1994). Thus, while LMT sectors may not dominate headlines, their role in sustaining innovation and facilitating widespread technological application is indispensable.

According to this background, the role of institutions and regulations becomes particularly significant in the diffusion of HT technologies, a factor that is crucial for LMT sectors amid increasing globalization and the rise of various international health and security policies (Rotaba and Beaudry, 2012). LMT industries are characterized by their reliance on external sources for innovation, particularly from suppliers who provide essential machines, equipment, and software. This dependency underscores the importance of embodied knowledge — the ability to adopt technical-organizational process components — in the innovativeness of LMT companies (Arundel *et al.*, 2008). The construction industry, which has historically been considered an LMT sector of activity, emerges as an excellent example of the ways in which companies operating in an LMT environment can benefit immensely from technologies and innovations produced by firms operating in HT sectors.

There is a growing body of digital technologies and innovations that are gradually being adopted by an equally expanding number of companies operating in different segments of the construction industry's vast supply chain. For example, BIM (Building Information Modeling) is becoming a critical tool to ensure that the planning, design, and construction of buildings are increasingly efficient and collaborative. If utilized to its maximum potential, BIM is a digital tool capable of linking all stakeholders involved in a construction project by allowing architects, engineers, general contractors, equipment manufacturers, and asset owners to interact with each other through all project stages via a 3D digital model of the building. Newer technologies such as drones, sensors, robots, systems that allow the remote operation of tower cranes, 3D printing, and cyber-physical systems that can be used as bi-dimensional connectors between virtual models of the building and their physical counterparts on-site are also starting to be adopted by the industry. By the same token, general contractors and all the other constitutive parts of the built environment sector will also take advantage of the benefits generated by Artificial Intelligence (AI) in areas such as resources and supply chain management, waste optimization, contract management, procurement, and safety management (Zhang *et al.*, 2023).

The role of LMT is particularly relevant also in the case of emerging economies. Knowledge generation through interaction within LMT sectors is a significant factor favoring economies that are catching up, as these economies are perceived to better facilitate the accessibility of funds for industrial growth, with notable implications for LMT sectors (Rotaba and Beaudry, 2012). It has been found that LMT industries are marked by process, organizational, and marketing innovations, with a reliance on external knowledge sources such as suppliers for their innovation capabilities (Heidenreich, 2009). Moreover, research shows that firms in LMT sectors often engage in search patterns focused on market knowledge, which differs from high-technology industries that concentrate more on technology sourcing (Grimpe and Sofka, 2009). Knowledge transfer within LMT sectors, particularly through informal local and global linkages, can lead to substantial improvements in technological capabilities (Chen, 2009). However, the dynamics of knowledge generation in LMT sectors suggest that these industries, while not traditionally seen as high-tech, play a crucial role in the broader innovation system. Industries traditionally labeled as 'low-tech' are now recognized for their complex and capital-intensive products and production processes, which are sometimes comparable to those found in high-tech sectors (Robertson *et al.*, 2009). The construction industry is an excellent example of such a change. As the industry becomes more digitized and building requirements more complex, the image and the perception that people have of the sector are changing fast. Still, it is important to recognize that the adoption of new technologies and digital tools, management practices, and construction methodologies vary widely across the industry. In fact, industry remains extremely heterogeneous and there are still a significant number of barriers preventing a more widespread transformation of industry. Among them, it is possible to identify regulatory barriers that may stifle competition and innovation in certain segments of the industry. A good example is the protection from which large general contractors benefit. Another factor typically associated with low adoption of new technologies and management practices is the rather conservative mindset of some business leaders. Finally, the cost of R&D is often too high for many companies, especially for SMEs such as small subcontractors.

Considering these insights, institutions specializing in LMT and export within economies striving to catch up are pivotal in broadening their global market presence. These entities not only comply with regulatory frameworks prior to commercialization but also strategically capture value from their innovations, safeguarding their outputs from being copied. While governments globally tend to focus on HT sectors, those in developing economies give special attention to LMT sectors, recognizing their critical role in economic advancement (Rotaba and Beaudry, 2012). Nevertheless, the formation of co-invention networks within LMT industries faces challenges, notably geographical constraints, which underscores the importance of regional policy measures to facilitate R&D collaboration across cities. Implementing such measures could enhance knowledge exchange and innovation renewal among LMT firms, boosting their competitiveness on an international scale (Chong and Liu, 2023).

3. Research Settings

China's construction industry, a critical sector within the LMT spectrum, has undergone significant transformation, paralleling the country's rapid economic expansion. Historically, as noted by Chen (1998), the industry has been a substantial contributor to the national economy, with an annual output of around USD 93 billion and employing over 24 million people. The sector's growth has been marked by an increasing involvement in international projects, with a cumulative overseas contract value reaching USD 38.3 billion by the end of 1994. China's construction industry, until recently perceived as an LMT sector, remains one of the main pillars of the country's economy. The sector has played a crucial role in the modernization and overall economic development of the nation. Since the years of the reform and opening era under the leadership of Deng Xiaoping, the construction industry enabled the transformation of China's physical infrastructure and became a major contributor to the country's astonishing process of urbanization. The remarkable development of Shenzhen from a small fishing village to a gleaming global metropolis and economic powerhouse, home of corporations such as Huawei and China's bustling tech industry, is in no small measure the product of the modernization of the design and engineering capabilities of indigenous firms (UN Habitat, 2019). Another example of the technological progress of China's construction capability can be seen in the country's impressive railway system which, at the end of December 2022, had about 42,000 km of track, about 13 times larger than Japan's shinkansen, which has around 3,300 km of tracks (Nikkei, 2023). To make sense of the place that the construction sector occupies in the Chinese economy, in the late 1990s, the industry's annual output was around USD 93 billion and employed over 24 million people. Fast-forward to 2022 and the industry's total output has reached USD 4.3 trillion and provided jobs to roughly 52 million people (Yiting, 2023; Chen, 1998). Like in many other prominent industries such as automotive or semiconductors, China's construction sector has benefited immensely from technology and knowledge transfer from foreign construction firms, mostly Western entities. In the 1980s and 1990s, it was common to see the construction of major infrastructure projects awarded to foreign construction firms. This was both because local construction firms lacked the project experience and engineering know-how to execute these projects and the Chinese provincial and municipal governments lacked the liquidity to finance them. In this context, the construction of the Shanghai No.1 Subway Line tells the story of a very different China from the one we know today. As JinDong and YiXin (1997) recount, although its construction was awarded to a cooperative venture formed by two German firms, Adtranz and Siemens, the project served as an investment magnet to more than 60 firms involved in subway construction from 12 countries around the world. Bidding sparked fierce competition in political, economic, and technological fields. Germany, France, Japan, and the United States were among the main competitors to secure the construction, financing, trains, and signaling technologies. Today, such a scenario is impossible to find as most infrastructure projects are awarded to China's large domestic general contractors. However, the entry of foreign contractors into the Chinese market has been limited, predominantly taking the form of joint ventures. The evolution of this sector is not just economic but also cultural and managerial. Recent research by Qin and Green (2022) sheds light on the internal tensions experienced by managers in the construction industry. These individuals often find themselves caught between dual identities: adhering to traditional practices and roles as "cadres of the party" while simultaneously aspiring to be modern entrepreneurs. This dichotomy reflects a broader struggle within the industry, balancing long-established practices with the pursuit of modernity and innovation. In the midst of significant industrialization, modernization, and urbanization, China is navigating a critical period of transformation (Wang and Zhang, 2011). This evolving landscape underscores the importance of innovation in construction, a sector where the success of projects is increasingly reliant on innovative approaches, as emphasized by Li (2008). Pinto and Covin (1989) categorize construction projects into two types: business and development (innovation) projects, highlighting the project-based and diverse nature of the industry (Ozorhon, 2013). The uniqueness of each project, according to Veshoskey (1998), presents ample opportunities for innovative behavior, a sentiment supported by Kulatunga *et al.* (2006, pp. 654–662). This tendency toward innovation is often most pronounced at the project level (Ozorhon, 2013; Winch, 2003; Widén *et al.*, 2013), with Ozorhon *et al.* (2014) identifying integration and leadership as key enablers. The success of construction innovation is not just about the innovation itself but also hinges on the ability to forge long-term, stable cooperation with suitable partners and to develop a conducive context using appropriate management skills (Cheng *et al.*, 2000). In this regard, the professionalism and credibility of partner firms become paramount, especially given the adversarial nature of many construction projects (Liu *et al*., 2014). Moreover, Liu *et al*. (2014) highlight that innovation-based cooperation extends beyond immediate project boundaries, encompassing long-term strategic collaboration within the entire innovation network. Currently, there are still many difficulties in the technological innovation of medium and small-sized enterprises (SMEs) in China, such as policy unavailability, fund shortage, training insufficiency, and so on. One of the most important reasons is that the intermediary service organization of science and technology cannot perform its function adequately between the government, academic institutions, and SMEs. Indeed, the construction industry is highly fragmented. A single construction project can easily have hundreds of stakeholders stretching from the construction materials suppliers and long lead equipment manufacturers all the way to architectural and engineering consultants, the general contractor, and the myriad of sub-contractors, many of them SMEs, that specialize in specific trades of the construction process such as pilling, civil and structural works, or mechanical and electrical activities to name only a few. For this reason, the technological transformation of the industry has been rather slow due to, in part, the challenges posed by the large number of agents involved in the delivery of a construction project as well as because of the pressures that project developers face to keep a lid on construction costs to simultaneously ensure the profitability and affordability of their investments.

Amidst this evolving landscape, the construction industry in China illustrates a complex interaction between traditional practices and modern technological demands, a dynamic shaped significantly by broader national policies and cultural factors. As Crupi (2021) elucidates, three distinct features of the Chinese scenario — cultural influences like guanxi, strong central technology transfer policies, and the ambitions of Chinese universities and technology-transfer entities — aim to position China as a global leader in science and technology. These elements have not only facilitated the flow of foreign expertise into China's construction sector but have also enhanced the capacity for domestic innovation. The strategic use of guanxi, or personal networks, has been instrumental in navigating the intricate political and social landscapes necessary for project approvals and collaborations. Coupled with robust governmental directives that prioritize technological advancement and the proactive stance of academic institutions in technology transfer, China is creating a fertile environment for transformative practices in construction. This unique blend of cultural, policy-driven, and academic influences is crucial as

China seeks to overcome challenges similar to those faced in advanced markets like Japan and Singapore, where the industry is driven by a combination of government initiative and cutting-edge technology. As China continues to refine its approach to integrating these elements, the potential for a more productive, safe, and sustainable construction industry grows, illustrating a critical shift from traditional methodologies to a more integrated, innovative approach. This transformation is essential as Chinese contractors increasingly engage with technology intermediaries to address the sector's pressing issues; mirroring efforts seen in other technologically advanced regions.

As in highly developed regional markets such as Japan and Singapore, which are at the forefront of technological innovation in the construction sector, Chinese general contractors in particular and the industry as a whole will have to deepen their collaboration with a number of technology intermediaries to address some of the most pressing challenges the sector currently faces. These include the industry's low levels of productivity, uneven enforcement of health and safety procedures, high levels of carbon emissions, frequent project delays, and cost overruns. To address these challenges, the Singapore government has recently launched the "Build Environment Industry Transformation Map" (BCA, 2022), an ambitious policy plan that seeks to foster collaboration between the key agents of the construction industry and other sectors of the economy to foster integrated planning and design of projects, accelerate the decarbonization of the industry's supply chain, promote the adoption of advanced manufacturing and off-site assembly to improve productivity, quality control and streamline logistical processes. In Japan, the rapid decline of the country's working-age population has long cemented its position as one of the government's top policy concerns. According to official estimates, by 2025 the number of workers at construction sites is forecasted to drop by 1.3 million, a problem that is expected to lead to rising costs, longer construction schedules, and lower productivity levels. As a result, the government has created a number of different policy initiatives to work with a number of different technology intermediaries and private enterprises to develop and implement new construction technologies using ICT tools and the use of robotic solutions (The Government of Japan, 2017; Hirikoshi, 2019). The country's "big five" general contractors — Kajima, Obayashi, Shimizu, Takenaka, and Shimizu — are expected to be the leaders of the industry's transformation, adoption of automation and ICT tools by making use of their experience, know-how, and the work of large research and development institutes (Hirikoshi, 2019; Bennett, 1993). In order to remain competitive with similar economies, the role of intermediaries becomes significant. Hou *et al.* (2019) highlight that the collaboration between industry and academia, facilitated by intermediaries, plays a vital role in improving industrial innovation performance in China. This is particularly true in the construction sector in China, where the complexity and scale of projects necessitate a diverse range of knowledge and expertise. Research by Xia and Chan (2012) underscores the multifaceted nature of project complexity, identifying factors such as project scale and environmental conditions as key measures of this complexity, thus highlighting the need for a broad spectrum of expert knowledge to manage the potential risks associated with such large-scale endeavors (Xia and Chan, 2012).

Further emphasizing this point, He *et al.* (2015) developed a model to measure the intricacies of mega construction projects, incorporating aspects like technological and organizational complexities, which are critical to the successful execution of these projects in the Chinese context (He *et al.*, 2015). These studies collectively affirm that the construction sector's expansion and complexity in China demand a multidisciplinary approach, integrating varied expertise to navigate the challenges presented by its dynamic growth. Similarly, Wu and Xu (2013) emphasize that technology intermediaries contribute positively to regional product-related innovation, indicating their importance in sectors like construction, which require continuous product and process innovation.

4. Innovation Intermediaries

Innovation intermediaries, as defined by Howells (2006, p. 720), are organizations or bodies that act as agents or brokers in various aspects of the innovation process between multiple parties. These intermediaries are pivotal in facilitating the innovation process, a role increasingly recognized in the literature (Boon *et al.*, 2011; Howells, 2006). They facilitate knowledge sharing and technology transfer, acting as matchmakers between supply and demand (Coppolino and Abbate, 2012). Moreover, these intermediaries are diverse, with different types serving different interests and imposing different conditions (Pollard, 2006). Their survival over time depends on their ability to adapt to changing conditions and their knowledge management capabilities (Kant and Kanda, 2019). The complexity of modern innovation processes, involving diverse actors, networks, and institutions, has led to the emergence of "systemic intermediaries" (van Lente *et al.*, 2003). These entities operate not just at the level of individual firms or projects, but across broader networks, within innovation systems or socio-technical transitions (Kivimaa, 2014; Klerkx and Leeuwis, 2009; van Lente *et al.*, 2003). Kivimaa (2014) underscores the importance of neutrality for the success and longevity of these intermediaries, emphasizing their independence from public administration, politics, finance, or technology. Kant and Kanda (2019) further elaborate that the survival of innovation intermediaries hinges on several factors, including neutrality, technological context, shared consensus, and internal value creation. The innovation intermediaries' context in China, even if is shaped by a legacy of central control and planned regional specialization, is still adept at supporting technology adoption and incremental innovation. However, it may face challenges in fostering innovation that transcends industrial or disciplinary boundaries or that deviates from the system's original design (Dalziel and Yao, 2010). In this complex environment, innovation intermediaries assume roles such as technology gatekeepers, technology spanners, technical problem solvers, and innovation resource integrators (Guo and Guo, 2013). At the technology acquisition stage within industrial clusters, they act as gatekeepers, introducing and integrating external knowledge into local systems. During the technology diffusion stage, they serve as spanners, transferring technology or ideas between firms. Finally, in the technology application stage, they emerge as problem solvers, offering customized solutions to accessibility-driven issues faced by cluster firms. However, regional disparities in China depict a complicated landscape. Indeed, as stated previously by Chong *et al.*, (2021), China lives a noticeable imbalance in regional economic development, with economic prosperity gradually diminishing from the eastern coastal areas to the inland regions. For instance, compared to northwestern regions like Shaanxi, southeastern coastal areas and Beijing have distinct location advantages in market mechanisms, international openness, and intellectual property rights protection. These regional differences in institutional environments are crucial in understanding how innovation intermediaries contribute to outbound open innovation through absorptive capacity. In this regard, Zeng *et al.* (2023) highlight that due to variations in resource endowment, geographical location, stage of economic development, and historical and cultural factors, there are significant disparities even in the level of smart city development across different regions.

Innovation serves as a vital catalyst for high-quality regional economic development. In recent years, the Chinese government has been actively seeking innovative approaches to enhance regional innovation levels. This subnational spatial heterogeneity means that different regions offer varying opportunities and constraints for construction firms (Li *et al.*, 2019; Hitt *et al.*, 2016). The construction of smart cities has been identified as a key initiative in the pursuit of an innovation-driven development strategy (Zeng *et al.*, 2023). This approach underscores the government's commitment to leveraging innovation as a means to address regional disparities and foster balanced economic growth across the country. It is necessary to clarify that due to this spatial heterogeneity, institutions can be broadly classified as formal and informal ones. Institutions govern societal transactions in the areas of politics (e.g., corruption and transparency), law (e.g., economic liberalization, regulatory regime), and society (e.g., ethical norms and attitudes toward entrepreneurship. (Peng *et al.*, 2008).

Institutional theory posits that these institutional environments significantly influence firm strategy and operations (Li *et al.*, 2019; Hitt *et al.*, 2016). Furthermore, even on a microlevel, the role of intermediaries becomes crucial; Marrone *et al.* (2007) highlight that in the interactions between providers and recipients of technology, teams dedicated to technology transfer employ external networks and boundary-spanning activities to fulfill their objectives. Consequently, it is imperative for intermediaries in technology transfer to acknowledge the significance of these boundary-spanning (TBS) activities, given their substantial contribution to enhancing team effectiveness and, in turn, team performance (Kaiji *et al.*, 2022). It is essential for these intermediaries to bolster their top-down management of tasks. The inclination of technology transfer intermediaries to partake in TBS activities is influenced by factors such as the interdependence of tasks, their complexity, and the pressure of time constraints. In scenarios where tasks are intricately interdependent, complex, and time-sensitive, intermediaries in technology transfer are naturally inclined to undertake TBS activities. Managers in this field should assess the need for such activities based on their understanding of the task's interdependence, complexity, and timing. Additionally, enhancing the team efficacy of members through the adoption of a flat organizational structure is crucial. This can be further augmented by forming a team of skilled technology transfer professionals, which would not only improve boundary-spanning communication skills among team members but also streamline communication with external partners (Kaiji *et al.*, 2022).

5. Methodology, Data Collection, and Analysis

This chapter employs an explanatory single case study approach to investigate the challenges and obstacles encountered by an international construction firm operating within the Chinese market. This method is particularly appropriate for exploring the complexities of innovation within the construction sector. The challenges inherent in fostering innovation in this sector necessitate a thorough exploration of the dynamics involving innovation intermediaries. Qualitative studies are essential for rendering these concepts actionable and relevant to real-world scenarios (Randhawa *et al.*, 2021). Additionally, given the continuous evolution of innovation intermediaries, this study seeks to illuminate the less-explored aspects of LMT industries, such as construction in China, and the specific challenges faced by foreign firms like the one examined here.

The study conducts an exploratory analysis of the international corporation's activities in the Chinese construction market. This case provides an ideal context to investigate the distinct challenges and strategies pertinent to foreign innovation intermediaries within the Chinese construction sector. An in-depth case study will yield valuable insights into the strategies and approaches employed by the corporation to navigate the complex market dynamics and regulatory landscapes in China. By analyzing how the corporation orchestrates innovation and manages its entry into the Chinese construction business environment, this study will make a significant contribution to the existing body of knowledge, particularly in the areas of cross-border market entry strategies and innovation management in emerging economies.

Building upon existing scholarship that examines the role of innovation intermediaries in LMT sectors, with a particular focus on the construction industry (Intarakumnerd and Chaoroenporn, 2013), this study adopted a dual approach to data collection: primary data through in-depth interviews and secondary data analysis. The latter involved extensive information gathered from the corporation's official channels, including website, social media platforms, press releases, and relevant news articles retrieved using Nvivo software. This secondary data was invaluable in understanding the initiatives of the corporation and the measures it undertakes to nurture and manage its relationships with innovation intermediaries.

The evaluation of gathered data employed a recursive method that progressively refined the theoretical framework based on empirical findings from the case study, following established qualitative research practices (Harrell and Bradley, 2009; Kallio *et al.*, 2016). The authors collectively synthesized the validated data. The initial stage involved hands-on categorization and contemplation of secondary source data. Through the process of qualitative coding, we translated raw data into basic constructs indicative of the case-relevant activities (Corbin and Strauss, 2014). This primary categorization drew on fundamental terms like "Innovation Intermediaries" and "Open Innovation" This was followed by an amalgamation and enhancement of the information arising from the secondary data with the primary data insights. In line with literature-derived concepts such as innovation intermediaries and open innovation, the analysis pinpointed concrete operations within the Corporation's innovation activities.

6. Discussion and Conclusions

China's construction market, characterized by its large, state-affiliated general contractors, operates within a framework deeply embedded in networks of political influence, known as guanxi. This traditional system of relationships is crucial for securing contracts for substantial infrastructure and transportation projects. During the 1980s and early 1990s, as China opened its market to foreign investments and strengthened ties with the United States, foreign contractors played a significant role in key infrastructure projects like the construction of Shanghai Metro's Line 1. However, this scenario has dramatically evolved, reflecting substantial progress within Chinese construction firms in methodologies, engineering, and technological capabilities. Chinese contractors now dominate the construction sector, benefiting from substantial public investments and legal protections that restrict foreign competition. This environment has facilitated extensive opportunities for local firms to gain project experience and knowledge through joint ventures and collaborations with foreign contractors. Consequently, foreign construction firms have adapted by carving out niches in the market, particularly targeting greenfield foreign direct investment projects from multinational corporations (MNCs).

The interplay between traditional practices and modern technological demands in the Chinese construction industry is significantly influenced by national policies and cultural factors. Guanxi remains instrumental in navigating the political and social landscapes necessary for project approvals and collaborations. This traditional network system, coupled with robust governmental directives and the proactive stance of academic institutions in technology transfer, has created a fertile environment for transformative practices in construction. China's transition from a factor-driven to an innovation-driven economy is pivotal for achieving its goal of becoming a global leader in innovation. Despite the progress, significant disparities remain between China's innovative cities and those in more developed nations. The construction sector, with its substantial role in urban development, significantly impacts China's socio-economic and environmental fabric. Effective management of this sector is crucial for driving technological innovations that promote resource-efficient and eco-friendly construction practices.

The importance of innovative cities in driving economic and social progress across China cannot be overstated. These cities are instrumental in setting standards, enforcing regulations, and fostering cooperation between industry stakeholders and academic institutions to promote sustainable practices and advance innovation within the construction industry. Intermediaries play a crucial role in this ecosystem, primarily focusing on fostering autonomous innovation and significant breakthroughs in key areas. Their strategies should be market-oriented, leveraging regional interactions and supported by a robust talent base. Innovation intermediaries are essential in bridging the existing gaps in technology adoption and enhancing the industry's capacity for innovation. Policy plays a critical role as an external factor influencing the construction sector. Policymakers must reevaluate regulations and market dynamics to create an environment that encourages technological progress. Environmental regulations at the city level are particularly crucial for boosting urban innovation capabilities and promoting sustainable practices, given China's status as the world's largest carbon emitter. Research has shown a significant reduction in carbon emissions following the adoption of innovative city construction strategies. While intermediaries are indispensable, Chinese firms must also cultivate the capabilities necessary for effectively identifying, assimilating, and commercializing external knowledge and technologies. This approach will maximize the benefits of openness and propel the country's innovative drive forward.

In the broader context of LMT sectors, the construction industry exemplifies how LMT environments can benefit from high-tech innovations. Building Information Modeling (BIM), drones, sensors, and AI are among the technologies gradually being adopted by construction firms, enhancing efficiency, safety, and sustainability. These technologies facilitate integrated planning, design, and execution of projects, fostering a collaborative approach among stakeholders. The role of LMT sectors in emerging economies is particularly relevant. Knowledge generation through interactions within these sectors significantly contributes to economic growth and technological advancement. LMT industries, while often overshadowed by high-tech sectors, play a crucial role in sustaining innovation and facilitating the widespread application of technologies. In China, the construction industry's transformation illustrates the critical role of LMT sectors in driving national development. Figure 1 shows a proposed integrative model for innovation in China's construction industry that encapsulates the dynamic interplay between government policies, innovation intermediaries, traditional practices, and modern technological demands. At its core, the model emphasizes the pivotal role of innovation intermediaries as facilitators of knowledge transfer, technology adoption, and collaboration across diverse stakeholders. Traditional practices, such as guanxi networks and the influence of state-affiliated contractors, are juxtaposed with modern technological advancements like BIM, drones, and AI, reflecting a sector in transition. Regional disparities further complicate the landscape, highlighting the uneven economic and technological development between coastal and inland regions. The collaborative ecosystem, comprising industry stakeholders and academic institutions, is crucial for driving innovation and addressing pressing challenges like productivity, safety, and sustainability. This model underscores the importance of a holistic approach, where coordinated efforts among government, industry, and academia can foster a more innovative, efficient, and sustainable construction industry in China.

The construction industry's evolution in China highlights the importance of institutions and regulations in facilitating technological diffusion. The dependency of LMT industries on external sources for innovation underscores the significance of embodied knowledge in their innovativeness. Institutions specializing in LMT and export within economies striving to catch up are pivotal in broadening their global market presence and ensuring compliance with regulatory frameworks prior to commercialization. The regional disparities within China present a complex landscape for innovation intermediaries. Economic prosperity and development levels vary significantly across regions, affecting the effectiveness of innovation intermediaries. Southeastern coastal areas and cities like Beijing have distinct advantages in market mechanisms, international openness, and intellectual property rights protection compared to northwestern regions.

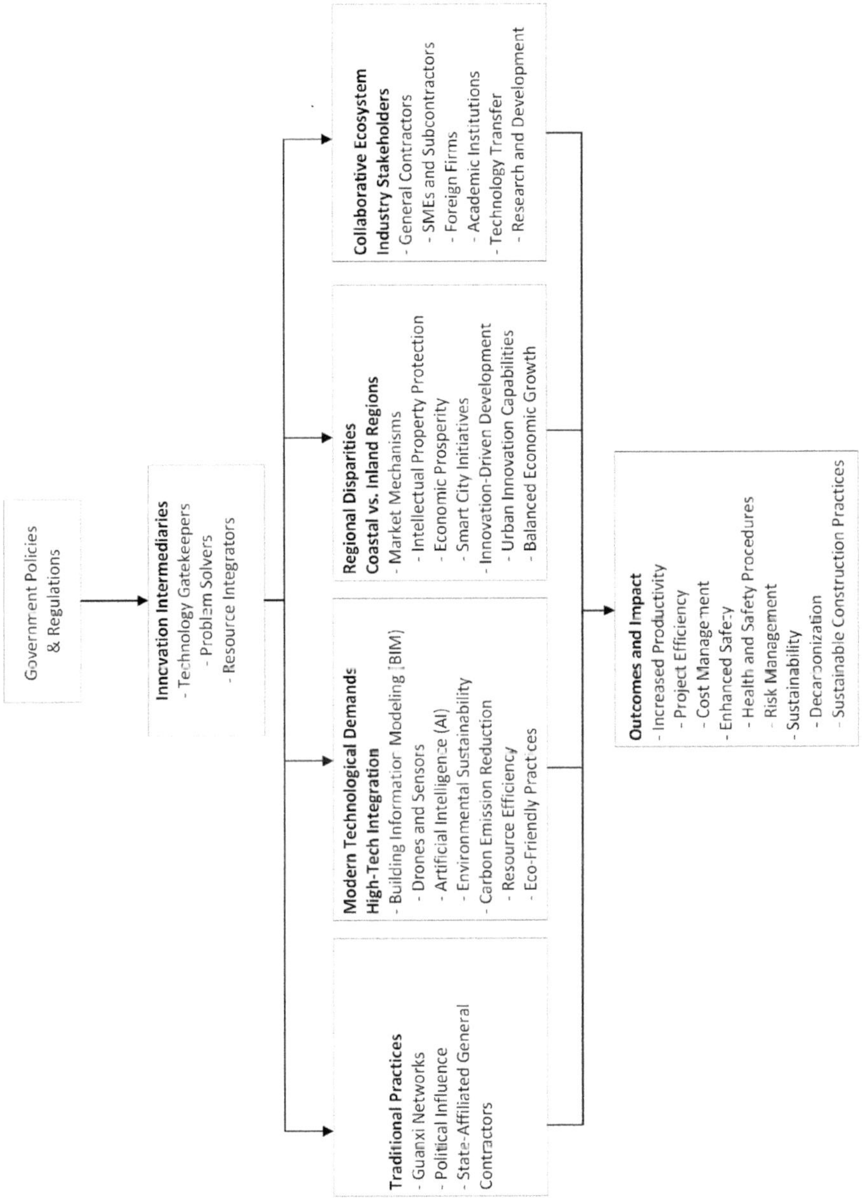

Figure 1. Integrative model for innovation in China's construction industry.

These regional differences influence how innovation intermediaries contribute to outbound open innovation through absorptive capacity. The construction of smart cities has emerged as a key initiative in promoting innovation-driven development in China. This approach underscores the government's commitment to leveraging innovation to address regional disparities and foster balanced economic growth. The spatial heterogeneity across China necessitates a nuanced understanding of institutional environments and their impact on firm strategy and operations.

Intermediaries must adapt to the evolving demands of the construction industry, characterized by increasing complexity and scale. They play critical roles in facilitating collaboration, knowledge transfer, and technology adoption. The success of construction projects increasingly relies on innovative approaches and long-term, stable cooperation with suitable partners. The professionalism and credibility of partner firms are paramount, particularly given the adversarial nature of many construction projects. The transformation of China's construction industry from a low to medium technology sector to one that increasingly integrates high-tech innovations underscores the critical role of innovation intermediaries. These entities facilitate knowledge sharing, technology transfer, and collaboration, driving the industry's evolution toward greater efficiency, safety, and sustainability. Policymakers, industry stakeholders, and academic institutions must continue to foster an environment conducive to innovation, ensuring that the construction sector contributes effectively to China's broader economic and technological aspirations.

References

Ahn, J. M., Minshall, T., and Mortara, L. (2017). Understanding the human side of openness: The fit between open innovation modes and CEO characteristics. *R&D Management*, 47(5), 727–740.

Almeida, F., Santos, J., and Monteiro, J. (2020). The challenges and opportunities in the digitalization of companies in a post-COVID-19 world. *IEEE Engineering Management Review*, 48, 97–103. https://doi.org/10.1109/EMR.2020.3013206.

Angelidou, M. (2015). Smart cities: A conjuncture of four forces. *Cities*, 47, 95–106.

Arundel, A., Bordoy, C., and Kanerva, M. (2008). Neglected innovators: How do innovative firms that do not perform R&D innovate? Results of an analysis of the Innobarometer 2007 survey No. 215. *INNO-Metrics Thematic Paper*.

Boon, W. P. C., Moors, E. H. M., Kuhlmann, S., and Smits, R. E. H. M. (2011). Demand articulation in emerging technologies: Intermediary user organisations as co-producers? *Research Policy*, 40, 242–252.

Chen, H. H., Chen, S., and Lan, Y. (2016). Attaining a sustainable competitive advantage in the smart grid industry of China using suitable open innovation intermediaries. *Renewable and Sustainable Energy Reviews*, 62, 1083–1091. https://doi.org/10.1016/j.rser.2016.03.008.

Chen, L.-C. (2009). Learning through informal local and global linkages: The case of Taiwan's machine tool industry. *Research Policy*, 38(3), 527–535.

Cheng, E. W., Li, H., and Love, P. E. D. (2000). Establishment of critical success factors for construction partnering. *Journal of Management in Engineering*, 16(2), 84–92.

Coppolino, R. and Abbate, T. (2012). Knowledge sharing and innovation: The contribution of innovation intermediaries. In *Information systems: Crossroads for organization, management, accounting and engineering: ItAIS: The Italian Association for Information Systems* (pp. 251–258). Physica-Verlag HD.

Crupi, A. (2021). Technology transfer and team boundary-spanning activities and their antecedents: Do the classic measures apply to China? *R&D Management*, 51(3), 260–272. https://doi.org/10.1111/RADM.12441.

Crupi, A., Del Sarto, N., Di Minin, A., and Kenney, M. F. (2022). Disentangling the importance of digital platforms and absorptive capacity in digital business ecosystems. In *Handbook on Digital Business Ecosystems* (pp. 40–49). Edward Elgar Publishing.

Crupi, A., Del Sarto, N., Di Minin, A., Gregori, G. L., Lepore, D., Marinelli, L., and Spigarelli, F. (2020). The digital transformation of SMEs-a new knowledge broker called the digital innovation hub. *Journal of Knowledge Management*. https://doi.org/10.1108/JKM-11-2019-0623.

Dalziel, M. and Yao, W. (2010). Innovation intermediaries in China. http://ssrn.com/abstract=2630739.

Demirkan, H., Spohrer, J. C., & Welser, J. J. (2016). Digital innovation and strategic transformation. *It Professional*, 18(6), 14–18.

Dente, B., and Coletti, P. (2011). Measuring governance in urban innovation. *Local Government Studies*, 37(1), 43–56.

Di Minin, A., Gregori, G. L., Spigarelli, F., Kenney, M., Lanzolla, G., Lepore, D., Nambisan, S., Tucci, C. L., Zahra, S. A., Crupi, A., Del Sarto, N., and Marinelli, L. (2019). Digital transformation & firms' innovative strategies: Capabilities, ecosystems, and business models. *Academy of Management Proceedings*, 2019(1), 14623. https://doi.org/10.5465/ambpp.2019.14623 symposium.

Duan, R. and Jin, L. (2021). The role of public innovation intermediaries plays in regional innovation: A comparative study of two regions in Japan. *Technology Analysis & Strategic Management*, 34(5), 578–593.

Eisenhardt, K. M. (1989). Building theories from case study research. *The Academy of Management Review*, 14(4), 532–550. doi:10.2307/258557.

Fang, C. Liu, Y., and Lin, Y. (2013). *Report on Development of Innovative Cities in China*. Beijing: Science Press, 2–3 (in Chinese).

Fang, C., Ma, H., Wang, Z., and Li, G. (2014). The sustainable development of innovative cities in China: Comprehensive assessment and future configuration. *Journal of Geographical Sciences*, 24(6), 1095–1114. https://doi.org/10.1007/s11442-014-1141-z.

Fang, C. and Xiong, S. (2014). A software for comprehensive evaluation and dynamic monitoring for Chinese innovative cities (V1.0), National Computer Software Certificate Registration No.2011SR082055. (in Chinese).

Freddi, D. (2009). The integration of old and new technological paradigms in low- and medium-tech sectors: The case of mechatronics. *Research Policy*, 38, 548–558.

Fukugawa, N. (2017). University spillover before the national innovation system reform in Japan. *International Journal of Technology Management*, 73(4), 206–234.

Gentile-Lüdecke, S., de Oliveira, R. T., and Paul, J. (2019). Does organizational structure facilitate inbound and outbound open innovation in SMEs. *Small Business Economics*. Published online: May 14, 2019.

Granstrand, O. and Holgersson, M. (2020). Innovation ecosystems: A conceptual review and a new definition. *Technovation*, 90, 102098.

Grimpe, C. and Sofka, W. (2009). Search patterns and absorptive capacity: Low- and high-technology sectors in European countries. *Research Policy*, 38(3), 495–506.

Guo, J. and Guo, B. (2013). How do innovation intermediaries facilitate knowledge spillovers within industrial clusters? A knowledge-processing perspective. *Asian Journal of Technology Innovation*, 21(sup2), 31–49. https://doi.org/10.1080/19761597.2013.819245.

Hansen, T. and Winther, L. (2015). Manufacturing in the knowledge economy: Innovation in low-tech industries.

Harrell, M. C. and Bradley, M. (2009). Data collection methods: Semi-structured interviews and focus groups. *RAND Corporation*.

Heidenreich, M. (2009). Innovation patterns and location of European low- and medium-technology industries. *Research Policy*, 38(3), 483–494.

Hirotsu, C. (2000). Statistical training of researchers in total quality management: The Japanese experience. *Training Researchers in the Use of Statistics IASE Roundtable Conference*. https://doi.org/10.52041/srap.00103.

Hitt, M. A., Li, D., and Xu, K. (2016). International strategy: From local to global and beyond. *Journal of World Business*, 51(1), 58–73.

Hou, B., Hong, J., Chen, Q., Shi, X., and Zhou, Y. (2019). Do academia-industry R&D collaborations necessarily facilitate industrial innovation in China?

The role of technology transfer institutions. *European Journal of Innovation Management*, 22(5), 717–746. https://doi.org/10.1108/EJIM-09-2018-0195.

Howells, J. (2006). Intermediation and the role of intermediaries in innovation. *Research Policy*, 35, 715–728.

Hua, L., Mei, L., and Mei, S. (2011). Shortcomings and innovative strategies of technology innovation in Chinese construction industry. *Journal of Engineering Management*, 25, 359–363.

Huang, F., Rice, J., and Martin, N. (2015). Does open innovation apply to China? Exploring the contingent role of external knowledge sources and internal absorptive capacity in Chinese large firms and SMEs. *Journal of Management and Organization*, 21(5), 594–613. https://doi.org/10.1017/jmo.2014.79.

Intarakumnerd, P., and Chaoroenporn, P. (2013). The roles of intermediaries and the development of their capabilities in sectoral innovation systems: A case study of Thailand. *Asian Journal of Technology Innovation*, 21(1), 99–114.

Iturrioz, C., Aragon, C and Narvaiza, L. (2015). How to foster shared innovation within SMEs' networks: Social capital and the role of intermediaries. *European Management Journal*, 33(2), 104–115.

Kagermann, H., Wahlster, W., and Helbig, J. (2013). *Recommendations for implementing the strategic initiative INDUSTRIE 4.0: Final report of the Industrie 4.0 working group*. Acatech.

Kaiji, X., Crupi, A., Di Minin, A., and Cesaroni, F. (2022). Team boundary-spanning activities and performance of technology transfer organizations: Evidence from China. *Journal of Technology Transfer*, 47(1), 33–62. https://doi.org/10.1007/s10961-021-09843-8.

Kant, M. and Kanda, W. (2019). Innovation intermediaries: What does it take to survive over time? *Journal of Cleaner Production*. https://doi.org/10.1016/j.jclepro.2019.04.213.

Kirner, E., Kinkel, S., and Jaeger, A. (2009). Innovation paths and the innovation performance of low-technology firms — An empirical analysis of German industry. *Research Policy*, 38(3), 447–458.

Kokshagina, O., Le Masson, P., and Bories, F. (2017). Fast-connecting search practices: On the role of open innovation intermediary to accelerate the absorptive capacity. *Technological Forecasting and Social Change*, 120, 232–239.

Kulatunga, K. J., Amaratunga, R. D. G., and Haigh, R. P. (2006). Construction innovation: A literature review on current research. Salford: *University of Salford.*

Lee, J., Suh, T., Roy, D., and Baucus, M. (2019). Emerging technology and business model innovation: The case of artificial intelligence. *Journal of Open Innovation: Technology, Market, and Complexity*, 5(3). https://doi.org/10.3390/joitmc5030044.

Li, B. C. (2008). Engineering innovation: The major battle field of innovative activities. *Chinese Soft Science*, (10), 44–51.

Li, B. C. (2010). *Engineering innovation: Break through the barriers and avoid the traps*. Hangzhou: Zhejiang University Press.

Li, Y., Song, Y., Wang, J., and Li, C. (2019). Intellectual capital, knowledge sharing, and innovation performance: Evidence from the Chinese construction industry. *Sustainability*, 11(9). https://doi.org/10.3390/su11092713.

Liu, G., Li, K., Zhao, D., Asce, A. M., and Mao, C. (2016). Business model innovation and its drivers in the Chinese construction industry during the shift to modular prefabrication. https://doi.org/10.1061/(ASCE)ME.1943-5479.

Liu, H., Wang, M., Skibniewski, M. J., He, J., and Zhang, Z. (2014). Identification of critical success factors for construction innovation: From the perspective of strategic cooperation. *Frontiers of Engineering Management*, 1(2), 202. https://doi.org/10.15302/j-fem-2014027.

Marozzo, V., Abbate, T., Cesaroni, F., Crupi, A., and Di Minin, A. (2023). Orchestrating an open innovation ecosystem in low-tech industries: The case of Barilla's Blu1877. *Technology Analysis & Strategic Management*, 1–16.

Matsuoka, Y. (2014). Building communications system: Takenaka's M2M platform for building management & application interface. *Proceedings of PICMET '14 Conference: Portland International Center for Management of Engineering and Technology; Infrastructure and Service Integration*, 1746–1758.

Mount, M., Milewski, S., and Fernandes, K. (2015). Exploring the knowledge complexities of innovation intermediaries: The case of nanotechnology in the UK. *International Journal of Technology Management*, 69(1), 20–37.

Ozorhon, B. (2013). Analysis of construction innovation process at project level. *Journal of Management in Engineering*, 29(4), 455–463.

Ozorhon, B., Abbott, C., and Aouad, G. (2014). Integration and leadership as enablers of innovation in construction: A case study. *Journal of Management in Engineering*, 30(2), 256–263.

Pan, W. and Li, K. J. (2016). Clusters and exemplars of buildings towards zero carbon. *Building and Environment*, 104, 92–101.

Patel, P. and Pavitt, K. (1994). The continuing, widespread (and neglected) importance of improvements in mechanical technologies. *Research Policy*, 23, 533–545. Pearson, M. (1994). The Janus face of business associations in China: Socialist corporatism in foreign enterprises. *The Australian Journal of Chinese Affairs*, 31, 25–46.

Peng, T. and Deng, H. (2020). Research on the sustainable development process of low-carbon pilot cities: The case study of Guiyang, a low-carbon pilot city in south-west China. *Environmental Development and Sustainability*, 23, 2382–2403.

Pflaum, A. and Golzer, P. (2018). The IoT and digital transformation: Toward the data-driven enterprise. *IEEE Pervasive Computing*, 17, 87–91.

Pollard, D. (2006). Innovation and technology transfer intermediaries: A systemic international study. In *Innovation through collaboration* (Vol. 12, pp. 137–174). Emerald Group Publishing Limited.

Randhawa, K., Wilden, R., and Gudergan, S. (2021). Innovation ecosystems: A conceptual review and a new definition. *Technovation*, 90, 102098.

Reier Forradellas, R. F. and Garay Gallastegui, L. M. (2021). Digital transformation and artificial intelligence applied to business: Legal regulations, economic impact and perspective. *Laws*, 10(3). https://doi.org/10.3390/laws 10030070.

Reuter, E. (2021). Hybrid business models in the sharing economy: The role of business model design for managing the environmental paradox. *Journal of Business Strategy and the Environment*, 31(2), 603–618.

Robertson, P. L., Pol, E., and Carroll, P. (2003). Receptive capacity of established industries as a limiting factor in the economy's rate of innovation. *Industry and Innovation*, 10, 457–474.

Robertson, P. L., Smith, K., and von Tunzelmann, N. (2009). Innovation in low- and medium-technology industries. *Research Policy*, 38(3), 441–446.

Robertson, P., Smith, K. and Tunzelman, N. (2009). Innovation in low and medium technology industries [Introduction]. *Research Policy*, 38, 441–446.

Ruslin, R., Mashuri, S., Rasak, M. S. A., Alhabsyi, F., and Syam, H. (2022). Semi-structured Interview: A methodological reflection on the development of a qualitative research instrument in educational studies. *IOSR Journal of Research & Method in Education (IOSR-JRME)*, 12(1), 22–29.

Sandven, T., Smith, K., and Kaloudis, A. (2005). Structural change, growth and innovation: The roles of medium and low-tech industries, 1980–2000. In H. Hirsch-Kreinsen, D. Jacobson, and S. Laestadius (Eds.), *Low-tech innovation in the knowledge economy* (pp. 31–59). Peter Lang.

Saklit, I. W. (2017). Pengaruh gaya kepemimpinan dan pengembangan karir terhadap intensi turnover: Kepuasan kerja sebagai mediator. *Jurnal Manajement*, 472–496. https://doi.org/10.24912/jm.v21i3.263.

Serger, S. S. and Breidne, M. (2007). China's fifteen-year plan for science and technology: An assessment. *Asia Policy*, 4, 135–164.

Sjoholt, O. (1997). A summary of project 189. *Building Research and Information*, 25(1), 3–4.

Smedlund, A. (2006). The roles of intermediaries in a regional knowledge system. *Journal of Intellectual Capital*, 7(2), 204–220.

Van Lente, H., Hekkert, M., Smits, R., and van Waveren, B. (2003). Roles of systemic intermediaries in transition processes. *International Journal of Innovation Management*, 7, 247–279.

Veshosky, D. (1998). Managing innovation information in engineering and construction firms. *Journal of Management in Engineering*, 14(1), 58–66.

Voss, C. (2010). Case research in operations management. In C. Karlsson (Ed.), *Researching operations management* (pp. 176–209). London, UK: Routledge.

Wåge, D. and Crawford, G. E. (2017). Innovation in digital business models. In *Proceedings of the 2017 XXVIII ISPIM Innovation Conference on Composing the Innovation Symphony*, Vienna, Austria, 18–21 June 2017.

Wang, M. J. and Zhang, Z. S. (2011). Analyse of the formation and operation mechanism for technological innovation network of major construction projects. *Chinese Engineering Science*, 13(8), 62–66.

Wang, N. (2014). The role of the construction industry in China's sustainable urban development. *Habitat International*, 44, 442–450.

Wang, M. and Yang, Q. (2022). The heterogeneous treatment effect of low-carbon city pilot policy on stock return: A generalized random forests approach. *Financial Research Letters*, 47, 102808.

Wei, C. and Kong, J. (2022). The effect of innovation city construction on carbon emissions in China. *Land*, 11(7), 1099; https://doi.org/10.3390/land11071099.

Westerman, G., Bonnet, D., and McAfee, A. (2014). *Leading Digital: Turning Technology into Business Transformation*. Boston: *Harvard Business Press*.

Widén, K., Olander, S., and Atkin, B. (2013). Links between successful innovation diffusion and stakeholder engagement. *Journal of Management in Engineering*, 30(5), (04014018)1–(04014018)7.

Winch, G. M. (2003). How innovative is construction? Comparing aggregated data on construction innovation and other sectors — a case of apples and pears. *Construction Management and Economics*, 21(6), 651–654.

Wu, J. and Xu, M. (2013). Technology intermediaries and regional innovation performance: An empirical study in China. *Asian Journal of Technology Innovation*, 21(1), 19–7.

Xia, B. and Chan, A. (2012). Measuring complexity for building projects: A Delphi study. *Engineering, Construction and Architectural Management*, 19, 7–24. https://doi.org/10.1108/09699981211192544.

Xiang, D., Zhao, T., and Zhang, N. (2021). Does public subsidy promote sustainable innovation? The case of Chinese high-tech SMEs. *Environmental Science and Pollution Research*, 28, 53493–53506. https://doi.org/10.1007/s11356-021-14555-5.

Xie, Y., Xu, K., and Huang, J. Q. (2020). How do innovation intermediaries influence outbound open innovation in China? A moderated mediation mechanism. *IEEE Transactions*.

Yang, H., Duan, Y., Song, W., and Zhao, H. (2018) A comparative study on the construction model of innovation-type provinces in China. *Current Urban Studies*, 6, 223–242. https://doi.org/10.4236/cus.2018.62013.

Zhang, Y., Zheng, J., and Darko, A. (2018). How does transformational leadership promote innovation in construction? The mediating role of innovation climate and the multilevel moderation role of project requirements. *Sustainability*, 10, 1506. https://doi.org/10.3390/SU10051506.

Zhao, N., Fan, D., Chen, Y., and Wu, C. (2023). Impact of innovation organization network on the synergy of cross-organizational technological innovation: Evidence from megaproject practices in China. *Journal of Civil Engineering and Management*. https://doi.org/10.3846/jcem.2023.18051.

https://doi.org/10.1142/9789819807611_0005

Chapter 5

Preparing Lab Technologies for the Market: Proof-of-Concept Centers in China

Xinhua Jiang*,‡ and Ya-Feng Zhang†,§

**Institutes of Science and Development, Chinese Academy of Sciences, Beijing, China*

†Faculty of Business, City University of Macau, Macau, China

‡jiangxinhua22@mails.ucas.ac.cn

§yfzhang@cityu.edu.mo (corresponding author)

Abstract

Technology transfer is a process of mutual integration of complex, multiple heterogeneous elements of innovation. Proof of concept (POC) is the latest attempt to promote technology transfer. The proof-of-concept center (POCC) is an innovation intermediary organization for the transfer of laboratory technologies to the market. This chapter provides a systematic overview of the evolution of POC in China. By examining the policies and practices associated with proof of concept, we find that China's POC practices have been driven mainly by top-down policies. In addition, we give examples of four types of POCCs and make a brief comparison with the U.S. and the EU. Based on an analysis and summary of typical cases, we outline the working process of POC and the effects of promoting technology transfer.

Keywords: Proof of concept, innovation intermediaries, technology transfer, technology commercialization.

1. Introduction

The commercialization of technologies from laboratories in universities is the key to realizing the value of R&D investment. Moreover, only commercialized technologies can be recognized as real innovations (Palmberg, 2006; Yi and Long, 2021). Technology transfer (TT) is a process of mutual integration of complex, multiple heterogeneous elements of innovation. The phase during which technologies are transferred from the laboratory to the market is referred to as the "valley of death," representing a critical juncture in the process of technology transfer (TT) (Son *et al.*, 2022). Technologies from universities are usually at an early stage of commercialization and require a long time to be used in products that can be put into the market (Jensen and Thursby, 2001; Son *et al.*, 2022). These technologies face various issues before they can be finally used. First, university researchers lack research commercialization experience and awareness (Battaglia *et al.*, 2021b). Their research capacity does not always allow their research results to develop in a commercially viable direction. Second, scientists lack social networks that can be tapped into for investment and also lack links with government departments and industries. Building connections with potential investors, government agencies, and industry partners is crucial for securing funding, accessing regulatory support, and identifying market opportunities (O'Reilly and Cunningham, 2017). However, it is difficult for scientists to access the necessary resources required for TT. Third, technologies in the lab stage have no clear product market or application scenario. Due to uncertainty and complexity in laboratory technology development (Markman *et al.*, 2008), stakeholders involved in the commercialization process may find it challenging to estimate a technology's commercial value (Siegel *et al.*, 2004). At the very forefront of the TT phase, factors such as information and resource asymmetry and institutional differences between universities and businesses contribute to increased risks and challenges. Proof-of-concept (POC) activities or the intervention of intermediary organizations, such as proof-of-concept centers (POCCs), can help alleviate these issues. A POCC is a common type of intermediary organization used to promote the commercialization of research results or the transfer of knowledge (Villani *et al.*, 2017). POC refers to the process of accelerating the commercialization of laboratory technologies by providing seed funding, business advisors, entrepreneurial education, and incubation space to validate whether a researcher's idea can achieve the desired results (Maia and Claro, 2013; Gulbranson and Audretsch, 2008; McAdam *et al.*, 2013; Hayter and Link, 2015; Munari and Toschi, 2021; Battaglia *et al.*, 2021a). POC serves to address uncertainties and risks at the front end of the TT process, providing an effective means to bridge the "valley of death" (Rasmussen and Sørheim, 2012; Battaglia *et al.*, 2021a; Passarelli *et al.*, 2020). POC is not about creating ideas but rather about working on an existing original idea, aiming to close the gap between scientific discovery and further development by reducing the technological risk and increasing the Technology Readiness Level (TRL) of laboratory inventions (Battaglia *et al.*, 2021a). POC facilitates the early-stage development and utilization of technology for SMEs, identifies intellectual property (IP) with potential commercial value, and clarifies the commercial value of technologies (Maia and Claro, 2013). To achieve its goal, a POC project usually consists of a collection of funding, industrial networks, and skills training aimed at verifying the idea and technical and commercial viability of scientific results.

POC in the U.S. and Europe has been in practice for a few decades and has attracted increased attention from scholars (Maia and Claro, 2013; Gulbranson and Audretsch, 2008; McAdam *et al.*, 2013; Bradley *et al.*, 2013; Hayter and Link, 2015; Munari and Toschi, 2021; Battaglia *et al.*, 2021a). POCCs established by universities, research institutes, enterprises, or other government entities represent a novel type of innovation intermediary organization that connects innovation subjects. They can provide support to commercially validate early-stage scientific results from laboratories (Maia and Claro, 2013), such as technical feasibility analysis, prototype testing, and business prospect validation. However, the state of POC in developing or emerging economies, e.g., China, has not been investigated. Although the history of POC in China is not extensive, it has attracted much attention in the last five to ten years. At the central government level, the State Council, the Ministry of Science and Technology (MOST), and the Ministry of Education (MOE) have stressed POC in their policy agenda; at the local government level, cities, including Beijing, Shanghai, Shenzhen, and Hangzhou, have issued policies related to POC to promote TT in universities and research institutes.

This chapter focuses on the practice of POC in China. In particular, this chapter introduces the features of POC in China. We present a systematic overview of the evolution of POC from perspectives of policy and organization practice and discuss typical cases of POCCs in China. We also outline the design of the POC process and the effects of POC. This chapter contributes to the literature on TT and POC, using China as the main context.

2. The Evolution of POC in China: Policy Perspective

In the policy practice of conducting POC activities in China, the government plays a key role. There are both top-down policy promotions in the vertical direction and mutual learning among local governments in the horizontal direction. Directional leadership is provided in science and technology policies at the national level, and specific policies are strongly supported at the regional level, which suggests that national-level policies guide local governments to put forward innovative initiatives accordingly. At the local government level, Beijing, the capital of China, was among the earliest regions to promote POC activities by the government, establishing a demonstration model for the other provinces and cities. In some provinces, specific provisions for POC were included in the 14th Five-Year Plan for Science, Technology, and Innovation as well as other TT policies. Some local governments have even formulated policies specifically for POC. The role of the government is to (1) promote the construction of POCCs and (2) provide financial support for POC.

2.1 *National-level policies*

National-level policies regarding POC include policies issued directly by the State Council or by the departments under the State Council.

State Council: "Proof of concept" first appeared in a national-level policy in 2017 when the State Council issued the policy *Plan for the Development of a National Technology Transfer System*. According to Table 1, the policy emphasized the need to strengthen the TT capacity of innovation and entrepreneurship platforms and to guide enterprises, universities, and research institutes to build professional innovation spaces to support TT activities, including proof of concept and commercial development. In September 2018, the policy titled *Opinions on Promoting the High-Quality Development of Innovation and Entrepreneurship and Creating an Upgraded Version of "Entrepreneurship and Innovation among All the People"* issued by the State Council proposed the joint establishment of service platforms for the transfer of basic research technology, including POCCs and incubation platforms.

Departments under the State Council: In 2020, the policy titled *Implementation Opinions on Further Promoting the Establishment and Development of Specialized Technology Transfer Bodies of Universities* issued by the MOST and MOE proposed that TT institutions should gradually develop POC service capabilities based on the TT fundamental capabilities. In particular, technology transfer organizations should possess the fundamental capabilities of implementing policies and regulations, assessing emerging technologies, managing intellectual property rights, evaluating scientific and technological advancements, analyzing market research, and negotiating legal agreements. Additionally, they should gradually develop service capabilities such as proof of concept, science and technology finance, enterprise management, and pilot testing. In 2022, a policy titled *Special Plan for the Market of Technical Factors for the 14th Five-year Plan* issued by the MOST proposed exploring differentiated financial support for various phases of technology, including POC, pilot testing, and industrialization. The importance of POC, as a stage of TT activities, is highlighted in national-level policies. In 2022, a report titled *"14th Five-Year Plan" of National High-tech Industrial Development Zone Development Plan* issued by the MOST proposed to support the zones to construct POCCs. The above policies are shown in Table 1.

2.2 *Regional-level policies*

As shown in Table 2, at the local level, the first policy that paid attention to POC was issued in Beijing. In 2018, the policy titled *Implementation Plan for Promoting the Technology Transfer of Colleges and Universities in Beijing* explicitly proposed promoting the construction of POCCs in

Table 1. National-level policy documents on POC.

Policy	Content
Plan for the Development of a National Technology Transfer System (State Council, 2017)	Focuses on the real economy and advantageous industries; provides service support for technology transfer activities such as proof of concept and commercial development.
Opinions on Promoting High-Quality Development of Innovation and Entrepreneurship and Creating an Upgraded Version of "Entrepreneurship and Innovation among All the People" (State Council, 2018)	Promotes universities, research institutes, and enterprises to jointly establish proof-of-concept centers, incubation centers, and other service platforms for the transfer of basic research results.
Implementation Opinions on Further Promoting the Establishment and Development of Specialized Technology Transfer Bodies of Universities (MOST & MOE, 2020)	Technology transfer agencies should gradually establish service capabilities such as proof of concept, technology finance, enterprise management, and technology maturity.
Special Plan for the Market of Technical Factors for the 14th Five-year Plan (MOST, 2022)	Explores differentiated financial support methods for scientific and technological achievements at different stages such as proof of concept, pilot testing, and industrialization.
"14th Five-Year Plan" of National High-tech Industrial Development Zone Development Plan (MOST, 2022)	Supports the zones in constructing professional technology transfer agencies, technology trading platforms, technology pilot service platforms, proof-of-concept centers, quality infrastructure service platforms, etc.

universities in Beijing. Beijing Zhongguancun Science City announced the first POC support plan in the country. The plan proposed to establish comprehensive dedicated funds worth 100 million yuan to support the implementation of regional POC projects and the construction of POCCs in universities and other institutes. In 2021, the policy titled *Outline of the 14th Five-Year Plan (2021-2025) for National Economic and Social Development and Vision 2035 of the Beijing Municipality* proposed to support the construction of many POCCs in the fields of integrated circuits, artificial intelligence, and biomedicine, among others. The report *Action Plan of Shanghai Municipality for Promoting the Transfer and Transformation of Scientific and Technological Achievements (2021-2023)* issued by the General Office of Shanghai Municipal People's Government in 2021 proposed to support specialized institutions in carrying out POC services and launch a pilot to establish POC funds. Since 2021, the Shanghai Municipal Science and Technology Commission has published criteria annually for the application of projects for POCCs.

With the promotion of a central policy and guidance from the two super first-tier cities of Beijing and Shanghai, seven provinces and municipalities — Tianjin City, Shanghai City, Shandong Province, Hubei Province, Fujian Province, Guangxi Province, and Beijing City — proposed to support the construction of POCCs in local technology innovation plans as part of the 14th Five-Year Plan. In June 2022, Beijing released a policy titled *The Measures of Zhongguancun National Innovation Demonstration Zone on Administration of Support Fund for Improving Entrepreneurship Service and Promoting Talent Development Environment (for Trial Implementation)*. On the one hand, it establishes a third-party POC platform around cutting-edge industries to provide POC services for universities, scientific research institutions, medical and healthcare organizations, and enterprises. On the other hand, it provides support to these innovation bodies in jointly carrying out collaborative cooperation and implementing POC activities, such as technological development, product validation, and market application research, centering on core technologies and high-value technological achievements. Shenzhen was the first city to issue a special policy targeting funding for POCCs, namely, *Measures for Shenzhen Municipality for Funding Proof of Concept Centers and Pilot Sites*. The policy noted that "a proof-of-concept center is a new carrier that relies on institutions of universities, research institutes, medical and healthcare institutions, enterprises and social organizations with basic research capabilities; gathers elements related to TT such as technology, talent, capital, and markets; and creates an ecosystem for POC to accelerate the excavation and release of the value of basic research." The policy titled *The Guidelines for Hangzhou Municipality for Work to Construct Proof of Concept Centers (for Trial Implementation) released by Hangzhou Municipal Science and Technology Bureau* makes specific provisions for the construction, application, and management of POCCs.

Table 2. Regional-level policy documents about POC.

Name	Department
Province-level policies mentioning POC	
Beijing: Implementation Plan for Promoting the Technology Transfer of Colleges and Universities in Beijing	The Department of Science and Technology of MOE, the Administrative Commission of Zhongguancun Science Park (2018)
Beijing: The Outline of the 14th Five-Year Plan (2021–2025) for National Economic and Social Development and Vision 2035 of the Beijing Municipality	The Beijing Municipal People's Government (2021)
Beijing: The Measures of Zhongguancun National Innovation Demonstration Zone on Administration of Support Fund for Improving Entrepreneurship Service and Promoting Talent Development Environment (for Trial Implementation)	Beijing Municipal Science and Technology Commission and the Administrative Commission of Zhongguancun Science Park (2022)
Shanghai: The Action Plan of Shanghai Municipality for Promoting the Transfer and Transformation of Scientific and Technological Achievements (2021–2023)	Shanghai Municipal People's Government (2021)
Shanghai: The "14th Five-Year Plan" for Constructing Science and Technology Innovation Centers with Global Influence of Shanghai Municipality	Shanghai Municipal People's Government (2021)
Tianjin: The Science and Technology Innovation Plan of Tianjin Municipality for the "14th Five-Year Plan"	Tianjin Municipal People's Government (2021)
Tianjin: Measures of Tianjin Municipality on Post-Subsidies for Promoting the Transformation of Scientific and Technological Achievements	Tianjin Municipal Science and Technology Bureau, Tianjin Finance Bureau (2022)
Shandong: The Science and Technology Innovation Plan of Shandong Province for the "14th Five-Year Plan"	Shangdong Municipal People's Government (2021)
Hubei: The Science and Technology Innovation Plan of Hubei Province for the "14th Five-Year Plan"	Hubei Municipal People's Government (2021)

Table 2. (*Continued*)

Name	Department
Guangxi: The Science and Technology Innovation Plan of Guangxi Zhuang Autonomous Region for the "14th Five-Year Plan"	The People's Government of Guangxi Zhuang Autonomous Region (2021)
Fujian: The Science and Technology Innovation Plan of Fujian Province for the "14th Five-Year Plan"	Fujian Municipal People's Government (2021)
Specialized POC policies	
Shenzhen: The Measures for Shenzhen Municipality for Funding Proof of Concept Centers and Pilot Sites	Science and Technology Innovation Committee of Shenzhen Municipality (2022)
Hangzhou: The Guidelines for Hangzhou Municipality for Work to Construct Proof of Concept Centers (for Trial Implementation)	Hangzhou Municipal Science and Technology Bureau (2022)
Wuhu: The Measures Wuhu Municipality for the Recognition of Proof of Concept Centers and Pilot Experiment Bases (for Trial Implementation)	Wuhu Municipal Science and Technology Bureau (2023)
Chengdu: The Measures for Chengdu Municipality for Funding Proof of Concept Centers and Pilot Platforms (for Trial Implementation)	Chengdu Municipal Science and Technology Bureau (2023)
Qingdao: The Measures for Qingdao Municipality for Recordation of the Construction of Proof of Concept Platform of Scientific and Technological Achievements Commercialization (for Trial Implementation)	Qingdao Municipal Science and Technology Bureau (2023)
Shanghai: The Measures for Baoshan District for the Management Proof of Concept Centers	Science and Technology Innovation Committee of Baoshan District (2023)
Jiangsu: The Guidelines for Jiangsu Province for Work to Construct Proof of Concept Centers (for Trial Implementation)	Jiangsu Science And Technology Department, Jiangsu Education Department, Jiangsu Finance Department (2023)

2.3 *POC supported by policies*

Policies stipulate the functional positioning, construction subject, application conditions, main duties, funding mechanism, and other aspects of the POCCs. According to the policies of the POCCs in Shenzhen, Jiangsu, Hangzhou, Chengdu, and Qingdao, the guiding principle for the construction of POCCs in China is a combination of government guidance and market leadership.

There are some differences in the local policies in terms of the support mode. Beijing municipality adopts the mode of pre-subsidy support. The support periods generally do not exceed 3 years, and the amount of support for a single platform does not exceed 15 million yuan. Shanghai municipality has proposed to set up special funds for POC. The aim is to attract investments from industry-leading enterprises, investment institutions, or technology transfer institutions to invest socialized capital. Shanghai has adopted non-fixed funding, with the funding amount for each project not exceeding 2 million yuan. Shenzhen municipality adopts the post-subsidy model of "build first, identify later" for qualified POCCs. Every year, the relevant departments choose superior departments for funding after identification and evaluation. The maximum amount of funding is not more than 5 million yuan. Hangzhou takes the approach of "create first, recognize later." The recognized POCCs will receive up to 5 million yuan according to their annual service performance.

Beijing: Since 2019, Zhongguancun Science City has collaborated with Beijing University of Aeronautics and Astronautics (BUAA), Tsinghua University (THU), the Chinese Academy of Sciences (CAS), Peking University (PKU), and the Beijing Institute of Jiaotong (BJTU) to conduct POC projects and establish POCCs through the implementation of a POC support plan. With the support of local policies, in December 2022, Beijing announced its intent to support 12 POC platform construction projects. In December 2023, the Beijing Municipal Commission of Science and Technology, Zhongguancun Science and Technology Park Administration, Tianjin Municipal Bureau of Science and Technology, and Hebei Provincial Department of Science and Technology issued a *List of Beijing-Tianjin-Hebei Proof-of-Concept Platforms and Pilot Maturation Bases (First Batch)*, indicating regional synergy to promote TT.

Shenzhen: In November 2019, the Innovation Proof Center of Shenzhen University aimed to industrialize technology by providing validation funds, supporting seed funds, expert consulting services, entrepreneurial talent training, incubation space, and other personalized support for innovation validation projects. In March 2023, Shenzhen awarded funding to 10 POCCs, relying on institutions such as the International Graduate School of Tsinghua University, the Shenzhen Research Institute of Sun Yat-sen University, and Shenzhen University.

Hangzhou: In November 2022, Hangzhou declared the establishment of the first batch of 15 POCCs. These centers were established in collaboration with relevant universities, institutes, and enterprises. Hangzhou set up a fund of 5 billion yuan for TT to create a national POC capital. In September 2023, a further plan for another 15 POCCs was made.

3. The Evolution of POC in China: Practice Perspective

POCCs in China began to emerge in 2018. The POCC at Xi'an Jiaotong University (XJTU) established in April 2018 was the first formal POCC in China; it relies on the university technology transfer office (TTO). At the end of the same year, the Global Innovation Capital Research Institute POCC of Shanghai Normal University was established; it focuses on key scientific fields such as new energy and new materials. Its purpose is to promote the transfer of technology, as well as enhance the performance of technology innovation and transfer in strategic emerging industries.

POCCs can be categorized into four types according to the host organization: university-hosted POCC (e.g., XJTU POCC), research institute-hosted POCC (e.g., CAS POCC), enterprise-hosted POCC (e.g., Hangzhou Delnor High-end Medical Device POCC), and government–university–enterprise joint mode (Hangzhou Qizhen POCC). This section details representative examples of these types of POCCs to understand their specifics.

Table 3 lists the status of POCCs in China (based on available data). We categorize POCCs into those that are initiated by organizations and those that are recognized by policies. Policy-recognized POCCs are those promoted by the local government or publicized by the local government's POC construction list. The number POCCs in China has grown quickly since 2022 due to the increase in the number of policy-recognized POCCs.

Table 3. List of POCCs in China.

Part 1: Organization-initiated POCC	
Name	**Host organization**
POCC	Xi'an Jiaotong University (2018)
POCC	Shanghai Normal University (2018)
POCC	Beihang University (2019)
Innovation POCC	Shenzhen University (2019)
Beijing Tsinghua Institute of Industrial Development POCC	Tsinghua Institute of Industrial Development and Haidian district government (2020)
Genfire Innovation Park of CAS	Chinese Academy of Science and Haidian district government (2020)
POCC for Clinical Medicine, Peking University Third Hospital	Peking University and Haidian district government (2022)
POCC	Beijing Jiaotong University and Haidian district government (2022)
Chengdu Electronic Information POCC	Shuangliu district government, Sichuan and Sichuan Science and Technology Collaborative Innovation Promotion Association (2022)
High-end medical device POCC	Guangzhou Medical University (2022)
Tongji Zhilan POCC	Tongji University (2023)
POCC	Shenzhen Research Institute, Northwestern Polytechnical University (2023)
POCC	Tsinghua University Shenzhen International Graduate School (2023)
POCC	Jilin University (2023)
Yuyue POCC	Huazhong University of Science and Technology (2023)
POCC	East China University of Science and Technology (2023)
Liaoning Shenyang Digital Technology POCC _	Dongbei University (2023)
POCC for Frontier Technologies for Future Industries	Shanghai Jiaotong University and Lingang Group (2023)

Table 3. (*Continued*)

Part 2: Policy-recognized POCC	
Location and number of POCCs	**Policy**
Beijing: 12	Notice of the Proposed List of Supported Projects for the Construction of Proof of Concept Platforms in 2022. (Beijing Municipal Science and Technology Commission and the Administrative Commission of Zhongguancun Science Park, 2022.)
Hangzhou: 15 (2022); 15 (2023)	The first batch of 15 Proof of Concept Centers in Hangzhou officially awarded licenses in 2022; Notice of the Proposed List of Proof of Concept Centers to be Established in Hangzhou in 2023. (Hangzhou Municipal Science and Technology Bureau.)
Shenzhen: 10 (2023); 9 (2024)	The Announcement of the Proposed Funding for Proof of Concept Centers and Small-scale Trial Bases Projects in Shenzhen in 2023; The Announcement of the Proposed Accreditation and Funding for the First Batch of Proof of Concept Centers and Small-scale Trial Bases in Shenzhen for the Period 2023–2024. (Science and Technology Innovation Committee of Shenzhen Municipality, 2024.)
Suzhou: 8	Suzhou High-tech Zone Science and Technology Innovation Conference and Industry Innovation Cluster Integration Development Promotion Conference. (Suzhou High-tech Zone Science and Technology Bureau, 2023.)
Hefei: 5	Conference on Technology Transfer in Hefei City and Launch Event of "Hefei Innovation Brain." (Hefei Municipal Science and Technology Commission, 2023.)
Chengdu: 10	The Announcement of Registration and Establishment Funding for Proposed Projects of Concept Centers and Pilot Platforms in Chengdu. (Chengdu Municipal Science and Technology Bureau, 2023.)
Tianjin: 18	List of Beijing-Tianjin-Hebei Proof-of-Concept Platforms and Pilot Maturation Bases (First Batch). (Beijing Municipal Commission of Science and Technology, Zhongguancun Science and Technology Park Administration, Tianjin Municipal Bureau of Science and Technology, and Hebei Provincial Department of Science and Technology, 2023.)
Shandong Province: 6	Notice on Issuing the List of Concept Validation Centers (Pilot) in Shandong Province. (Shandong Provincial Department of Science and Technology, 2024.)

3.1 *Xi'an Jiaotong University POCC*

The XJTU POCC was the first POCC at any university in China. The POCC is an independent institution under the TTO of XTJU, with a full-time director, several part-time deputy directors, and 2–3 project managers. The project managers of the POCC are supposed to have the certification of technology managers and play a professional role during the POC activities. The POCC focuses on small early-stage technology investments and professional management, with an investment amount of 100,000–200,000 yuan. The project investment cycle is generally about one year. The target is to verify concept and produce prototypes, and the technology is transferred when it is mature, which is then taken over by angel funds or social capital. On the one hand, the POCC collaborated with the university and industry to initiate a 10 million yuan business incubation fund. On the other hand, the fund was established jointly with enterprises to create the XJTU TTO Tiankui Biotechnology Research Institute.[1]

In terms of organizational structure, the center is subordinate to the TTO. The TTO is a comprehensive service organization engaged in TT, capital management, and industry–university–research cooperation on behalf of XJTU. The TTO consists of a technology development office, a regional management office, an intellectual property operation office, a science and technology finance office, etc. The multi-departmental structure can help the POCC access resources, policies, finance, etc., which facilitates an orderly and efficient POC process. Additionally, the POCC can obtain a large number of research results from universities and has a stable source of POC projects.

3.2 *Chinese Academy of Sciences POCC*

In July 2019, the CAS POCC was established with the support of the Science and Technology Innovation Development Center of the CAS and the Haidian District Government. The center relies on the CAS Genfire Innovation Park and aims to build a CAS POC system. The CAS POC Program supports and incubates some early-stage technologies from the laboratory to the market by providing seed funding, business consulting, entrepreneurship education, industrial resource matching, investment and

[1] https://news.xjtu.edu.cn/info/1033/21602.htm.

financing services, incubation space, etc. The POCC has developed a full-process management system, constructed a project evaluation system, launched the POC innovation competition, released the POC online service platform, and carried out technology manager partner programs. As of December 2023, the Proof-of-Concept Program has supported the launch of 40 projects. Of these, 13 have established industrialization companies and 7 have secured social financing, attracting a total of 370 million yuan in social capital. The current cumulative valuation of these projects is 3 billion yuan.[2]

In terms of operational structure, the CAS POCC uses a combination of the director responsibility system and the partner system. The director is responsible for the decision-making and management of the center and regularly reports to researchers on the progress of the project. The partner system refers to a partnership that relies on external expertise in various fields. A team of partners comes together in an informal, unfixed way to maintain a certain size and plays an advisory role in project selection, evaluation, and commercialization. As a core institution of the research system, CAS possesses a wealth of research resources and projects from subordinate research institutions. The POCC has established seed funds to support diverse projects in various areas.

3.3 *Hangzhou Dinova high-end medical device POCC*

The Hangzhou Dinova high-end medical device POCC was founded by Hangzhou Dinova Ruihua Medical Technology Co. Relying on the innovation ecosystem and market experience of the Dinova Medical Enterprise, the center aims to promote the connection of the innovation chain, industrial chain, and market demand. The center provides validation services from the initial idea to clinical solutions, combining patient needs with clinical treatment concepts and product design. It provides technical support for product design, validation, and clinical trials from a clinical perspective, establishing a significant connection in TT that unites medicine, industry, and science. It has formed three types of project validation systems and has validated multiple projects, with a total of six validated to date.[3]

---

[2] https://www.eeo.com.cn/2023/1211/618384.shtml.

[3] https://kjt.zj.gov.cn/art/2023/11/15/art_1229225188_59009951.html.

Unlike POCCs hosted by universities and research institutes, the enterprise-hosted POCC operates on a market-oriented basis with better cognitive proximity to industry. The center can obtain more information and resources from the market and verify and develop technologies based on enterprise demand. It specializes in aligning with market demands, emphasizing the application value and commercialization potential of technologies, and is dedicated to converting innovations into products or services with market value.

3.4 *Hangzhou Qizhen Innovation POCC*

The Hangzhou Qizhen Innovation POCC was jointly established by the Xihu District, Zhejiang University (ZJU), and ZJU Holding Group Co. The center follows a TT path that includes original innovation, POC project incubation, and industrialization. The center acquires the technologies from ZJU and other universities and research institutes, utilizes the POC fund to conduct prototype tests and R&D pilots, and incubates the technologies through ZJU Science Park. The center aims to promote TT activities in key areas, such as advanced equipment manufacturing, biomedicine, and optoelectronic information. The center has formed a team consisting of experts from three fields: technology, industry, and investment. Project applicants must submit an application form, which will be reviewed by the center's expert committee. The expert committee evaluates the projects based on objective criteria such as TRL, market acceptance, commercial value, industrialization speed, and market scale. As of November 2023, the center has received over 100 project applications. After thorough screening and evaluation, more than 30 projects applications were accepted, with 9 projects having completed the validation process.[4]

The center, as a market-oriented operating body, has established a center director, a management committee, and an expert committee to oversee project solicitation, screening, incubation, and investment. The collaboration between government, universities, and enterprises promotes heterogeneous resource sharing. The Xihu District should provide financial, administrative, and innovation ecosystem support. ZJU should increase the supply of high-quality technologies and contribute talent teams to enhance the center's innovative capacity. The ZJU Holding Group should promote the market-oriented and professional operation of the center, integrating related innovation elements.

[4] *Ibid.*

3.5 *A comparison with the U.S. and Europe*

The U.S. and Europe are pioneers in conducting POC activities and establishing POCCs. In the U.S., POC is viewed from an institutional perspective. POCCs are organizations established within or in cooperation with universities to provide financial, mentoring, and educational support for TT activities (Maia and Claro, 2013; Battaglia *et al.*, 2021b). U.S. POC activities are an expansion of the university entrepreneurship service system. POCCs in the U.S. are typically established based on universities. Examples include the POCC at Columbia University and the Deshpande Center at MIT. The primary purpose of POCCs is to offer commercialization support and training for early-stage innovations, verify the commercial feasibility of technologies, and reduce the uncertainty of commercialization.

In Europe, POC is a collection of resources and services implemented through the European Research Council's (ERC) POC program (Munari *et al.*, 2016; Battaglia *et al.*, 2021a). POC grants, an expansion of ERC-funded projects, aim at exploring the commercial or societal innovation potential of the results of frontier research.[5] The goal is to facilitate the advancement of ERC-funded concepts from groundbreaking research to innovation.

POC in China is carried out mainly by funding POCCs or POC projects. The practical exploration of China's POCCs draws mainly on the U.S. experience, beginning within universities and gradually expanding to other organizations. POCCs integrate the innovation chain, capital chain, industrial chain, and talent chain by funding research teams, providing business consultants, and conducting entrepreneurial training. Further, some organizations have begun to establish POC funds. The Hangzhou Research Institute of Xi'an University of Electronic Science and Technology established the POC fund in 2022. The fund is intended for graduate supervisors and faculty members at Hangzhou Research Institute who intend to industrialize and commercialize their innovations. Shenzhen Bay Laboratory initiated the POC project declaration in 2023. The fund focuses on the laboratory's key tasks and assists in the transfer of basic research.

---

[5]ERC offers four types of frontier research grants: Starting Grants, Consolidator Grants, Advanced Grants, and Synergy Grants. https://erc.europa.eu/apply-grant/proof-concept.

In China, POCCs differ from those in the U.S. in that they extend beyond universities to include research institutions and enterprises as organization hosts. In addition, considering the difference in regime between Chinese and U.S. universities, POCCs are hosted by university-related enterprises to achieve market-oriented operations. The organizational forms of China's POCCs mainly include entity organizations established by enterprises and nonentity organizations relying on universities or their TTOs. University-hosted and research institute-hosted POCCs can gain access to a wider range of technological and talent advantages, as well as high-quality source innovations. Enterprise-hosted POCCs have more experience with market-oriented operations and access to a wider range of market innovation elements. The government–university–enterprise joint mode can efficiently integrate government, industry, and academic resources to promote TT.

The differences in policy and institutional frameworks between China and the United States have significant implications for the organizational structure and operation of POCCs. First, multiple organization hosts mean that POCCs have access to a wider range of resources. The broader inclusion reflects China's concerted effort to leverage the expertise and resources available across various sectors to drive innovation and technology transfer. Second, POCCs in China, particularly those hosted by university-related enterprises or other enterprises, prioritize market-oriented operations to a greater extent than their U.S. counterparts. POCCs hosted by enterprises that are familiar with industry are better able to facilitate the successful commercialization of laboratory technologies. Third, the joint collaboration between the government, universities, and enterprises promotes efficient integration and synergy of resources. This integration can accelerate the technology transfer process and promote the development and commercialization of innovative products in the market. In contrast, POCCs in the United States may require more effort to coordinate cooperation among different stakeholders, which can lead to delays or complications in the transfer process.

4. The Working Process and Effects of the POC

Building upon the insights gleaned from both the policy and practice perspectives, this section delves into the operational aspects and outcomes of POC initiatives in China. It elucidates the working process of POC, which encompasses proof of ideas, proof of technical feasibility, and proof of commercial viability. The POCC is a novel type of innovation intermediary organization. It aims to identify technological breakthroughs with market potential at an early stage and establish an effective connection between the innovation chain, the capital chain, and the industrial chain. By outlining the working process and effects of POC in China, this chapter aims to provide a comprehensive understanding of how these initiatives facilitate early-stage identification of marketable technological breakthroughs and foster synergies between the innovation, capital, and industrial chains.

4.1 *Working process of POC*

The working process of POC can be summarized as shown in Figure 1, with the processes of screening of projects, verification of projects, and commercialization of technology as described in the following:

(1) Screening of projects
POCCs are supposed to establish a project evaluation system, including TRL, industrialization speed, and market value. The center calls for projects in key areas and organizes experts to screen projects with commercial potential. The experts combine the market demand, clarify the validation objectives, and formulate the validation program. A POC expert panel, composed of experts from academia, industry, and the investment sector, is responsible for validating and assessing the technological maturity, market value, and commercialization potential of research outcomes.

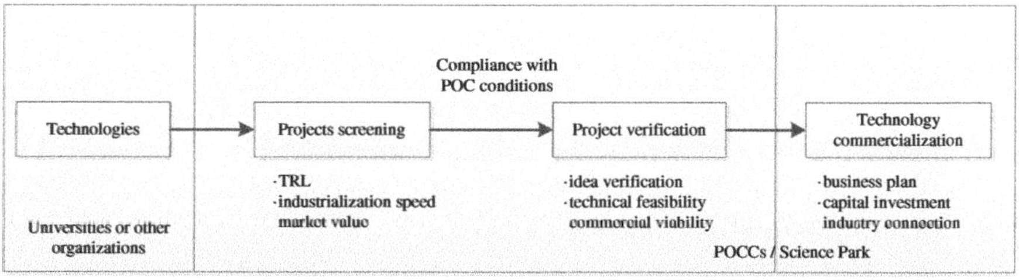

Figure 1. The working process of POC.

(2) Verification of projects

Project verification refers to the verification of ideas, technical feasibility, and commercial viability. The POC provides funds to carry out validation work, as a key financial support for researchers in the early stage of R&D. The funds can come from the university, government, or social capital. The POCC collaborates with innovation entities across the upstream and downstream of the industrial chain to validate the feasibility of ideas, provide prototype testing for technologies, and ultimately produce a project feasibility analysis report. Furthermore, POC can optimize the design of the commercialization path, application scenarios, IP rights, business models, and team building.

(3) Commercialization of technology

At the stage of commercialization, technologies are brought from the laboratory to the market. After finishing the project review, POCCs help researchers complete business plans, acquire social capital, and connect industry resources. Finally, the project ends in technology transfer, licensing, or the establishment of start-ups. At this stage, the university's science and technology park or the enterprise's scientific and TT platform should be relied upon.

4.2 *The effects of POC*

The main effects of POC can be divided into the three aspects of resource acquisition, social network matchmaking, and IP management as detailed in the following:

(1) Resource acquisition

POCCs can access and integrate various resources to support the validation and development of technologies or products. These resources include talent, IP rights, funds, equipment, and other innovation elements. Teams with multidisciplinary and comprehensive backgrounds can provide reliable POC services. They can also offer financial support for inventions to carry out validation tests and support TT.

(2) Social network matchmaking

POC can bridge the gap between researchers, potential investors, and potential users. The POCCs assist in creating an external cooperation network for the transfer of lab technologies. Entrepreneurial experts with rich technology and market experience provide consulting and training services to researchers, conduct market analysis and business planning, and enhance the commercial awareness of researchers. Additionally, POCCs establish long-term links with the government and incubation platforms to support the subsequent incubation of technologies and products. They also establish cooperative relationships with venture capitalists to provide the necessary social capital for the investment and financing requirements for the commercialization of lab technologies.

(3) IP management
The POCCs implement extensive IP protection measures (Passarelli *et al.*, 2020), encompassing not only patents but also other forms of IP, such as trade secrets and copyrights. They promote the protection of technologies from the outset through the disclosure of inventions while enhancing the quality of patents through prepatent application assessments. In cases where projects have not yet been patented, the POCCs foster the creation of new IP rights. For patented technologies, technology commercialization can be facilitated through technical and commercial feasibility validation. A patent layout strategy is adopted to support the commercialization process of IP rights by focusing on specific fields. They apply for patents in the core and peripheral technology of the project through a patent layout and construct high-value patent clusters.

5. Conclusions

China has implemented an innovation-driven development strategy. However, despite the increasing investment in R&D and the rapid growth in the number of research outcomes, TT remains challenging, with low efficiency. This has become a bottleneck for innovation and industrial development. POC is the latest attempt to facilitate the translation of innovations into productivity, and POCCs are important intermediary organizations for promoting the transition from laboratories to market.

In this chapter, we outline the policies and practices related to POC in China and describe the evolution of POC and its characteristics. Typical cases of China's POCCs are presented, and the working process and main effects of POC are summarized. Notably, China's POC practices draw heavily from the experience of the U.S., yet they exhibit distinct features shaped by the country's unique socio-economic context.

The host organizations of POCCs include universities, research institutions, enterprises, and other innovative organizations. China's POCCs focus on key strategic research areas to establish a TT service system that reflects their unique characteristics.

One significant implication of China's POC practices for academic and research institutions lies in the expansion of their role in the innovation ecosystem. Traditionally focused on academic research, these institutions have now expanded to actively engage in the translation of their discoveries into tangible societal benefits. In particular, the performance of research institutions is more prominent. While universities tend to focus on verification in a specific field and extending the innovation chain, research institutions focus on POC in a broader field. POCCs verify projects from many research institutes under the Chinese Academy of Sciences with market-oriented service capabilities to ensure their industrialization and feasibility. Unlike the bottom-up development paths in the U.S., China's POC practices have been driven mainly by top-down policies. Local governments have responded in innovative manners to the call to action by the central government, along with mutual learning. Besides, the principle behind China's POCC operation is market-dominated. China's POCCs have developed a process that includes project screening, project verification, and technology commercialization. They provide laboratory technology for the market through resource acquisition, social network matching, and IP management (Munari *et al.*, 2016).

Moreover, the operation of China's POCCs reflects a dual framework guided by government intervention and market forces. This hybrid approach empowers universities, research institutions, and enterprises to navigate the complexities of technology commercialization while ensuring alignment with broader economic objectives. Through processes such as project screening, verification, and commercialization, organizations can leverage POCCs to enhance the visibility and impact of their research outputs.

In summary, China regards POC as a catalyst for innovation, which helps laboratory technology go to market. By aligning research priorities with commercialization imperatives, academic and research institutions can leverage POCCs as strategic partners in translating research excellence into tangible societal benefits. As China continues to refine its POC practices, academic and research institutions stand poised to play a pivotal role in driving the country's innovation agenda forward.

References

Battaglia, D., Paolucci, E., and Ughetto, E. (2021a). The role of proof-of-concept programs in facilitating the commercialization of research-based inventions. *Research Policy*, 50(6), 104268.

Battaglia, D., Paolucci, E., and Ughetto, E. (2021b). Opening the black box of university proof-of-concept programs: Project and team-based determinants of research commercialization outcomes. *Technovation*, 108, 102334.

Bradley, S. R., Hayter, C. S., and Link, A. N. (2013). Proof of concept centers in the United States: An exploratory look. *The Journal of Technology Transfer*, 38, 349–381.

Gulbranson, C. A. and Audretsch, D. B. (2008). Proof of concept centers: Accelerating the commercialization of university innovation. *The Journal of Technology Transfer*, 33, 249–258.

Hayter, C. S. and Link, A. N. (2015). On the economic impact of university proof of concept centers. *The Journal of Technology Transfer*, 40, 178–183.

Jensen, R. and Thursby, M. (2001). Proofs and prototypes for sale: The licensing of university inventions. *American Economic Review*, 91(1), 240–259.

Maia, C. and Claro, J. (2013). The role of a proof of concept center in a university ecosystem: An exploratory study. *The Journal of Technology Transfer*, 38, 641–650.

Markman, G. D., Siegel, D. S., and Wright, M. (2008). Research and technology commercialization. *Journal of Management Studies*, 45(8), 1401–1423.

McAdam, M., McAdam, R., Galbraith, B., and Miller, K. (2010). An exploratory study of principal investigator roles in UK university proof-of-concept processes: An absorptive capacity perspective. *R&D Management*, 40(5), 455–473.

Munari, F. and Toschi, L. (2021). The impact of public funding on science valorisation: An analysis of the ERC proof-of-concept programme. *Research Policy*, 50(6), 104211.

Munari F, Sobrero M, Toschi L. (2016). Financing technology transfer: assessment of university-oriented proof-of-concept programmes. *Technology Analysis & Strategic Management*, 29(2), 233–246.

O'Reilly, P. and Cunningham, J. A. (2017). Enablers and barriers to university technology transfer engagements with small- and medium-sized enterprises: Perspectives of principal investigators. *Small Enterprise Research*, 24(3), 274–289.

Palmberg, C. (2006). The sources and success of innovations — determinants of commercialisation and break-even times. *Technovation*, 26(11), 1253 1267.

Passarelli, M., Landi, G. C., Cariola, A., and Sciarelli, M. (2020). Open innovation in the new context of proof of concepts: Evidence from Italy. *European Journal of Innovation Management*, 24(3), 735–755.

Rasmussen, E. and Sørheim, R. (2012). How governments seek to bridge the financing gap for university spin-offs: Proof-of-concept, pre-seed, and seed funding. *Technology Analysis & Strategic Management*, 24(7), 663–678.

Siegel, D. S., Waldman, D. A., Atwater, L. E., and Link, A. N. (2004). Toward a model of the effective transfer of scientific knowledge from academicians to practitioners: Qualitative evidence from the commercialization of university technologies. *Journal of Engineering and Technology Management*, 21(1–2), 115–142.

Son, H., Chung, Y., and Yoon, S. (2022). How can university technology holding companies bridge the Valley of Death? Evidence from Korea. *Technovation*, 109, 102158.

Villani, E., Rasmussen, E., and Grimaldi, R. (2017). How intermediary organizations facilitate university–industry technology transfer: A proximity approach. *Technological Forecasting and Social Change*, 114, 86–102.

Yi, W. and Long, C. X. (2021). Does the Chinese version of Bayh-Dole Act promote university innovation? *China Economic Quarterly International*, 1(3), 244–257.

https://doi.org/10.1142/9789819807611_0006

Chapter 6

Navigating Transnational Innovation: Best Practices in Academic Cooperation between Italy and China

Marco Begani[*,], Marco Bonaglia[†,††], Michele Bonino[*,‡‡], Anna Facchinetti[‡,§§], Antonio Frisoli[§,¶¶], Lorenzo Gonzo[¶,‖,‖‖], and Maria Gottardo[‡,***]**

[*] *Politecnico di Torino, Italy*

[†] *Chongqing University, China*

[‡] *University of Bergamo, Italy*

[§] *Sant'Anna School of Advanced Studies of Pisa, Italy*

[¶] *Fondazione Bruno Kessler, Trento, Italy*

[‖] *International Cooperation at the International Technology Transfer Network, Hong Kong*

[**] *marco.begani@polito.it*

[††] *marco.bonaglia@hotmail.it*

[‡‡] *michele.bonino@polito.it*

[§§] *Anna.facchinetti@gmail.com*

[¶¶] *antonio.frisoli@santannapisa.it*

[‖‖] *lorenzo.gonzo@outlook.com*

[***] *maria.gottardo@unibg.it*

Abstract

Italy and China boast a long history of scientific collaborations. In recent decades, several Italian universities have launched double degree programs, opened offices, exchanged students and professors, signed agreements, and together contributed to the production of research and publications that, thanks to the expertise of both parties, have been cited countless times by the scientific community in both countries.

This chapter is the result of a concerted effort by three research groups. It aims to provide an overview of different actors in Sino-Italian academic cooperation over more than a decade, studying how the Galileo Galilei Italian Institute of the Sant'Anna School in Pisa, based in Chongqing, the "China Center" of the Politecnico di Torino, and the "China–Italy Joint Laboratory on Advanced Manufacturing (CI-LAM)" of the University of Bergamo have played a role in such Sino-Italian scientific exchange.

In particular, this chapter focuses on the role of these three realities as intermediaries for Innovation between Italy and China. It will showcase the results achieved during the golden years of Sino-Italian cooperation and will attempt to provide an analysis of the post-pandemic recovery and the strategies implemented.

Through scientific diplomacy, these intermediary entities (Galilei Institute, China Center, CI-LAM) have brought together minds, experiences, and stories and played an innovative and fundamental connecting role.

Keywords: Academic cooperation, Italy-China relations, scientific diplomacy, Galileo Galilei Italian Institute, China Center, CI-LAM, Sant'Anna School of Advanced Studies, Chongqing University, Polytechnic of Turin, Qinghua University, University of Bergamo, COVID-19, post COVID-19

1. Introduction

Italy and China are linked by centuries of cooperation ranging from culture and economy to diplomatic relations. In particular, as regards scientific cooperation, the two countries have been able to count on innovative ambassadors and visionaries who have contributed to mutual development and cooperation. Starting from the Jesuits, the two countries have then opened up to each other (De Giorgi and Samarani 2011; Pini, 2011;

Bertuccioli and Masini, 2011) and more and more Universities over the last decades could build academic cooperation projects. This is the case of the realities described in this chapter.

Over the past decades, and in particular since the beginning of the twentieth century, Italian Universities have launched mutual academic cooperation projects with Chinese counterparts. The cases presented in this research show two things: from one side, how Italian Universities have developed innovative transnational academic Institutes and Research Center, acting as tools for implementing and realizing goals and projects with the support of Chinese colleagues. On the other side, creativity and diverse approaches have led to the establishment of different managerial realities.

Our research team developed this work with three main aims in mind.

The first was to present examples of successful academic cooperation projects, active in different parts of China, to understand whether or not there was a cooperation model developed over the years, or whether the three actors were instead differently structured and managed by academic actors involved. A second goal was to analyze the achievements of the different case studies presented, to understand whether or not we were faced with real academic "innovation intermediaries" between Italy and China, and to understand how these case studies worked and survived the COVID-19 pandemic. Finally, the last of our objectives was to contribute to the varied and multifaceted framework of relations between Italy and China, focusing on the academic side of it, providing useful information that could be used for future researchers and also to implement a more efficient "model" for academic cooperation between Chinese and Italian universities.

Our aims have been achieved by presenting three case studies, active in different parts of China and managed by Italian Universities present in different regions. Through our analysis of these centers' historical developments, their main activities and results over the years, and their dynamic response to the difficult pandemic years, we have brought attention to managerial differences and operational similarities that are existing in the complex and multifaceted area of Sino-Italian academic cooperation activities. In the final part of our chapter, we put emphasis on the "lessons learned" and we bring suggestions for the development of a more coherent and efficient model of academic cooperation between Italy and China's universities.

The chapter is divided into three main parts. The first is an explanation of the evolution of Italian–Chinese relations in academic and scientific cooperation over the years. The second is the presentation of the three case studies (China Center of the Polytechnic of Turin, Galileo Galilei Italian Institute of Sant'Anna School of Advanced Studies of Pisa, and the cooperation activities launched and implemented by the University of Bergamo). The third and final part collects the main consideration stemming from the analysis of our case studies and brings our research team suggestions for a more efficient and dynamic cooperation.

2. The Evolution of Italian–Chinese Relations in Academic and Scientific Cooperation

In 2022, the expenditures in R&D in China reached Euro 401.42 billion corresponding to 2,54% of GDP%, ranking second at the global level, after the US, in terms of absolute value and 13th in terms of percentage. In the last six years, such expenditures increased by over 10% yearly. Private sector contributes to this amount by 77%, the remaining being left to the public sector. Overall, only 6,02% is devoted to basic science research.[1]

By contrast, according to the Italian Institute of Statistics, in 2021, the national expenditure in R&D reached Euro 25,992 billion, corresponding to 1,51% of GDP, with the private sector contributing nearly 60%, while public and private research organizations contributing the remaining 40%. Expenditure in basic science research reached 23%.[2]

From the academic point of view, according to Times Higher Education in 2023,[3] 11 Chinese Universities entered the top 200 while three are represented with two (three) Universities within this range. There are several academic ranking agencies and, depending on the evaluation parameters, a given university may classify differently; however, this example can be taken as a reference for defining a strategy for collaboration on science and technology (S&T) with China.

By the end of 2023, according to the Cineca database, the cumulative number of collaboration agreements between Italian and Chinese

[1] www.gov.cn.

[2] All this information can be found on the ISTAT website, available at this link, www.istat.it.

[3] https://www.timeshighereducation.com/world-university-rankings/2023/world-ranking.

Universities amounted to 1049, involving 69 Italian and 266 Chinese institutions. In the last 5 years, over 250 joint collaboration agreements were signed.[4] These are important figures that rank China at the 5th place in the Italian international collaborations on S&T, after France, Spain, and the US, and before Brazil and way more distant Germany.

Quite in general, when establishing and carrying out successful collaboration on S&T with other countries and specifically with China, several best practices and essential instruments shall be considered. Particularly when it comes to the establishment of Joint R&D laboratories, structural frameworks for cooperation, funding of mobility programs, focusing on priority areas and shared challenges, IPR management, and regular dialogue and exchange programs are the few instruments that matter. Those instruments typically are contained in a national strategy on international cooperation on S&T and education.

Given the dimensions and the importance of the bilateral collaboration with China, over the years, the Italian Government has been elaborating and adopting such a strategy, depending on the specific national needs, interests, and geopolitical situation.

Italy–China collaboration on S&T dates back to 1978 when, also pioneering other European countries, the first intergovernmental Agreement of cooperation was signed. Successively, a new Agreement, updating and replacing the former one was signed in Beijing in 1998. The new Agreement marked a pivotal step in strengthening scientific and technological collaboration, laying a foundation for future cooperation projects.

In the following years, the collaboration between Science and Technology flourished. In 2010, within the framework of the "Triennial Joint Plan of Action", a further bilateral mechanism, specifically on S&T cooperation, was agreed. Three Joint Research and Innovation (R&I) Centers, involving sectors of Design, e-Government and Technology Transfer, were established as well as an exchange platform named China–Italy Innovation Forum which to time has become famous as the "China–Italy Science, Technology, and Innovation Week", whose 12th edition was held by end of November 2023.[5]

---

[4] https://accordi-internazionali.cineca.it.

[5] The english version of the website of the 12th edition of the "China–Italy Science, Technology, and Innovation Week" is available at this link, https://www.ciiw.com.cn/EN.

In 2014, the Ministry of Foreign Affairs and International Cooperation (MAECI) in coordination with other relevant Ministries and the national public research system set up the platform "Tavolo Cina". It aimed to define national priority sectors of cooperation on S&T as well as the background for a national strategy. The platform kept working until 2020, when, through a consultation process with the main national stakeholders, a document "Piano d'Azione Italia-Cina per la Collaborazione Scientifica e Tecnologica verso il 2025" was approved and adopted.

The plan was intended as a guideline on specific priority sectors of national interest to be developed in collaboration with Chinese entities through the already consolidated Executive Protocols of Bilateral Collaboration on Science and Technology coordinated by MAECI for the Italian side and the Ministry of Science and Technology as well as the National Natural Science Foundation for the Chinese side.

In 2016, the network of the Italian Science and Technology Attache' in China was established by opening, besides the already consolidated office at the Italian Embassy in Beijing, two new positions at the General Consulates of Italy in Shanghai and Chongqing, respectively.

In the above contest, the three examples of innovation intermediaries, described in the following sections, are expressions of three different approaches to the bilateral collaboration on S&T with China. Each example shares common goals and aims at results of national interest, leveraging on knowledge and experiences exchanges with relevant Chinese institutions.

3. Three Innovation Intermediaries of Sino-Italian Academic Cooperation

In this paragraph, we present the three case studies we collected for analyzing new ways of cooperation and innovation between academic institutions in China and Italy. For each of the case studies, we bring a short introduction to the development of the cooperation, then we focus on the main tools (Galilei Institute, China Center, and CI-LAM) that implemented the cooperation and developed specific projects. These "tools", with their uniqueness and diversification, represent, in our opinion, true cases of transnational innovation.

3.1 *Galileo Galilei Italian Institute: Sant'Anna School of Pisa*[6]

3.1.1 *Introduction to the cooperation between China and Sant'Anna School*

Chongqing, Chinese megalopolis and one of the world's most populated urban areas, is currently the city carrying the highest potential for economic growth in the whole country (+10.7 % GDP in 2016) (Bonaglia, 2019b). Chongqing is the focal point of the "Go West Policy" and the "Western Development Strategy", China's economic policies launched to reduce imbalances between coastal regions and its internals, recently promoted by the Chinese central government, which is transforming the Municipality into a major economic, industrial and infrastructural hub in inland China (Bonaglia, 2020). Conceived as the nodal point of the New Silk Road, Chongqing has seen the emergence of numerous Economic and Technological Development Zones (Bonaglia, 2019a), as well as the creation of a freight railway directly linking China and Europe. The new international airport operates dozens of routes out of China, with direct links also to Rome.

Until recent years, the Italian presence in Chongqing consisted of a dozen residents and a limited number of industrial activities. Sant'Anna School of Advanced Studies has been a pioneer in establishing a connection between China and Italy, giving birth to a new institute there, active since 2007. Official cooperation started some years earlier: in fact, Sant'Anna School of Advanced Studies and Chongqing University (CQU), officially signed a cooperation agreement in December 2004 during the visit of the then Italian President Carlo Azeglio Ciampi to China. Thanks to the continued support of its Chinese partner, the Galileo Galilei Italian Institute (since now simply the "Galilei") has increasingly expanded and diversified its activities.

---

[6]Official website of the Galileo Galilei Italian Institute, https://www.galileiinstitute.it/;

Official page of the Galileo Galilei Italian Institute on Sant'Anna School website, https://www.santannapisa.it/en/galileo-galilei-italian-institute;

Galileo Galilei YouTube official presentation, https://www.youtube.com/watch?v=5RhGDfTNvqk&t=293s;

Official page of the "China Studies" programme at the Institute of Management, https://www.santannapisa.it/en/institute/management/china-studies.

Since that time, the Galilei has been developing a systemic multifaceted project, involving not only those fields in which Italy is traditionally outstanding (fashion, food and beverage, design), but investing also in areas with the highest innovative content, such as scientific research and academic cooperation. The strong partnership with Chongqing University — the most important and prestigious university in the city — gives the Galilei great visibility and allows it to have an effective impact. Making symmetrical and synergic the collaboration with the Galilei, is the presence, since 2008, of the Confucius Institute in Pisa, hosted by Sant'Anna School of Advanced Studies. The Confucius Institute, in charge of promoting Chinese culture and language, is co-directed by professors of the School and Chongqing University.

The main objective of the Galilei is the strengthening of joint research projects on areas of expertise shared by Sant'Anna and CQU. These include Innovation Management, Health and Wellbeing Management, Augmented Reality and Bio-robotics, Photonics, Software Engineering and Telecommunication Engineering, Biotechnology, Economics, Legal and Institutional Systems. In order to improve the acceleration of research projects, the Galilei facilitates interaction opportunities between academics, researchers, and scholars of Sant'Anna and Chongqing University.

Thanks to its well-established presence on the Chongqing University campus, the Galilei is able to keep in active and constant contact with the most innovative departments and laboratories of the Chinese university. Therefore, the Galilei is always up-to-date on the latest research outcomes and research projects, the new priorities identified by the central government, as well as the projects where Sant'Anna can provide complementary expertise. To date, the Galilei is running several successful projects in partnership with the School of International Education, the International Office, the School of Economics and Business Administration of CQU, and has launched many academic exchange dialogues between individual professors of the two universities.

Apart from monitoring the academic dimension, the Galilei has a proactive stance with regard to the different opportunities that may arise from the development and investment agendas promoted by public institutions and private entities (new R&D centers, technology parks, and technology investment projects).

The Galilei, serving as a research platform, offers support not only for the endeavors of the Institute of Management and all the other institutes at Sant'Anna but also as an active contributor within the Academic Italian system in China. When feasible, it strengthens scientific collaboration between Italy and China. For instance, this was exemplified in a prior initiative known as the Sino-Italian Innovation Base Camp (Bani *et al.*, 2018), initiated in 2017, where numerous Italian universities were able to engage and receive support from the Galilei. The Galilei celebrated its first ten years of activities in the same year, with many events in Chongqing realized with the support of the Consulate General of Italy and Chongqing University (Di Minin, 2017).

3.1.2 *Main activities of the Galilei Institute over the years and main achievements*

The Galilei provides consultancy services and assistance to the Chinese delegations of entrepreneurs or academics planning a mission to Italy, as well as to the Italian delegations visiting Chongqing. The Galilei also facilitates the realization of training and student exchange programs between Italy and China, especially with CQU. Furthermore, the Institute acts as the front desk for Sant'Anna School's training courses and research opportunities and promotes the enrolment of the best students of CQU into the academic programs of Italian Universities.

The Galilei has also produced hundreds of articles and insights on Chongqing, SouthWestern China, and China as a whole. Its "Missiva Galileiana" is a newsletter offering a weekly overview of news and events relevant to the Italian and Chinese communities, providing its readers with a calendar of the upcoming initiatives taking place both in Chongqing and Italy. Inside the newsletter, readers can find the *Galileo weekly Observer*,[7] a space to keep an eye on the institutional and socio-economic scenario of contemporary China, and *Chongqing stories*,[8] a section that puts a light on expats and local people's lives in Chongqing. *China Through the Telescope*[9] is a series of research seminars organized, coordinated, and moderated by the Institute, concentrating on topics of strategic relevance to contemporary China in the areas of economic, business, and policy cooperation.

The Galilei has also been a point of reference with regard to the teaching of Italian language in Chongqing and the sharing of Italian culture in

---

[7]All the articles of the Galileo Weekly Observer column can be found at this link, http://www.galileiinstitute.it/category/galileo-observer/.

[8]All the articles of the Chongqing Stories column can be found at this link, http://www.galileiinstitute.it/category/chongqing-stories/.

[9]All the events under the label of "China Through the Telescope" series can be found at this link, http://www.galileiinstitute.it/category/china-through-the-telescope/.

the Municipality. The Institute is also the first ever CILS examination center active in South-Western China and over the years, thanks to the cooperation with the Università per Stranieri di Siena, there have been hundreds of Chinese and international students taking the exam in the offices of the Galilei.

The Sino-Italian Innovation Base-Camp Project (SIIB-C) developed and designed in the years between 2017 and 2019, represented the biggest project of the second decade in the life of the Galilei. It stemmed from the cooperation between Sant'Anna School of Advanced Studies in Pisa, Chongqing University, and Bishan District — a district in Chongqing Municipality which hosts a National High-Tech Zone (Fasulo, 2018; Di Minin and Caluti, 2017; Redazione Pisa Today, 2017; Sabbadin, 2017).

The trilateral agreement was signed in February 2017 in the presence of Presidents Sergio Mattarella and Xi Jinping, and aimed at the creation of the Sino-Italian Innovation Base-Camp (SIIB-C), which should have realized over 3 km^2 of land in Bishan. The project was covered extensively by the online resource "Sant'Anna Magazine" and by many Italian digital newspapers (*Sant'Anna Magazine*, 2017a, 2017b, 2017c) and it gave new energy to academic exchanges between Pisa and Chongqing, putting the Institute under the spotlight (*Sant'Anna Magazine*, 2018a, 2018b). Synergies with the Consul General of Italy led by Consul Filippo Nicosia led to a fruitful cooperation and many activities with a bigger team of Italians and Chinese personnel.

3.1.3 *The years of the pandemic and future perspectives*

The pandemic brought a sudden and unexpected stop to the evolution of the project. Its team had to reinvent itself in many ways, facing daily challenges. Part of the staff was blocked in Italy and no delegations were possible for almost three years. The project nevertheless was kept alive thanks to the mutual cooperation between its Italian and Chinese supporters (Di Minin and Fasulo, 2023a).

In 2023 delegations could restart and the visits of Professor Di Minin, Professor Frisoli, and Miss Ida Fiore (program manager of the Confucius Institute of Pisa) could keep the dialogue between Sant'Anna and Chongqing University alive, opening a new phase for the Institute and new step forward in its almost twenty-year long history.

At the beginning of 2024, the Galilei supported the official mission led by Professor Frisoli and Professor Dario from the Institute of Mechanical Intelligence and the Institute of Biorobotics, to strengthen the cooperation between Sant'Anna and Chongqing University from an academic, scientific, and cultural point of view.

3.2 *China center: Politecnico di Torino*[10]

3.2.1 *Introduction to the cooperation between China and the Politecnico di Torino*

The history of the relations between the Politecnico di Torino and China has a significant starting point in 2005 with the Politong program, which involved PoliTO, Tongji University (Shanghai), and Politecnico di Milano. Stemming from intergovernmental dialogue between Italy and China, the project was funded by the Italian Ministry of Education, Universities and Research (MIUR) until 2013 and subsequently primarily by China. Over the years, more than 1000 students have benefited from the program in Information and Communication Engineering, Mechanical and Production Engineering, and Systemic Design (Di Minin and Fasulo, 2019, 2023b; Bonaglia, 2023).

During this period, Chinese universities had already begun to ascend in the international rankings, to invest substantial resources (Fedasiuk *et al.*, 2022), and to gradually develop a more structured capability to dialogue with foreign universities. Many academics and managers involved in the cooperation with foreign Universities had gained previous experience abroad. On the Country's policy front, initiatives such as the Double First Rate University Plan[11] granted a selected group of Chinese universities special resources and a strategic role in implementing governmental policies in education and research.

During this period, the number of Chinese students enrolled at the Politecnico significantly increased, to a maximum of almost 1.300 in 2017 and decreasing afterward to the current 850 students, reflecting the trend of young Chinese people studying abroad.[12]

At the same time, on the PoliTO side, between 2010 and 2015 some academics established and developed relationships with relevant Chinese

---

[10] Official page of the China Center at Polytechnic of Turin website, https://www.polito.it/en/polito/international-campus/politecnico-around-the-world/china-center; Official website of the Project, https://chinaroom.polito.it/.

[11] http://www.moe.gov.cn/srcsite/A22/s7065/202202/W020220214318455516037.pdf; http://www.moe.gov.cn/srcsite/A22/moe_843/201709/t20170921_314942.html.

[12] https://www.researchgate.net/figure/Number-of-Chinese-students-studying-abroad-and-returned-Source-Ministry-of-Education_fig1_351072413.

universities such as Tsinghua University, Shanghai Jiaotong University, Xi'an Jiaotong University, and South China University of Technology, with the support of PoliTO dedicated funds for internationalization of research. The South China–Torino Collaboration Lab of 2015, an outcome of this kind of experience having premises in Torino and Guangzhou, was focused on cooperation in the field of architecture and, through the partnership with SCUT, offered PoliTO the opportunity to take part in competitions and gain contacts with non-University local entities.

3.2.2 *Main activities of the China center*

In consideration of the increasing number of activities and relations with Chinese HEIs, the development of the Chinese university system, and the opportunities for cooperation with governmental and industrial institutions, in 2016, the Politecnico outlined a first strategic plan for China, appointed a Delegate of the Rector for relations with China, allocated a specific budget for activities in China through the International Relations Office, and provided support for the 3-years mobility of four researchers (two in Engineering, two in Architecture) specifically dedicated to the cooperation with Chinese HEIs. The plan restricted the number of key partner HEIs to 8top institutions.

The PoliTO China Center, approved by the Board of Governors in 2017 and started in 2018, was a natural continuation and development of the idea of 2016. The China Center has been approved three times since, each one corresponding to a three-year project period: 2018–2020; 2021–2023; 2024–2026.

The China Center introduced several structural aspects to PoliTO's approach to China:

- a project approach encompassing the entire cycle of activities, from setting goals to planning, implementation, and monitoring;
- an integrated approach between the academic and the administrative components, reflected by its governance structure;
- an advisory board providing advice on the general trends of cooperation with China, on its risks and opportunities; the board includes experts in fields that traditionally do not belong to PoliTO, such as economics and political sciences;
- the creation, in 2023, of a regional manager position within the administration.

In this view, the China Center serves as a hub for the activities of the PoliTO having China as the main focus of interest. In particular, the CC

- supports the PoliTO leadership in defining the strategy and making decisions regarding its operations in China;
- sets goals, activities, timing, and results for the activities and describes the interactions among the academic and administrative areas involved;
- promotes and manages the relations with Chinese partners, including the organization of incoming as well as outgoing delegations;
- promotes, coordinates, and facilitates (and in some cases financially supports, at least for the mobility aspects) the relation between the PoliTO Depts. and the entities of China involved in research cooperation, or potentially interested, in cooperation with PoliTO, such as HEIs, local agencies, industry, consortia, research institutes, and others;
- supervises the definition of agreements and promotes, plans, and manages collaborative education programs such as exchange and double degree programs at bachelor and master levels, including the recent collaborative sino-foreign programs promoted by the Chinese MOE;
- together with the PhD School, promotes and manages PhD agreements and programs including full-degree and visiting PhD students mobility, as well as the relation with CSC: China Scholarship Council;
- manages a Chinese intermediary company appointed in 2021 for legal, financial and business development services;
- supports the Communication Dept. in institutional communication related to China, including the Official WeChat Account started in 2022 (13.000+ followers as of March 2024) and the development and maintenance of the CC website;
- supports the promotion of the PoliTO teaching offer in China, with the support of the China Polito Alumni Association started in 2020;
- monitors and evaluates results and sensitive/critical issues, updating the executive plan accordingly.

As shown by this description, the China Center is not conceived as a Research or an Innovation center but rather as a facilitator/promoter of the research and training activities conducted by the PoliTO departments in cooperation with Chinese partners. The China Center supports specific research groups such as the China Room,[13] established in 2016, dedicated to

[13] https://chinaroom.polito.it/.

urban and architecture studies in China, or the Automotive Group, recently enriched with a specific headquarters dedicated to Chinese collaborations and supporting various individual researchers or small groups as well.

3.2.3 *Main results achieved*

Since its start in 2018, the China Center[14] has contributed to achieve different results alongside with the implementation of traditional education programs in partnership with top partner HEIs, such as bilateral Student Exchange agreements and Double Degree agreements at all levels.

Here below are listed a few[15] (Table 1):

Table 1. Main results achieved and implemented by China Center from 2018 to 2023.

Start year	Area	Project/Program/ Topic	Partner	Financial support
2018	Education/ Research	Joint PhD in Architecture	Tsinghua University	Bilateral
2018	Joint competition	Solar Decathlon China: Project for an energy-efficient building powered by solar energy — 1st prize	South China University of Technology (SCUT)	SD organizing committee
2019	PhD / Research	Agreement on scholarships for full-degree and visiting PhD students	China Scholarship Council (CSC)	CSC
2020	Education	DD Master of Science in Urban Design (30 students/cycle)	South China University of Technology (SCUT)	SCUT

[14] https://www.polito.it/ateneo/campus-internazionale/il-politecnico-nel-mondo/china-center.

[15] All this information can be found on the PoliTo official page of the China Center, at this link, https://www.polito.it/en/polito/international-campus/politecnico-around-the-world/china-center.

Table 1. (*Continued*)

Start year	Area	Project/Program/Topic	Partner	Financial support
2021	Applied research	Concept Design for Big Air building — Winter Olympic Games, Beijing 2022	Design Institute of Tsinghua University (THAD)	THAD
2021	Joint competition	Lishui Mountain Dwellings Urban Design Prize	South China University of Technology (SCUT)	Organizer
2021	Applied research	Vehicle EMC	China Automotive Research Institute (CAERI)	CAERI
2022	Applied research	Inverter for e-mobility	New Energy Vehicle Innovation Center (NEVC)	NEVC
2022	Communication	WeChat Official Account (13.000+ followers to date)	—	PoliTO
2022	Management	Intermediation for legal, financial, and business development services	—	PoliTO
2023	Applied research	Architectural project	CMAD design studio	Yatong group
2023	Applied/bilateral research	New Energy Vehicle	New Energy Vehicle Innovation Center (NEVC)	NEVC

3.2.4 *The China Center as a developer of relations*

The resumption of mobility to and from China has enabled PoliTO academics and managers, since spring 2023, to visit partners again and explore new cooperation and business opportunities. In some cases, intermediary consulting companies have supported PoliTO in these meetings. In 2023, alongside the projects mentioned earlier, Politecnico metcompanies of particular interest in the NEV (New Energy Vehicles) sector. The outcome of these meetings is still to be determined, but for Politecnico, these encounters represent an interesting context, not only because they may lead to research and development projects, both bilateral and applied, but also because dialogue with these industrial entities can contribute to increasing the understanding of Politecnico and its stakeholders of technological and market phenomena that are currently evolving rapidly in China.

Similarly, in the field of Architecture, PoliTO has had the opportunity to develop contacts not only with large public institutions, like Universities and their design institutes, but also with private firms, which have led to significant design opportunities. These opportunities are not only meant as business opportunities but can help PoliTO understand a rapidly transforming reality. In some cases, these relations have involved other entities in the Turin area which PoliTO collaborates with, and in particular, some architectural firms involved in international collaboration, especially in China, with PoliTO through an agreement signed in 2019 with the Torino Council of Architects.

3.2.5 *The years of the pandemic and future perspectives*

The spread of COVID-19 and its impact on international mobility significantly affected Politecnico's position regarding its operations in China (Di Minin, Fasulo 2023b). In 2021, Politecnico decided to promote itself through widely distributed online tools. Unable to meet with partners and promote its activities in China, between 2021 and 2022, PoliTO started to invest in its remote presence in China. On the one hand, it enhanced its online communication by opening an official WeChat account and dedicating personnel to its management. On the other hand, it extended the legal and financial intermediary service provided since 2019 by a company based in China to the sphere of business development. Both of these activities yielded interesting results and, regardless of COVID, they now represent a significant value for Politecnico's operations in China. The existence of a China Center allowed for a rapid study of the feasibility of these initiatives and helped to address contingent difficulties, developing tools that not only proved useful at the time but also continue to be of great support today.

In conclusion, the PoliTO China Center — that is, a structure with governance, resources, and project vision — has proven to be an effective tool, within the domain of relations with China, to define strategies and activities, to promote relationships and projects, to support the interaction between academic and managerial areas, to define strategies and activities, to promote relationships and projects, to support the interaction between academic and managerial areas, and to address unexpected changes of the geopolitical landscapes (such as the one imposed by COVID, but the recent conflicts are another example) more quickly, critically, and effectively.

Considering the University as a safe, privileged place for dialogue between countries, cultural contexts, and political visions, such an approach seems to be worth maintaining, and this is even more true looking at a future where instability and tensions are growing.

Amid these tensions, technology and the sharing of research activities and results seem to become increasingly sensitive topics. In this consideration, the Politecnico di Torino underlines the importance of keeping and further developing the scientific interaction and mutual understanding between Italy and China.

3.3 *China–Italy Joint Laboratory on Advanced Manufacturing (CI-LAM): University of Bergamo*[16,17]

3.3.1 *Introduction to the cooperation between China and the University of Bergamo*

The University of Bergamo has carried out a successful international strategy toward China that has evolved through the years until the inauguration of a liaison office of the University of Bergamo in Beijing in

[16] Official website of the project available at this link, https://www.cilam.org/.

[17] Official page on the University of Bergamo website, https://www.unibg.it/internazionale/destinazione-unibg/programmi-congiunti-e-summer-school-unibg/ci-lam-china-italy.

December 2023: a *leap forward* in the cooperation between the two municipalities.

The China–Italy Technology Transfer Centre (CITTC) represented the first step toward the establishment of a stable platform connecting Bergamo and Beijing's science and innovation clusters.[18] The CITTC was aimed at promoting internationalization activities in the research-industry system between China and Italy and was supported in Italy by the former Ministry of Education, University and Research (MIUR) and in China by the Ministry of Science and Technology (MOST) and the Beijing Municipal Science and Technology Commission (BMSTC). The CITTC represented the technical partner of Chinese and Italian institutions for the organization of research valorization activities and provided support in the bilateral technology transfer.

The CITTC had an office in Beijing and two technical secretariats in Italy, situated in Bergamo and Naples, respectively, supervised by the University of Bergamo at the Kilometro Rosso Innovation District[19] — a science park in Bergamo municipality where both private companies and research institutions carry on research and development activities — and by Fondazione Idis-Città della Scienza with the participation of the University of Naples Federico II. At national level, CITTC could also count on the support of Netval, the Network for the Valorisation of Research, active throughout Italy. The services provided by CITTC included: partner scouting, support for business matching, valorization of intellectual property rights, organization of roadshows, thematic symposia, industrial visits for foreign delegations, and mobility programs for students and professionals. The underlying idea was that of promoting the creation of scientific and industrial partnerships to encourage mutual investment and talent training in the field of technological innovation, which found a very fertile ground in Bergamo's innovation ecosystem.

Against the background of the CITTC, another initiative was launched in 2017 which, during the COVID-19 period, essentially replaced the CITTC: the China–Italy Laboratory on Advanced Manufacturing (CI-LAM). CI-LAM is a bilateral platform established for the promotion and valorization of the research and development activities jointly carried on by its partners in the field of smart and advanced manufacturing. CI-LAM is meant to combine the resources of universities and enterprises to run joint

---

[18] Official website, http://www.cittc.it/.

[19] Official website, https://www.kilometrorosso.com/en/.

research and development activities for product application and innovation, in so doing also supporting manufacturing stakeholders in both countries, especially SMEs and start-ups, to adopt new paradigms and industrial technologies.

CI-LAM initiative has been coordinated, on the Italian side by the Universities of Bergamo together with the University of Naples Federico II while, on the Chinese side, by Tsinghua University in Beijing. It has been supported from the very beginning also by industrial partners in both countries, with Campania NewSteel Srl and China Science and Technology Automation Alliance as founding members in 2017.

The initiative is part of the internationalization efforts and cooperation action that the University of Bergamo is carrying out on various fronts, from scientific research to training and technology transfer, and represents an effective bridge of collaboration between China and Italy in the sector of advanced production systems. In this sense, advanced training is meant to bring industrial and academic realities closer together and create the conditions for collaboration and sustainable development.

CI-LAM was also mentioned in the "Action Plan towards 2025 between Italy and China on scientific and technological cooperation" drawn up by the Italian Ministry of Foreign Affairs and International Cooperation as a practical contribution to the bilateral cooperation in the field of advanced manufacturing.[20]

3.3.2 *Main activities and achievements*

The main activities organized to date under the framework of CI-LAM are the following:

- **CI-LAM Summer School:** two-week course dedicated to master's and doctoral students organized annually in Italy or China at one of the partner universities and open to external students. The Summer School includes lectures and industrial visits and has now reached its sixth edition.

[20] Italia-Cina: collaborazione scientifica e tecnologica. Piano d'Azione verso il 2025. Ministero degli Affari Esteri e della Cooperazione Internazionale. Direzione Generale per il Sistema Paese, https://www.esteri.it/mae/resource/doc/2020/03/piano_dazione_st_verso2025r.pdf.

- **Innovation Webinar Series:** a series of seminars on topics addressed to professionals and managers related to advanced manufacturing technologies, including manufacturing system, Energy, Predictive maintenance, AI and Big Data, Cobotic, Cybersecurity, DC connections Grid, and 5G, all seen from the perspective of Industry 4.0.

  In each webinar, a keynote speaker provided an overview of the state of the art on the specific technology, followed by the presentation of four case studies of SMEs or start-ups from the Italian and Chinese innovation ecosystem.
- **2023 China–Italy Science, Technology and Innovation Week:** CI-LAM was one of the organizers of the Smart Manufacturing Forum in the 2023 edition of the China–Italy Science, Technology and Innovation Week, organized by Italy's MUR and China's MOST.

3.3.3 *The years of pandemic and future perspectives*

The spread of the pandemic certainly affected the mobility exchanges with China, but didn't stop the bilateral activities: the Summer School went online in 2020 and 2021, actually allowing a larger participation than a physical version would have, and was held in a hybrid mode in 2022. The University and the municipality of Bergamo in general have been deeply affected by COVID-19, but after the first reaction of stigmatization of the management of the pandemic in the North of Italy that went on the Chinese media in 2020, Bergamo found itself closer to China than one would expect: the first batch of masks and medical devices that arrived during the emergency was shipped from China and the local institutions in Bergamo are still grateful for it.

With the resumption of mobility and of normal activities, the leadership of the university prepared its first mission to China after COVID-19. The result of which was that, on 4 December 2023, a liaison office of the University of Bergamo and a liaison CI-LAM office were inaugurated in Beijing, inside the Zhongguancun (E-Town) International Robot Industrial Park of the Beijing Economic-Technological Development Area. The two offices extend over an area of approximately 100 square meters, offering a physical space to the Laboratory which until then has only been virtual, with the aim of giving new impetus to the initiative.

A key factor in reaching this milestone were the relations built with authorities of Beijing Municipality, especially with the former Vice Mayor Yu Yingjie, who visited Bergamo in September 2023.

In April 2024, a delegation from Bergamo University visited again Beijing on the occasion of the important Zhongguancun Forum, a national-level open innovation platform and an international forum that takes place in Zhongguancun, China's first national high-tech industrial development zone, also known as "China's Silicon Valley". The University Rector joined a session on China–Italy Intelligent Technology Innovation Cooperation, which was the opportunity to showcase the role played by the University of Bergamo in the local innovation ecosystem and its approach to innovation cooperation with China: one of the main elements is the ability of bringing together and coordinating different stakeholders, therefore including the whole local industrial fabric; the university engages in projects and initiatives as part of an innovation ecosystem, sharing common values and specialization.

The mission to Beijing was also the opportunity to renew CI-LAM agreement and open it to new partners. In this new phase, the three universities — the University of Bergamo, Tsinghua University, and the University of Naples Federico II — remain the core members of the initiative, ensuring that shared research interests underpin all joint activities.

The main goal of CI-LAM is indeed to promote and enhance the results of joint cutting-edge research made by universities, research institutions, and enterprises and to develop collaboration within the field of smart and sustainable manufacturing systems, including mutual technology transfer, demonstrative applications, and commercialization, with a win-win approach.

The synergy of CI-LAM activities with the whole innovation ecosystem in both countries is made possible thanks to the other partners joining the initiative. As a matter of fact, each research institution also brings in an industrial partner: Intellimech — a private consortium of enterprises based in Bergamo and aimed at interdisciplinary research in the mechatronic field, China Science and Technology Automation Alliance — a professional association based in Beijing and dedicated to advancing science and technology innovation with automation technology and promoting integration between the above two, and SPICI Srl — Society for Innovation, Cooperation and Internationalization in Naples.

Among the new partners joining CI-LAM starting from April 2024 are Capital Normal University, Hangxing China–Italy Innovation Incubator, and Tus-Caohejing (Shanghai) Management & Operation Co., Ltd.

The Beijing liaison offices will soon have resident Chinese and Italian staff and host on-site seminars, conferences and webinars, training courses, and promotional activities in conjunction with fairs and other events, and will offer support and space to Italian experts visiting Beijing. The idea is to create opportunities for connecting Italian and Chinese companies in robotics, advanced manufacturing, and other areas, with special regard to the areas of Bergamo and Beijing. Simultaneously, the joint research activities and visiting exchanges between the University of Bergamo and Tsinghua University are being incremented.

The CI-LAM aims to be an effective collaboration bridge between China and Italy, first in the field of advanced manufacturing, but its goal is to expand to other fields of mutual interest, such as those of sustainability and longevity, topics of great interest in the Bergamo ecosystem. The CI-LAM will serve as a platform for the involvement of other scientific and industrial entities, including enterprises, consortia, industrial districts and scientific parks, universities and research institutions, associations, and other organizations, public or private, that are interested in engaging in research, didactic and exchange programs between China and Italy.

As the first step in this direction, the university is organizing an upcoming visit from the leaders of Zhongguancun (E-Town) International Robot Industrial Park to Bergamo, especially thinking of creating a direct connection with Kilometro Rosso Innovation District and bringing the two innovation ecosystems of Beijing and Bergamo closer.

To reach these goals, CI-LAM will rely on two main bodies: a Steering Committee to define its strategies and enact its activities, and a Board of CI-LAM Members, to provide advisory support and ensure that all partners are listened to in the definition of strategic objectives.

In general, the university's collaboration approach with China well aligns with its Third Mission, terms which refer to the activities of scientific, technological, and cultural transfer and productive transformation of knowledge, taking place via direct interaction of the university with civil society and the industrial sector, with the aim of promoting economic, social and cultural development. This approach of engaging the whole innovation ecosystem, rather than focusing strictly on the collaboration between higher institutions has proven successful for Bergamo. Over the years, the joint training and research activities and the mobility initiatives between Bergamo and Beijing have ensured a constant transfer of scientific and technological knowledge between the two countries, keeping the industrial partners engaged, with the University of Bergamo playing the role of intermediary for scientific and innovation cooperation.

In this period of geopolitical tensions, initiatives like the one of CI-LAM and the role played by universities and their science diplomacy are crucial as they have proven to be gateways to support and encourage China–Italy cooperation in innovation.

4. Conclusions and Future Perspectives

At the end of this research, having presented the three case studies of transnational innovation academic actors, we would like to summon, as stated in the introduction and in the list of the main aims of our research, the main results of our analysis, the similarities, differences and innovative elements of our findings. At the same time, in the final of our conclusions, we focus on the future of the Sino-Italian academic cooperation framework, bringing some suggestions.

4.1 *There is no standard model for academic cooperation between Italian and Chinese universities (for now)*

In general, the three cases of innovation intermediaries in academic and scientific cooperation between Italy and China are different but also complementary. In fact, they are active in different parts of China (Beijing, Chongqing) and have or do not have staff in China (Sant'Anna has been able to count on three Chinese resources present on site since the beginning of the pandemic, while PoliTo and UniBg have set up several delegations but not have a fixed presence in the country) and have been active in various sectors (between many, Pisa has supported cooperation activities with a special focus on management and hard sciences, Turin has achieved significant results on architecture and design, while Bergamo has invested in advanced manufacturing).

At the same time, the three case studies acted as "pioneers" in their cooperation stories. In fact, in all three cases, they did not count on a previous and already steady presence, but instead inaugurated the cooperation for their universities, and then structured and improved it over time. They were born thanks to the visions and interest toward China by Professors and researchers that truly represent an immensely rich capital of stories, exchanges, and learning activities that go beyond academia but were able to change lives and the history of these people.

At the moment therefore, at least based on what has been analyzed in our chapter, we can affirm that there is no common paradigm for academic cooperation, but different models active in China communicating with each other, essentially different and autonomous.

4.2 *The pandemic had a great impact and represented a major challenge, but it is now over*

The pandemic represented a significant turning point in the history of these academic cooperation projects. In all three cases, the pandemic blocked the exchange of delegations for some years and physically distanced the people working from Italy and China. The different teams faced the challenge with tenacity, relying on technologies to stay connected, and developing different activities compared to pre-pandemic years. 2023 was the year of the true restart, while 2024 has seen several new projects and agreements implemented, while Italian and Chinese delegations were able to travel again and to restart cooperation activities on site.

4.3 *The three case studies represent intermediaries of innovation for academic cooperation*

Each of the three projects has created its own way of developing cooperation over the years, becoming, in all respects, examples of innovation in the academic field. The three cases of cooperation have developed their own innovative and hybrid language, halfway between Italy and China, counting on Italian and Chinese resources. In a factual way, the three case studies represent a wealth of skills, from a human, linguistic, and strategic point of view, which we believe can be useful in strengthening relations between Italy and China not only in the scientific field but in the bigger picture of the Sino-Italian relations.

Innovative ways of cooperating between the members of the teams and the leaders of the projects were indispensable during the pandemic years: technologies such as WeChat, Tencent Meetings, and Tencent Clouds were essential on a daily basis to find new ways of working together. Trust (but also friendship and mutual understanding) became the key in many moments of challenge, and the investments in human capital in the pre-pandemic years truly paid off.

4.4 *Future of Sino-Italian academic cooperation must move from innovation to implementation*

The three cases described in this chapter represent, on the one hand, successful innovation intermediaries between Chinese and Italian universities, and on the other, cases of innovation in the scientific and management fields spanning two worlds. Our final advice, dedicated to colleagues working in not only the academic sector but also institutions and companies, and other key players of the "Italian System" operating in China, is to keep in mind these case studies, which bring with them human capital, successful results and countless elements of linguistic and cultural interpenetration between Italy and China, and to capitalize on it, if possible, to build in the hopefully not too distant future a cooperation model that can be implemented in a strategic and widespread way.

References

Bani, M., Di Minin, A., and Facchinetti, A. (2018). Belt and Road Initiative e trasferimento tecnologico, alcune chiavi di lettura. *Mondo Cinese*, 165–166, 75–88.

Barbatelli, C. and Cavalieri, R. (Eds.). (2015). *La Cina non è ancora per tutti: Dialoghi sul mercato cinese*. Edizioni Olivares.

Bertuccioli, G. and Masini, F. (2011). *Italia e Cina*. L'asino d'oro edizioni.

Bonaglia, M. (2019a, October 10). "Chongqing Model" and the shift towards innovation. *Galilei Institute*. http://www.galileiinstitute.it/chongqing-model-and-the-shift-towards-innovation/.

Bonaglia, M. (2019b, November 26). Industrial parks and incubators in Chongqing: The case of Xiantao Big Data Valley. *Galilei Institute*. http://www.galileiinstitute.it/industrial-parks-and-incubators-in-chongqing-the-case-of-the-xiantao-big-data-valley/.

Bonaglia, M. (2020, September 9). From quantity to quality — The impact of the Western Development Strategy. *Galilei Institute*. http://www.galileiinstitute.it/western-development-strategy-chongqing-development/.

Bonaglia, M. (2023, March 28). Galilei Circle of Friends — Interview with Michele Bonino. *Galilei Institute*. http://www.galileiinstitute.it/galilei-circle-of-friends-michele-bonino-and-the-shougang-oxygen-factory-experience/.

Bonino, M., Bruno, E., Armando, A., and Durbiano, G. (2022). *The story of a section: Designing the Shougang Oxygen Factory*. ORO Editions.

De Giorgi, L. and Samarani, G. (2011). *Lontane, vicine, le relazioni fra Italia e Cina nel Novecento*. Carocci editore.

Di Minin, A. (2017, December 27). Celebrating Istituto Galilei 10th Anniversary. *Diminin.it.* http://www.diminin.it/2017/12/celebrating-istituto-galilei-10th-anniversary/.

Di Minin, A. and Caluti, E. (2017, March 25). Dove far germogliare i semi della Terza Missione? I 40 ettari del Sino-Italian Camp di Chongqing. https://albertodiminin.nova100.ilsole24ore.com/2017/03/25/germogliare-chongqing/.

Di Minin, A. and Fasulo, F. (2019, April 9). #ChinaIssues con Michele Bonino: La più grande urbanizzazione. *Il Sole 24 Ore.* https://albertodiminin.nova100.ilsole24ore.com/2019/04/08/chinaissues-con-michele-bonino-la-piu-grande-urbanizzazione/.

Di Minin, A. and Fasulo, A. (2023a, March 6). #China Issues con Marco Bonaglia: Cooperazione accademica tra Pisa e Chongqing: l'esempio dell'Istituto Galilei. *Il Sole 24 Ore.* https://albertodiminin.nova100.ilsole-24ore.com/2023/03/06/cooperazione-accademia-italia-cina-caso-galilei/.

Di Minin, A. and Fasulo, F. (2023b, March 27). Il Politecnico di Torino in Cina. *Il Sole 24 Ore.* https://albertodiminin.nova100.ilsole24ore.com/2023/03/27/china-issues-con-michele-bonino-politecnico-torino-cina/.

Fasulo, F. (2018, June 5). SIIB-C: "Diplomazia Hi-Tech a Bishan". *ISPI Online.* https://www.ispionline.it/it/pubblicazione/siib-c-diplomazia-hi-tech-bishan-20722.

Fedasiuk, R., Omar, A., Martinez, L., and Puglisi, A. (2022). A competitive era for China's universities: How increased funding is paving the way. *CSET Data Brief.* https://cset.georgetown.edu/publication/a-competitive-era-for-chinas-universities/

Forina, C., Bruno, E., and Bonino, M. (2024). Digging cultures of production using design practice: Transforming the Main Oxygen Factory Workshop in Shougang, Beijing. In G. Botti, E. Mangi, and H. Shinohara (Eds.), *Building Technology and Culture in the Asia-Pacific Region: Transnational Histories of Design Cultures and Production.* Springer. https://doi.org/10.1007/978-981-97-1794-1_10.

Pini, M. F. (2011). *Italia e Cina, 60 anni tra passato e futuro.* L'Asino d'oro edizioni.

Politecnico di Torino. (2023, July 19). Politecnico reinforces its partnerships in China. https://www.polito.it/en/polito/communication-and-press-office/poliflash/politecnico-reinforces-its-partnerships-in-china.

Redazione Pisa Today. (2017, February 22). Cooperazione scientifica Italia-Cina: Accordo del Sant'Anna con la Chongqing University. *Pisa Today.* https://www.pisatoday.it/cronaca/cooperazione-scientifica-italia-cina-accordo-san-tanna-chongqing-university.html.

Redazione Scuola. (2023, July 14). Inaugurata la Summer School promossa da Unibg, Unina e Tsinghua University. *Il Sole 24 Ore.* https://www.ilsole24ore.

com/art/inaugurata-summer-school-promossa-unibg-unina-e-tsinghua-university-AF8L9AE.

Sabbadin, D. (2017, October 26). Little Italy a Chongqing. *La Nuova Ecologia.* https://www.lanuovaecologia.it/little-italy-chongqing/.

Sant'Anna Magazine. (2017a, May 2). Sant'Anna works to develop a stronger partnership with China: Opening ceremony of the "time gallery" to celebrate the 10th anniversary of "Galileo Galilei Institute in Chongqing". https://www.santannapisa.it/en/news/santanna-works-develop-stronger-partnership-china-opening-ceremony-time-gallery-celebrate-10th.

Sant'Anna Magazine. (2017b, November 13). Italy-China Cooperation: Minister Valeria Fedeli awarded Sant'Anna School professor the Italy China Research and Innovation Cooperation Award. https://www.santannapisa.it/en/news/italy-china-cooperation-minister-valeria-fedeli-awarded-santanna-school-professor-italy-china.

Sant'Anna Magazine. (2017c, November 21). Italy China partnership: Sant'Anna School has played a leading role in the development of the Chongqing "Galileo Galilei" Institute over the past 10 years. https://www.santannapisa.it/en/news/italy-china-partnership-santanna-school-has-played-leading-role-development-chongqing-galileo.

Sant'Anna Magazine. (2018a, October 30). Relazioni Italia Cina: l'ex Presidente del Consiglio Matteo Renzi in visita al Galileo Galilei Italian Institute di Chongqing gestito dall'Istituto di Management della Scuola Sant'Anna. https://www.santannapisa.it/en/node/42075.

Sant'Anna Magazine. (2018b, November 14). Italy-China relationship: Italian parliamentary delegation visits the Galileo Galilei Italian Institute in Chongqing. https://www.santannapisa.it/en/news/italy-china-relationship-italian-parliamentary-delegation-visits-galileo-galilei-italian.

https://doi.org/10.1142/9789819807611_0007

Chapter 7

How to Improve Open Innovation in China's SMEs? The Role of Open Innovation Networks and Platforms

Nan Wang[*,‡] **and Liya Wang**[†,§]

[*]*Beijing Technology and Business University, Fucheng Road, Haidian District, Beijing, China*

[†]*Beijing Jiaotong University, Beixiaguan Road, Haidian District, Beijing, China*

[‡]*wangnan5819356@163.com*
[§]*wly199410@126.com*

Abstract

Facing rapid technological advancements and fierce market competition, the traditional closed innovation model is insufficient for achieving sustainable competitive advantage. Open innovation (OI), which involves searching and integrating external knowledge and resources, emerges as a crucial strategy for enterprises to improve innovation capabilities and maintain a leading position in the market, especially for small and medium-sized enterprises (SMEs). Open innovation networks (OINs) are essential for these SMEs to access the necessary innovation knowledge and resources to overcome resource and capability limitations.

By constructing and maintaining OI network platforms, enterprises can collaborate with a variety of external entities such as suppliers, customers, universities, and research institutions to form a robust innovation ecosystem.

Within this context, this chapter considers the combination of digital technology and corporate innovation as a means to improve the efficiency and effectiveness of the innovation process. Especially digital platforms as innovation intermediaries and digital innovation ecosystems can enable SMEs to transcend organizational boundaries to achieve cross-border cooperation and value co-creation, ultimately facilitating the sustainable development of enterprises in a fiercely competitive market environment.

Keywords: Open innovation; open innovation network; digital platform; digital innovation ecosystems

1. Introduction

With the rapid development of digital technology and increasingly fierce market competition, innovation has become a complex activity (Yoo *et al.*, 2010; Fichman *et al.*, 2014). Enterprises relying on their own strength to focus on internal R&D can hardly meet the needs of innovation, and it is difficult to adapt to the fast-developing market demand and the increasingly fierce competition among enterprises.

In this context, open innovation (OI), which involves searching for and acquiring new knowledge from the outside, has become the dominant mode for enterprises to gain sustainable competitive advantages (Chesbrough, 2003). OI is an innovation model that opens up a firm's traditionally closed innovation model and introduces external innovation resources. OI emphasizes that enterprises can benefit from the integration of internal R&D knowledge with external knowledge, and jointly form the foundation of innovation. At the same time, OI actively seeks appropriate business models such as joint ventures, technology licensing, outsourcing research, technology partnerships, strategic alliances, or venture capital to turn innovative ideas into real products and profits as soon as possible (Ferreras-Méndez *et al.*, 2015). Such an OI model helps enterprises to bridge organizational boundaries to make up for the lack of internal resources, improve innovation efficiency, reduce the cost and risk of independent research and development, improve the success rate of innovation, and help enterprises to better grasp the market opportunities and improve their competitiveness and sustainable development capabilities. Therefore, the OI of enterprises has gradually become a research hotspot in the field of innovation management.

China is in the midst of an economic transformation, and in recent years, a large number of technology-based small and medium-sized enterprises (SMEs) have emerged. Unlike large mature enterprises, SMEs are relatively limited in terms of resources and capabilities, making it difficult for them to conduct large-scale R&D investment and technological innovation.

In the context of OI, SMEs need to keep up with the latest technologies to maintain a leading position in the competition. SMEs can collaborate with external institutions and enterprises to obtain more external technical support and new knowledge to compensate for their own shortcomings, improve their technological level and innovation ability, and enhance their competitiveness and market position. At the same time, OI can help SMEs share R&D resources and knowledge through collaborative R&D, reduce R&D costs, and shorten R&D cycles.

Thus, an OI strategy is an inevitable choice for SMEs to cope with market changes and enhance their competitiveness. However, resource-constrained SMEs are prone to certain negative impacts of OI due to the existence of transaction costs, management costs, information search costs, and technology leakage (Chen *et al.*, 2011). The OI models and experiences of large mature enterprises cannot be fully applied to these small and medium-sized enterprises.

Therefore, the question: "how can SMEs improve their sustainable competitive advantages in OI?" has become an important issue that needs to be solved urgently. Thus, it is necessary to carry out research on OI of SMEs in China.

This chapter reviews the paradigm of OI for SMEs within China's transformation context by considering the role of OI network and platforms as relevant innovation intermediaries.

2. Building OI Networks to Boost OI in SMEs

Due to the limited innovation resources available to SMEs, most SMEs are unable to support the entire innovation process of the enterprise or, even if they have completed the technological development of a new product, it is difficult for them to complete the entire process from production to sales completely independently. In the context of OI, the boundaries of enterprises are relatively blurred, and a relatively open network is formed between different organizations (Akbar and Giuseppe, 2009).

The knowledge and resources needed by enterprises to support innovation come from not only within the enterprise but also the external network in which the enterprise is located, which is an important way for enterprises to obtain the knowledge and resources they need. OI networks (OINs) are formal or informal innovation cooperation networks of mutual trust, long-term cooperation, and mutual benefit formed by various innovation agents through contractual relationships or based on repeated transactions in the process of technological innovation by an enterprise (Ndou *et al*., 2011). Therefore, SMEs must establish links with other organizations (e.g., suppliers, customers, competitors, universities, research institutes, investment banks, and government departments) and achieve sustainable development by embedding themselves in OINs in order to access the knowledge, information, and other resources needed for innovation.

OINs provide a smooth and organized innovation platform for SMEs implementing technological innovation. The OINs can be composed of innovative subjects from other enterprises, higher education institutions, research institutes, etc. SMEs can obtain a wider range of innovation resources through cooperation and communication with external partners, universities, research institutes, and other innovation intermediaries, and then effectively utilize these resources to carry out product R&D, and technological improvement to realize breakthroughs in technological innovation. For example, as one of China's strategic emerging industries, the new energy automobile industry relies mainly on cooperative innovation in the form of industrial alliances, which cover enterprises, universities, and research institutions.

With the increasingly close connection between industrial alliances, the cooperative innovation relationship between enterprises not only is limited to the internal industrial alliance but also presents a complex network structure of vertical and horizontal intertwining. By constructing, integrating, and maintaining the OI network, enterprises can effectively integrate the technical knowledge and market knowledge in the innovation network, and continuously improve their own technological capability and market capability, so as to enhance their catching-up ability.

(1) **Construction and integration of OI platforms:** SMEs can absorb external innovation resources and promote their own innovation development by building and integrating an OI platform. On the one hand, SMEs build their own OI platforms and encourage their internal

employees and external innovators to participate in their OI activities. On the other hand, SMEs can join existing OI platforms, such as open-source software platforms and technology innovation platforms. Through OI platforms, SMEs can establish partnerships with large enterprises, universities, research institutions, etc., and jointly participate in OI (Chen *et al.*, 2011). Through cooperation, SMEs can obtain more resources and technical support to improve their innovation ability. SMEs need to clarify their own position in the OINs, as well as their advantages and shortcomings. According to their own characteristics, they choose suitable ways to participate in OI, such as providing innovation resources and participating in open-source projects. In addition, the OI network is an ever-changing innovation ecosystem, and SMEs need to maintain a state and attitude of continuous learning and improvement to constantly understand industry dynamics and technological development trends, optimize their own innovation strategies, and improve their own competitiveness. Organizational learning theory suggests that SMEs' organizational learning capability is an important guarantee for transforming existing resources into applicable resources (Gebauer *et al.*, 2012). In order for a company to maintain an undefeated competitive advantage and strengthen in the competition, it is necessary to give assurance within the organization through continuous learning. Organizational behavior is also continuously adjusted with the process of organizational learning and further influences the innovative development of the firm. Organizational learning can help enterprises make better use of the knowledge gained in the network and convert it into applied knowledge to improve the efficiency of the use of resources gained in the network, at the same time, organizational learning is an important guarantee to enhance the motivation of organizational technological innovation and improve the vitality of organizational innovation. The more network-embedded SMEs are, the easier it is for them to learn externally through knowledge-sharing mechanisms in their interactions. SMEs can acquire resources by embedding themselves in the network, and after integrating and reorganizing the acquired resources, they can carry out technological innovations to enhance their sustainable competitive advantages.

(2) **Maintain of OI network:** Maintaining OI networks is crucial to the long-term development of SMEs. First of all, SMEs need to optimize the OI network structure and network dynamics. OI culture is one of

the key factors to promote the development of an innovation network. Enterprises themselves need to cultivate a culture of openness, inclusiveness, and collaboration and encourage their employees to actively share knowledge and technology, participate in external cooperation, and accept new challenges and opportunities. This will help increase employee motivation and creativity and promote the rapid development of OI networks to maintain the vitality and attractiveness of OI networks. Meanwhile, as an OI network is a dynamic process, it needs to be optimized and expanded continuously. Enterprises should understand the needs and dynamics of their partners and adjust their cooperation methods and strategies in a timely manner. Moreover, they need to actively seek new partner nodes and relationships to expand the coverage and influence of OI networks to enhance the diversity and vitality of OI networks. Second, it is crucial for firms to establish trusting relationships and long-term communication mechanisms in OI networks. By improving their ability to manage innovation partnerships, firms can maintain timely and efficient communication with partners, external innovators, and other stakeholders. According to structural hole theory, SMEs build deep relationships with external search sources, and this strong relationship facilitates a large flow of high-quality information, enabling firms to gain a deeper understanding of their partners' expertise. The establishment of a deep trust relationship also leads to the maintenance of a pattern of interaction over time between the firm and the external search source, resulting in common practices and treaties (Jack, 2005). Based on mutual trust, information shared between the two will be more reliable and accurate.

3. Exploring OI Models Suitable for SMEs in OINs: The Case of China

China's unique market system determines that local firms may have different innovation behavior patterns from those of Western firms, and we should try to explore an OI model suitable for Chinese SMEs.

As a result, how Chinese SMEs develop OI strategies in OI networks has become the focus of attention. As a new mode of information and knowledge transfer, OI encompasses the whole process of searching, analyzing, internalizing, and reorganizing external resources, which provides external support for organizations to occupy a sustainable competitive advantage in the market (Chesbrough and Crowther, 2006). Based on the scope and depth of the search for external information and resources, Laursen and Salter (2006) proposed the concept of "openness to innovation", which divides OI into breadth and depth of openness to innovation, with the breadth of openness to innovation reflecting the breadth of cooperation between an enterprise and an external innovation body, and depth of openness to innovation indicating the extent of cooperation between an enterprise and an external innovation body, and the depth of openness to innovation indicating the depth of cooperation between an enterprise and an external innovation body. The breadth of innovation openness reflects the extensive degree of cooperation between the enterprise and external innovation subjects, while the depth of innovation openness indicates the close degree of cooperation between the enterprise and external subjects. The breadth and depth of openness determine the quantity and quality of the organization's access to external resources. The wider the degree of innovation openness, the more conducive it is for enterprises to obtain differentiated and diversified knowledge or information from the outside, which can help the organization understand market demand more accurately, jump out of the original technological trajectory in time, and break the path dependence of inter-organizational cooperation and innovation. The greater the depth of innovation openness, the more conducive to the establishment of a relationship of trust between the two parties, the more knowledge an enterprise obtains from a limited number of cooperative partners through repeated cooperation, the formation of cooperation practices, the reduction of cooperation costs, and the promotion of the transfer of tacit knowledge to promote the development of enterprise innovation.

However, as the goals and preferences of the breadth and depth of openness to innovation do not coincide, the resource constraints and attention scarcity of SMEs, in particular, may exacerbate the contradiction between the breadth and depth of openness to innovation, resulting in a certain degree of tension between the two. When the enterprise carries out too extensive OI, it may cause the enterprise's external resource cost to rise, information overload, innovation path dependence and the conflict of new and old knowledge, etc., while excessive innovation open depth may make the enterprise fall into the "integration-oriented" inertia and path dependence, which may have the effect of "too much is not enough". These situations are especially significant for resource-constrained SMEs. Therefore, how to coordinate and balance the breadth and depth of innovation openness is an urgent challenge for enterprises.

To avoid an imbalance toward one extreme in the OI process, SMEs need to choose the right balance of openness to innovation, i.e., a balance between expanding the scope of OI and deepening the degree of openness to innovation in order to optimize access to external resources. Drawing on the organizational duality of "exploration-exploitation" (March, 1991), there are two modes of "punctuated equilibrium" and "simultaneous equilibrium" between the breadth of openness to innovation and the depth of openness to innovation. "simultaneous equilibrium" and "punctuated equilibrium" between the breadth and depth of innovation openness. "Simultaneous equilibrium" refers to the synergistic and complementary effects of the breadth and depth of openness to innovation in parallel sequential extension. On the one hand, the depth of innovation openness deeply masters and optimizes existing knowledge and technology, but the knowledge source obtained at a deep level may not be able to meet the dynamic demand of SMEs for continuous innovation, at this time, the breadth of innovation openness can precisely provide enterprises with diversified knowledge sources and complementary knowledge; on the other hand, the breadth of innovation openness is able to introduce a large amount of heterogeneous knowledge for the enterprise, but it also brings a greater degree of uncertainty for the enterprise, at this time On the other hand, the breadth of innovation openness can introduce a large amount of heterogeneous knowledge to the firm, but it also creates greater uncertainty for the firm, and then the depth of innovation openness can build up the strength of the firm's extensive search for knowledge through the "quick realization" of innovation results (Voss and Voss, 2013).

"Punctuated equilibrium" is a certain sequence in which firms dominate the implementation of the breadth and depth of innovation openness, focusing their attention on only one of the innovation openness strategies for a certain period of time (Gupta *et al*., 2006; Kang and Kim, 2020). In fact, in the current state of China where SMEs dominate and most enterprises are in high resource scarcity, the breadth and depth of innovation openness are faced with the competition effect of enterprises' attention allocation and competition for scarce resources being further highlighted, then the balance theory of innovation openness dominated by the competition effect of competition for scarce resources under the condition of resource scarcity is a localized theoretical innovation issue with important research value. The punctuated equilibrium model assumes that there are inherent inconsistencies and conflicts between the two types of innovation openness strategies, resulting in a possible mutually exclusive relationship between them. In the punctuated equilibrium model, the phases of change are relatively compact, and there is flexible switching between the breadth and depth of innovation openness activities, so as to avoid falling into the "trap" of over-emphasizing a single innovation strategy, and thus achieve better efficiency (Turner *et al.*, 2013). On the one hand, enterprises adopting the punctuated equilibrium strategy can concentrate their scarce resources on the breadth or depth of innovation openness at a specific stage, accelerating the learning curve in "focusing on one thing" and improving the efficiency of innovation activities. On the other hand, SMEs can give full play to their advantage of "small and flexible" strategic flexibility, which can be utilized by SMEs in their innovation activities. On the other hand, SMEs can take advantage of their "small and flexible" strategic flexibility to ensure the effectiveness of their innovation activities by adjusting the focus of their innovation strategies at the right time.

Enterprises' OI activity is a dynamic process, and the equilibrium model will evolve with the change of resource constraints. Whether it is simultaneous or punctuated equilibrium, it is necessary to view the transformation and synergistic relationship between the dual behaviors of enterprise OI from the perspective of "global" and "dynamic". Based on the enterprise life cycle theory, enterprises, like living organisms, go through different stages from birth to decay, during which there are great differences in their own characteristics and capabilities (Huergo and Jaumandreu, 2004), resulting in different resource endowments and operational experiences, which will inevitably affect the innovation output of enterprises. Therefore, enterprises may have different choices of innovation open balance models at different stages of development, and the matching law between innovation open balance models and SMEs' stages of development should be actively explored.

In the growth stage, enterprises are often subject to greater resource and capacity constraints, endogenous development momentum is insufficient, and innovation openness breadth and innovation openness depth are more likely to show a binary substitution effect, at this time, the enterprise adopts the "punctuated equilibrium" innovation and openness mode to better avoid the loss of the competition between the two innovation and openness strategies and can give full play to the technological advantages in a single field of innovation openness breadth or depth, thus promoting enterprise development (Chang and Hughes, 2012). In this case, enterprises adopting the "punctuated equilibrium" innovation openness model can better avoid the losses caused by the competition effect between the two innovation openness strategies and can utilize the technological advantages in a single field of innovation openness breadth or depth, thus promoting the development of the enterprise (Chang and Hughes, 2012). The breadth of innovation openness emphasizes a broader vision, open-mindedness, and risk-taking, while the depth of innovation openness focuses more on deepening and developing existing knowledge, and the difference in mindset between the "simultaneous equilibrium" innovation openness balancing strategy makes it difficult for firms to coordinate the two types of activities. It is difficult for startups to have sufficient resources and energy to balance the breadth and depth of innovation and openness at the same time. Therefore, at this stage, firms are more inclined to switch between the two openness-to-innovation strategies according to the needs of the situation by means of "intermittent balancing" to meet their innovation needs (Gillbert, 2005). At the same time, compared with large enterprises, SMEs have a sharper sense of the market, and the organization is more flexible and other unique advantages, which is more conducive to enterprises in the process of fierce market competition and flexible innovation open strategy switching (Wenke *et al.*, 2021).

When SMEs enter the maturity stage, the organizational structure of the enterprise becomes more and more perfect, the management experience becomes more and more mature, and the stock of assets stabilizes at a high level, the constraints of resource scarcity on SMEs' innovation and openness strategies will gradually diminish. Enterprises in the maturity stage have sufficient heterogeneous resources of their own, which can effectively alleviate the competition for scarce resources between the two innovation and openness strategies and promote the synergistic relationship between the two innovation and openness strategies, therefore, it is more beneficial for enterprises to choose the "simultaneous equilibrium" innovation and openness model for their development. Although the breadth and depth of innovation openness require different concepts and mental models, at this stage, SMEs already have the resources and ability to balance the two types of innovation openness strategies simultaneously, and enterprises are able to deploy and apply sufficient productive resources to extend both the breadth and depth of innovation openness at a higher level.

In addition, with the development of the enterprise, when the enterprise enters the recession period, the enterprise asset size and cash flow continue to shrink, and resource redundancy is constantly compressed, but because the enterprise in the recession period through many times with the external dynamic environment interaction already has a high degree of adaptive experience accumulation, which makes the enterprise innovation open balance strategy choice more proactive. By estimating the complex interaction between the breadth of innovation openness, the depth of innovation openness and the time of transformation, it can maximize the effect of innovation. Enterprises in a recession can strengthen the development of idle redundant resources to further release the redundant innovation capacity of the enterprise, give full play to the synergistic effect of the two innovation openness strategies, reduce the replacement cost of innovation, and help to promote SMEs to enter a new enterprise life cycle. Therefore, it is more beneficial for enterprises in recession to choose the "simultaneous equilibrium" innovation and openness model.

To summarize, in a market environment of increasingly fierce competition and rising technological complexity, SMEs should dynamically adjust the balance model of innovation search strategy and formulate a reasonable balance strategy of innovation openness according to their own innovation needs and life cycle, so as to balance the expansion of the scope of OI search and the deepening of the degree of innovation openness. On the one hand, it should strengthen the connection with external organizations and adjust the resource allocation and strategic objectives to discover and integrate the possible innovation opportunities. On the other hand, strengthen the in-depth communication with the existing external channels to avoid superficiality, so that the organization can obtain accurate information and cutting-edge key knowledge at a lower cost in the deep integration, thus promoting the enhancement of the stock of knowledge and the expansion of organizational knowledge in the direction of specialization, complexity, and other in-depth directions, in order to promote the sustainable and healthy development of the enterprise. By comprehensively utilizing innovation intermediary resources such as different partners, universities, research institutions, customers, and users, as well as industry associations and alliances, we can obtain more comprehensive and in-depth external knowledge and information so as to better support the innovation activities of enterprises.

4. Digitalization for OI in SMEs

The improvement of enterprise digitization improves OI capabilities and accelerates the deep integration of enterprise technological innovation and digital technology (Yoo *et al.*, 2010). On the one hand, the development of the digital economy provides broader innovation space and opportunities for SMEs to build OINs, enabling enterprises to better utilize external resources for OI and enhance their competitiveness and innovation capabilities. With the support of digital technology, digital platforms can connect multilateral markets and break through temporal, spatial, and organizational boundaries to support resource exchange among stakeholders (Constantinides *et al.*, 2018). The decentralized and boundary-less characteristics of digital platforms enhance knowledge flow and value spillover within the platform (de Reuver *et al.*, 2018), allowing enterprises to acquire and deploy resources at an unprecedented scale and speed. This helps platform participants leverage digital technology to achieve rapid information exchange and co-create value (Cenamor *et al.*, 2019), bringing diversity and heterogeneity of external knowledge sources to platform participants (Ahmed *et al.*, 2022), greatly enhancing the OI capabilities of enterprises. For example, the emergence of crowdsourcing platforms and OI communities has helped enterprises draw resources from a broader external environment, further enhancing the value of OI (Wang *et al.*, 2022). At the same time, digital technologies provide strong momentum and support for the development of digital platforms. Big data analysis helps enterprises efficiently and rapidly obtain and analyze external information to better understand market and industry dynamics, providing a more accurate direction and basis for SMEs' OI (Lepore *et al.*, 2023b). This enables enterprises to more widely absorb external innovative resources and wisdom, integrate open resources, obtain rich complementary resources, and ultimately achieve value co-creation (Khan and Tao, 2022). Cloud computing offers enterprises flexible computing and storage resources, enabling them to scale up or down their digital platforms as needed. Through cloud computing, businesses can rapidly deploy and update applications, enhancing their ability to respond to market changes. Moreover, digital technology also reduces the cost of information transmission and storage, making communication and interaction more convenient. Enterprises interact in real-time with multiple subjects such as customers, suppliers, competitors, and virtual communities to widely utilize information and data in the external environment, continuously acquire various innovative information and knowledge, and conduct OI (Spigarelli *et al.*, 2024).

On the other hand, the development of digital economy helps enterprises explore suitable OI strategies. Digital technologies such as big data, cloud computing, and artificial intelligence can effectively promote resource integration and reorganization in the process of enterprise R&D innovation by efficiently identifying innovative opportunities and unique resources (Huang *et al.*, 2017; Tumbas *et al.*, 2018), achieving the infiltration of OI for enterprises. Therefore, the high complementarity between enterprise OI strategies and digitalization levels will enable enterprises to achieve higher innovation efficiency. The higher the level of digitalization, the easier it is for enterprises to quickly grasp external market information and understand the latest trends in technology development. This improves the responsiveness and flexibility of enterprises and helps them make scientific decisions. Digital enterprises, digital markets, digital users, and governments have formed a digital ecosystem that interacts and shares resources online and offline (Lepore *et al.*, 2023a), providing efficient search paths and methods for enterprises to access various heterogeneous knowledge, and supporting the internalization and reuse of heterogeneous knowledge (Gao *et al.*, 2022; Teece, 2018), which helps reduce the negative impact caused by excessive openness. At the same time, enterprises with high digitalization levels can effectively use digital technologies such as big data analysis and cloud computing to improve the efficiency of information exchange between knowledge modules and accelerate knowledge integration and reorganization. This enabling effect helps enterprises integrate internal innovation resources at lower costs, reducing the negative impact of deep-level OI. Therefore, it can be seen that enterprises with higher digitalization levels are more suitable for "simultaneous balance". Optimizing the efficiency and effectiveness of enterprise OI through digital technologies such as big data analysis, cloud computing, and digital platforms. The enhancement of the synergistic complementary effect between innovation openness breadth and innovation openness depth under digital scenarios can promote the high-quality development of enterprises.

5. Conclusions

This chapter provided a comprehensive analysis of the role of OI strategy in Small and Medium-sized Enterprises (SMEs), particularly within the context of China's economic transformation.

It argues that, due to limited internal resources and capabilities, SMEs must leverage OI to maintain competitiveness and foster technological advancement. Additionally, it emphasizes that the construction of OI networks (OINs) is a critical mechanism for SMEs to access external knowledge and resources, which is essential for sustainable development.

In the OINs, we advocate for a dynamic adjustment of OI strategies for SMEs, choosing the right balance model of OI to optimize resource acquisition and innovation outcomes. Meanwhile, innovation strategies should adapt to the trend of digital transformation, efficiently utilizing digital platforms as relevant innovation intermediaries, and digital innovation ecosystems to enhance the OI capabilities of enterprises, ultimately promoting sustainable and healthy business growth.

References

Ahmed, A., Bhatti, S. H., Gölgeci, I., *et al.* (2022). Digital platform capability and organizational agility of emerging market manufacturing SMEs: The mediating role of intellectual capital and the moderating role of environmental dynamism. *Technological Forecasting & Social Change*, 177, 121513. https://doi.org/10.1016/j.techfore.2022.121513.

Akbar, Z. and Giuseppe, S. (2009). Network evolution: The origins of structural holes. *Administrative Science Quarterly*, 54(1), 1–31.

Cenamor, J., Parida, V., and Wincent, J. (2019). How entrepreneurial SMEs compete through digital platforms: The roles of digital platform capability, network capability and ambidexterity. *Journal of Business Research*, 100, 196–206.

Chang, Y. Y. and Hughes, M. (2012). Drivers of innovation ambidexterity in small to medium-sized firms. *European Management Journal*, 30(1), 1–17.

Chen, J., Chen, Y., and Vanhaverbeke, W. (2011). The influence of scope, depth, and orientation of external technology sources on the innovative performance of Chinese firms. *Technovation*, 31(8), 362–373.

Chesbrough, H. (2003). *Open Innovation: The New Imperative for Creating and Profiting from Technology*. Harvard Business School Press, Boston.

Chesbrough, H. and Crowther, A. K. (2006). Beyond high tech: Early adopters of open innovation in other industries. *R&D Management*, 36(3), 229–236.

Constantinides, P., Henfridsson, O., and Parker, G. G. (2018). Platforms and infrastructures in the digital age. *Information Systems Research*, 29(2), 381–400.

de Reuver, M., Sorensen, C., and Basole, R. C. (2018). The digital platform: A research agenda. *Journal of Information Technology*, 33(2), 124–135.

Ferreira, J. J. M., Fernandes, C. I., and Ferreira, F. A. F. (2019). To be or not to be digital, that is the question: Firm innovation and performance. *Journal of Business Research*, 101, 583–590.

Fichman, R. G., Nambisan, S., and Halpern, M. (2014). Configurational thinking and value creation from digital innovation: The case of product lifecycle management implementation. In *Digital innovation and entrepreneurship*. Palgrave Macmillan.

Gao, H., Deng, X., and Wu, S. (2022). Impact of knowledge search on product and process innovation: Mediating role of absorptive capacity and moderating role of IT capability. *European Journal of Innovation Management*, 25(2), 325–346.

Gebauer, H., Worch, H., and Truffer, B. (2012). Absorptive capacity, learning processes and combinative capabilities as determinants of strategic innovation. *European Management Journal*, 30(1), 57–73.

Gilbert, C. G. (2005). Unbundling the structure of inertia: Resource vs. routine rigidity. *Academy of Management Journal*, 48(5), 741–763.

Gupta, A. K., Smith, K. G., and Shalley, C. E. (2006). The interplay between exploration and exploitation. *Academy of Management Journal*, 49(4), 693–706.

Huang, J., Henfridsson, O., Liu, M., *et al.* (2017). Growing on steroids: Rapidly scaling the user base of digital ventures through digital innovation. *MIS Quarterly*, 41(1), 301–314.

Huergo, E. and Jaumandreu, J. (2004). How does probability of innovation change with firm age. *Small Business Economics*, 22(3-4), 193–207.

Jack, S. L. (2005). The role, use and activation of strong and weak network ties: A qualitative analysis. *Journal of Management Studies*, 42(6), 1233–1259.

Kang, J. and Kim, S. J. (2020). Performance implications of incremental transition and discontinuous jump between exploration and exploitation. *Strategic Management Journal*, 41(6), 1083–1111.

Khan, A. and Tao, M. (2022). Knowledge absorption capacity's efficacy to enhance innovation performance through big data analytics and digital platform capability. *Journal of Innovation and Knowledge*, 7(3), 100201. https://doi.org/10.1016/j.jik.2022.100201.

Laursen, K. and Salter, A. (2006). Open for innovation: The role of openness in explaining innovation performance among UK manufacturing firm. *Strategic Management Journal*, 27(2), 131–150.

Lepore, D., Vecciolini, C., Micozzi, A., *et al.* (2023b). Developing technological capabilities for Industry 4.0 adoption: An analysis of the role of inbound open innovation in small and medium-sized enterprises. *Creativity and Innovation Management*, 32(2), 249–265.

Lepore, D., Dolui, K., Tomashchuk, O., *et al.* (2023a). Interdisciplinary research unlocking innovative solutions in healthcare. *Technovation*, 120, 102511. https://doi.org/10.1016/j.technovation.2022.102511.

March, J. G. (1991). Exploration and exploitation in organizational learning. *Organization Science*, 2(1), 71–87.

Ndou, V., Vecchio, P. D., and Schina, L. (2011). Open innovation networks: The role of innovative marketplaces for small and medium enterprises' value creation. *International Journal of Innovation and Technology Management*, 8(3), 437–453.

Spigarelli, F., Compagnucci, L., and Lepore, D. (2024). Blockchain unlocking collaborative opportunities for environmental sustainability through innovation intermediaries. *Journal of Technology Transfer*. https://doi.org/10.1007/s10961-024-10106-5.

Teece, D. J. (2018). Profiting from innovation in the digital economy: Enabling technologies, standards, and licensing models in the wireless world. *Research Policy*, 47(8), 1367–1387.

Tumbas, S., Berente, N., and Brocke, J. (2018). Digital innovation and institutional entrepreneurship: Chief digital officer perspectives of their emerging role. *Journal of Information Technology*, 33(3), 188–202.

Turner, S., Mitchell, W., and Bettis, R. (2013). Strategic momentum: How experience shapes temporal consistency of ongoing innovation. *Journal of Management*, 39(7), 1855–1890.

Voss, G. B. and Voss, Z. G. (2013). Strategic ambidexterity in SMEs: Implementing exploration and exploitation in product and market domains. *Organization Science*, 24(5), 1459–1477.

Wang, N., Yin, J., Ma, Z., *et al.* (2022). The influence mechanism of rewards on knowledge sharing behaviors in virtual communities. *Journal of Knowledge Management*, 26(3), 485–505.

Wenke, K., Zapkau, F. B., and Schwens, C. (2021). Too small to do it all? A meta-analysis on the relative relationships of exploration, exploitation, and ambidexterity with SME performance. *Journal of Business Research*, 132, 653–665.

Yoo, Y., Henfridsson, O., and Lyytinen, K. (2010). The new organizing logic of digital innovation: An agenda for information systems research. *Information Systems Research*, 21(4), 724–735.

https://doi.org/10.1142/9789819807611_0008

Chapter 8

Building an AI Open Innovation Ecosystem: The Case of Baidu

Jacopo Cricchio[*,‡], Alberto Di Minin[*,§], and Dominique Lepore[†,¶]

[*]*Sant'Anna School of Advanced Studies Pisa, Institute of Management, Italy*

[†]*Department of Economics, Statistics and Business, Universitas Mercatorum, Italy*

[‡]*jacopo.cricchio@santannapisa.it*

[§]*alberto.diminin@santannapisa.it*

[¶]*dominique.lepore@unimercatorum.it*

Abstract

Partnerships and solid institutional support are fundamental in Artificial Intelligence (AI) developments. This chapter demonstrates the role of innovation intermediaries in the AI specialization in China by considering the exemplary case of Baidu.

The case of Baidu provides insights to understand how the creation of an open innovation ecosystem can drive AI advancements through a broad range of partnerships and involvements in national policies. Above all, Baidu's role as an orchestrator in this ecosystem highlights the importance of collaboration between government, academia, and industry in accelerating AI.

Based on the key initiatives of Baidu, policy implications and future research perspectives are drawn.

Keywords: Open innovation, artificial intelligence, innovation ecosystem, ecosystem orchestrator

1. Introduction

Since the initiation of opening-up reforms in 1978, China has gradually emerged as a major player in technological innovation, recognized as a key driver for Chinese economic development (Fu *et al.*, 2021). The role of firms in developing new technologies and carrying out the innovation process of the nation has been very important for the overall development of the country, historically leading to the coexistence of highly dynamic firms and hugely inefficient ones, with the role of the State always central in steering the development on one way or another (Brandt *et al.*, 2021).

In the fields of digital technology and digital transformation, China has experienced a sharp development of new products, processes, and business models in the last two decades (Liebenau *et al.*, 2019). Successful examples can be found in the cases of telecommunications, smartphones, integrated circuits, and cloud computing (Yu *et al.*, 2021). Among technologies crucial for global innovation leadership, China has also heavily invested in artificial intelligence (AI), formulating an ambitious roadmap for AI innovation with the ultimate goal of positioning the nation as a global AI innovator by 2030 (Cricchio *et al.*, 2023).

The Chinese strategy for achieving its AI-related goals is to build a robust AI innovation ecosystem by strengthening the collaboration between universities, firms, and governmental entities at both regional and national levels (Jacobides *et al.*, 2021). This approach has historically been crucial for the overall innovation strategy of China (Fu *et al.*, 2011), which has relied upon the development of an open innovation ecosystem (Fu *et al.*, 2016). The concept of Open Innovation (OI), which was crafted to describe a business strategy "that assumes that firms can and should use external ideas as well as internal ideas, and internal and external paths to market, as the firms look to advance their technology" (Chesbrough *et al.*, 2003), has been employed as a strategy to develop open innovation policies capable of boosting the overall national system (Di Minin *et al.*, 2024). In fact, enhancing AI capabilities requires collaboration across societal sectors, involving policymakers, universities, and companies to develop effective policies for regulating, improving, and disseminating AI technologies (Agrawal *et al.*, 2019).

In China, the "National New Generation Artificial Intelligence Open Innovation Platforms" (AIOIPs) policy, introduced by the Ministry of Science and Technology (MOST) in 2019, has established fifteen platforms led by industry leaders. These platforms focus on enhancing specific AI sub-segments nationwide. Central to this policy is the role of industry leaders as orchestrators in fostering an integrated AI ecosystem, facilitating the exchange of intellectual assets, knowledge, and technological advancements among various stakeholders (Wu *et al.*, 2020).

Baidu has been identified by the AIOIP policy as one of the national champions with the goal of focusing on developing autonomous driving. In fact, the "Apollo Project", launched in 2017, aims to provide a comprehensive software platform for partners in the automotive and autonomous driving industry (Apollo, n.d.). As a major player in China's tech scene alongside Alibaba and Tencent, Baidu pioneers cutting-edge technologies and offers AI platforms for third-party applications that go beyond the autonomous driving platform. For instance, Baidu Brain integrates deep learning algorithms, data models, and GPU-parallel computing (Yu *et al.*, 2021). For these reasons, this chapter examines Baidu's role as a key knowledge broker within China's AI ecosystem, analyzing its function as an orchestrator within the Open Innovation framework and how the company evolved over time. Policy and research implications are suggested.

2. Background: Open Innovation Ecosystem

The definition of OI revolves around the deliberate exchange of knowledge both within and outside organizational boundaries to enhance innovation strategies. This approach demonstrates the importance of collaboration with external partners to drive successful innovation outcomes. Simultaneously, the concept of ecosystems emphasizes the interconnectedness of various actors working collectively to create value. These ecosystems can range from broad industry networks to more focused market segments controlled by a single entity (West *et al.*, 2024).

Scholars in the field of innovation management and applied economics have increasingly focused on strategies related to innovation ecosystems (Holgersson *et al.*, 2018). These strategies play a crucial role in advancing open innovation ecosystems and are gaining traction on global policy agendas. In today's rapidly evolving landscape, innovation initiatives are seldom isolated, necessitating strategic alignment within broader ecosystems (Adner, 2017). An open innovation ecosystem prioritizes collaborative approaches, viewing knowledge sharing and cooperation as essential drivers of innovation. However, understanding the intricacies of interactions within specific innovation ecosystems remains a challenge. While some studies offer generalized frameworks or focus on specific interaction models, there is a clear need to delve deeper into the dynamics of information exchange and collaboration within these ecosystems (Autio *et al.*, 2014).

In essence, the convergence of Open Innovation and ecosystems offers a promising framework for navigating the complexities of the digital economy. By embracing collaborative strategies and leveraging external networks, organizations can position themselves to thrive amidst ongoing technological disruptions and drive sustainable growth (West *et al.*, 2024). The emergence of ecosystems is driven by multilateral firms with modular complementarities (Jacobides *et al.*, 2018). Various types of modularity explain variations in resource and knowledge flows within ecosystems, with different organizations linked by a system-level architecture (Kapoor, 2018). It becomes then necessary for an ecosystem to rely on an orchestrator that needs to understand and manage the interdependent activities required to foster innovation (Autio, 2022). As such, ecosystem research emphasizes the intentional knowledge-sharing and mutual adjustment among organizations to create value (Kapoor *et al.*, 2013).

China's adoption of OI reflects a global trend, with OI positively impacting digital technology innovation (Radziwon *et al.*, 2024). China has adeptly utilized OI domestically (Xie *et al.*, 2017) and internationally (Brem *et al.*, 2021) and empirical studies within Chinese firms highlighted the benefits of OI in various innovation modes (Chen *et al.*, 2011). The diverse OI practices in China have been historically supported by government policies promoting OI activities (Chesbrough *et al.*, 2021).

The AIOIP policy, to which Baidu is included as an orchestrator, integrates orchestrated leadership with OI principles, strategically aligning to maximize AI's potential nationally and establish an ecosystem-based standard (Nylund *et al.*, 2023). This alignment resonates with research highlighting the benefits of OI ecosystems and cross-boundary knowledge sharing (Nambisan *et al.*, 2018). In fact, knowledge transfer within OI networks often empowers central actors to drive economic development as representative open innovators, particularly crucial for technology upgrading and productivity growth (Huggins *et al.*, 2020).

3. The Case of Baidu: The Road Toward an AI Orchestrator

3.1 *Presentation of the case*

Baidu was established in the early 2000s in Beijing by Li Yanhong (Robin Li) and Xu Yong (Eric Xu), a period coinciding with the nascent stages of the Internet's proliferation and a surge in foreign investment within China, fostering the emergence of its private sector. Two decades hence, Chinese entrepreneurial endeavors exhibit a discernible trajectory toward technological innovation, notably in domains such as information and communication technology (ICT) and professional services. These advancements signify a noteworthy paradigm shift toward economic upgrading within the Chinese entrepreneurial landscape (Gao *et al.*, 2021). Baidu has been one of the technological pioneers fostering this change in China and together with Alibaba and Tencent, the so-called BAT. Within less than two decades, these three organizations have grown into one of the largest business ecosystems, with a combined estimated market capitalization of over 500 billion USD (Greeven *et al.*, 2017).

Both of Baidu's founders pursued their education in the United States and initiated the establishment of Baidu with the aid of 1.2 million dollars secured from Silicon Valley venture capital firms (Barboza, 2006). Throughout its nascent stages, Baidu underwent a gradual transition from providing search services for other enterprises to becoming an autonomous search engine. Initially, it specialized in music search services, a venture that inadvertently resulted in copyright infringements with major Western music publishers (Dong *et al.*, 2013). Nevertheless, the company successfully navigated these challenges by comprehending the needs of local users and employing labor-intensive sales tactics to gain potential advertisers, such as door-to-door visits and cold calls (Yeo, 2022). Furthermore, the strategic alliances forged with foreign internet players over the years have contributed significantly to Baidu's ability to increase its market share in the search engine market, reaching 64% by 2010, kicking its major international competitor, Google, out of Chinese market (Chao, 2010). However, internally, Baidu still faces great competition coming primarily from Tencent, Alibaba, Sogou, and Qihoo (Yeo, 2022). As shown in Table 1, with USD 18.96 billion in revenue and USD 2.86 billion in net income for 2023, the company demonstrates solid profitability. Above all, the company allocated USD 3.41 billion to R&D, which is

Table 1. Baidu basic information.

Business origin	**Internet search engine**
Core Founder	Li (Robin) Yanhong
Year of Establishment	2000
Number of Employees	41,300
Revenues (2023, USD billion dollars)	18.96
Net Income (2023, USD billion dollars)	2.86
R&D expenses (2023, USD billion dollars)	3.41
Number of Scientific Publications (2023)	2,128
Number of Patent Applications (2023)	24,498

Source: Baidu annual financial report, Orbis, Orbis IP, Web of Sciences.

approximately 18% of its revenue. This is a significant percentage, showing a strong commitment to innovation and technological development.

3.2 *Specialization in AI*

As a consequence of this strong market competition, Baidu started to diversify its core business, and this led to its orchestration role in the field of AI. Since 2013, Baidu has been investing heavily in AI, establishing the Institute of Deep Learning (IDL) and four other internal AI labs. These efforts led to the creation of Baidu Cloud and Baidu Brain, with over 370,000 developers and partners utilizing the platform daily (Jia *et al.*, 2018). In 2017, the company also launched the self-driving platform "Apollo" and became in the following years a leading patenting company in AI (China Internet Watch, 2020). According to Baidu's latest financial annual report, their intelligent driving system has provided about 839 thousand rides in the fourth quarter of 2023, up 49% year over year (Baidu Inc., 2024). Their robotaxi autonomous driving services are successfully employed in 10 Chinese cities including Beijing, Shanghai, and Chongqing, the most populated cities in the world (Baidu Apollo, n.d.). The designation of Baidu as the primary orchestrator of the national AIOIP focusing on autonomous driving comes as no surprise. Presently, the platform boasts a consortium exceeding 200 partners, including domestic and international entities, ranging from corporations to academic institutions (Apollo, n.d.). Baidu's intermediary role is based on fostering an open innovation approach within its business activities, spanning from software to hardware development. In particular, the Apollo auto development center, for instance, offers a repertoire of eight open and complimentary tutorials on its website aimed at nurturing software developers. Embracing open-source principles, the platform grants universal access to its software, comprising over 700 thousand lines of code, engaging over 80 thousand developers worldwide (Yeo, 2022). Furthermore, the Apollo partnership program boasts over 100 global members, including BMW, Daimler, Ford, Honda, Toyota, and Volkswagen, alongside 74 hardware members featuring prominent entities like Pioneer, Nvidia, and Texas Instruments. Noteworthy, software members include major corporations such as Microsoft and LG (Zhang *et al.*, 2021). Additionally, establishing collaborative ties with governmental bodies, both at the national and local levels, has facilitated Baidu's authorization for testing autonomous vehicles across key Chinese urban centers. More recently, through its collaboration with Geely in electric vehicle production, Baidu has lent support to a nascent startup, Jidu Automotive, dedicated to the production of autonomous electric cars, which was formally launched in 2022 (Smith, 2023). Part of this intermediary role in the open innovation ecosystem is directed toward attaining profitability.

3.3 *Institutional role*

Arguably, one of the most potent immediate advantages lies in Baidu's operational focus predominantly within China, a jurisdiction conducive to autonomous vehicle deployment, undergirded by robust governmental backing (Zhang *et al.*, 2021).

Indeed, Baidu's growth is not solely contingent upon its technical innovations; rather, it crucially hinges on China's evolving political economy. Specifically, the expansion of Baidu's industrial AI ventures and autonomous driving initiatives necessitates robust public infrastructure, urban planning reforms, and the establishment of new regulatory frameworks. Building an ecosystem that includes the local institutions, it then becomes an essential strategic decision.

Having the governmental bodies profoundly committed to advancing AI-enabled automobiles, which is Baidu's core AI venture, occupies a central position within China's strategic innovation policy and infrastructure development. Besides the already mentioned AIOIP policy in which

Baidu is central, another example showcasing the existence of a strong open innovation ecosystem in which Baidu is one of the leading companies and orchestrators is the 14th Five-Year Plan (FYP) (State Council of the PRC, 2022).

The plan prioritizes digitizing autonomous driving and smart transportation, identifying them as crucial areas for advancement. The plan outlines initiatives to develop autonomous travel services, facilitate vehicle-road collaboration, implement intelligent highway systems, synchronize traffic signal operations, prioritize bus traffic, and construct smart parking facilities. Baidu has become instrumental in executing this strategy and has engaged in collaborative efforts with local governments to invest in AI infrastructure, particularly in support of the AIOIP's development (Larsen, 2019).

4. Conclusions and Implications

Baidu's evolution into a key orchestrator within China's AI ecosystem demonstrates the success of an open innovation model in driving technological leadership. Baidu by leveraging collaboration with government bodies, international corporations, and academic institutions, Baidu has positioned itself at the forefront of AI development, especially in autonomous driving.

The company's integration into national strategies like the AIOIP and China's Five-Year Plans highlights the critical role of state-supported ecosystems in fostering innovation.

Moreover, the case examined shows that Baidu's success is dependent on the broader political economy, emphasizing the need for robust infrastructure, regulatory frameworks, and urban planning reforms to fully realize the potential of AI-enabled technologies.

As for research implications, the case demonstrates the need for further exploration of open innovation ecosystems in non-Western contexts, particularly in emerging economies like China, where state-driven innovation policies play a focal role. Research could investigate how the unique state-business-academia collaboration model in China compares to those in other regions, providing insights into how different governance structures influence innovation outputs.

Second, the role of orchestrators in innovation ecosystems, as demonstrated by Baidu, requires deeper analysis. Researchers could focus on how orchestrators facilitate knowledge sharing, coordinate activities across various stakeholders, and manage intellectual property within open innovation frameworks. In Baidu's case, its role in autonomous driving and AI platforms serves as an example of how companies can leverage open-source initiatives to create collaborative innovation environments. Further research could explore the conditions that make these orchestrator roles successful across different types of industries.

Finally, there is a need to investigate the long-term impact of national AI strategies, such as China's AI roadmap, on both economic development and technological leadership. This includes studying the effectiveness of policies like AIOIP in fostering innovation.

References

Adner, R. (2017). Ecosystem as structure: An actionable construct for strategy. *Journal of Management*, 43(1), 39–58.

Agrawal, A., Gans, J., and Goldfarb, A. (2019). Economic policy for artificial intelligence. *Innovation Policy and the Economy*, 19(1), 139–159.

Autio, E. (2022). Orchestrating ecosystems: A multi-layered framework. *Innovation*, 24(1), 96–109.

Autio, E. and Thomas, L. D. W. (2014). Innovation ecosystems: Implications for innovation management. In M. Dodgson, N. Philips, & D. M. Gann (Eds.), *The Oxford Handbook of Innovation Management* (pp. 204–228). Oxford University Press.

Baidu Apollo. (n.d.). [Apollo Go] Baidu's autonomous ride-hailing service provider-autonomous driving travel services.

Baidu. (2024). Baidu Announces Third Quarter 2024 Results. Investor Overview | Baidu Inc. Available at: https://ir.baidu.com/news-releases/news-release-details/baidu-announces-third-quarter-2024-results, last accessed: 10 April 2024.

Barboza, D. (2006). The Rise of Baidu (That's Chinese for Google). *The New York Times*. Available at: https://www.nytimes.com/2006/09/17/business/yourmoney/17baidu.html, last accessed: 9 April 2024.

Brandt, L. and Thun, E. (2021). The great dialectic: State versus market in China. In X. Fu, B. McKern, & J. Chen (Eds.), *The Oxford Handbook of China Innovation*. Oxford, EN: Oxford University Press. https://doi.org/10.1093/oxfordhb/9780190900533.013.31.

Brem, A. and Nylund, P. A. (2021). Maneuvering the bumps in the New Silk Road: Open innovation, technological complexity, dominant design, and the international impact of Chinese innovation. *R&D Management*.

Chao, L. (2010, April 26). Google Loses Chinese Market Share. *Wall Street Journal*. Available at: https://www.wsj.com/articles/SB10001424052748703465204575207833281993688, last accessed: 9 April 2024.

Chen, J., Chen, Y., and Vanhaverbeke, W. (2011). The influence of scope, depth, and orientation of external technology sources on the innovative performance of Chinese firms. *Technovation*, 31(8), 362–373.

Chesbrough, H. (2003). *Open Innovation: The New Imperative for Creating and Profiting from Technology*. Boston, MA: *Harvard Business Review Press*.

Chesbrough, H., Heaton, S., and Mei, L. (2021). Open innovation with Chinese characteristics: A dynamic capabilities perspective. *R&D Management*, 51(3), 247–259.

China Internet Watch. (2020). Baidu holds the most AI-related patents in China.

Cricchio, J. (2023). Policy comes first: Verso una sistematizzazione dell'ecosistema innovativo di intelligenza artificiale cinese. *OrizzonteCina*, 14(2), 121–126.

Di Minin, A. and Cricchio, J. (2024). Open innovation policy: The outline-inspire-promote spinner. In H. Chesbrough, A. Radziwon, W. Vanhaverbeke, & J. West (Eds.), *The Oxford Handbook of Open Innovation*. Oxford University Press.

Dong, X. "Snow", and Jayakar, K. (2013). The Baidu music settlement: A turning point for copyright reform in China? *Journal of Information Policy*, 3, 77–103.

Fu, X. and Xiong, H. (2011). Open innovation in China: Policies and practices. *Journal of Science and Technology Policy in China*, 2(3), 196–218.

Fu, X., McKern, B., and Chen, J. (2021). Introduction: China's journey to innovation. In X. Fu, B. McKern, & J. Chen (Eds.), *The Oxford Handbook of China Innovation* (pp. 1–26). Oxford: *Oxford University Press*.

Fu, X., Woo, W. T., & Hou, J. (2016). Technological innovation policy in China: The lessons, and the necessary changes ahead. *Economic Change and Restructuring*, 49(2), 139–157.

Gao, J. and Mu, R. (2021). Mass entrepreneurship and mass innovation in China. In X. Fu, B. McKern, and J. Chen (Eds.), *The Oxford Handbook of China Innovation*. Oxford University Press.

Greeven, M. J., & Wei, W. (2017). *Business Ecosystems in China: Alibaba and Competing Baidu, Tencent, Xiaomi and LeEco*. Routledge.

Holgersson, M., Granstrand, O., and Bogers, M. (2018). The evolution of intellectual property strategy in innovation ecosystems: Uncovering complementary and substitute appropriability regimes. *Long Range Planning*, 51(2), 303–319.

Huggins, R., Prokop, D., and Thompson, P. (2020). Universities and open innovation: The determinants of network centrality. *Journal of Technology Transfer*, 45(3), 718–757.

Jacobides, M. G., Brusoni, S., and Candelon, F. (2021). The evolutionary dynamics of the artificial intelligence ecosystem. *Strategy Science*, 6(4), 412–435.

Jacobides, M. G., Cennamo, C., and Gawer, A. (2018). Towards a theory of ecosystems. *Strategic Management Journal*, 39(8), 2255–2276.

Jia, K., Kenney, M., Mattila, J., and Seppala, T. (2018). The application of artificial intelligence at Chinese digital platform giants: Baidu, Alibaba and Tencent.

Kapoor, R. (2018). Ecosystems: Broadening the locus of value creation. *Journal of Organization Design*, 7(1), 12.

Kapoor, R. and Lee, J. M. (2013). Coordinating and competing in ecosystems: How organizational forms shape new technology investments. *Strategic Management Journal*, 34(3), 274–296.

Larsen, B. C. (2019). China's national AI team: The role of national AI open innovation platforms. *AI Policy and China: Realities of State-Led Development*, 16–20.

Liebenau, J., Yu, J., and Lee, H. (2019). Introduction: Special issue on digital economy in East Asia. *Technological Forecasting and Social Change*, 139, 73–74.

Nambisan, S., Siegel, D., and Kenney, M. (2018). On open innovation, platforms, and entrepreneurship. *Strategic Entrepreneurship Journal*, 12(3), 354–368.

Nylund, P. A. and Brem, A. (2023). Standardization in innovation ecosystems: The promise and peril of dominant platforms. *Technological Forecasting and Social Change*, 194, 122714.

Radziwon, A. and Chesbrough, H. (2024). Open innovation as a field of knowledge. In H. Chesbrough, A. Radziwon, W. Vanhaverbeke, & J. West (Eds.), *The Oxford Handbook of Open Innovation*. Oxford University Press.

Smith, C. S. (2023). Baidu and Geely will mass-produce an autonomous EV: The Chinese tech giants aim for a fully self-driving car. *IEEE Spectrum*, 60(1), 36–37.

State Council of the PRC [国务院]. (2020). 中共中央关丁制定国民经济和社会发展第十四个五年规划和二〇三五年远景目标的建议 [Recommendations of the Central Committee of the Communist Party of China on formulating the 14th Five-Year Plan for National Economic and Social Development and Long-term Goals for 2035]. *Gov.Cn*. Available at: https://www.gov.cn/zhengce/2020-11/03/content_5556991.htm, last accessed: 5 March 2024.

West, J. and Olk, P. (2024). Open innovation, innovation in ecosystems, and innovation beyond the firm. In H. Chesbrough, A. Radziwon, W. Vanhaverbeke, & J. West (Eds.), *The Oxford Handbook of Open Innovation*. Oxford University Press.

Wu, F., Lu, C., Zhu, M., Chen, H., Zhu, J., Yu, K., Li, L., Li, M., Chen, Q., Li, X., Cao, X., Wang, Z., Zha, Z., Zhuang, Y., and Pan, Y. (2020). Towards a new generation of artificial intelligence in China. *Nature Machine Intelligence*, 2(6), 312–316.

Xie, X., Zeng, S., Zang, Z., and Zou, H. (2017). Identifying the factors determining cooperative innovation effect in emerging economies: Evidence from Chinese firms. *Chinese Management Studies*, 11(3), 366–386.

Yeo, S. (2022). *Baidu: Geopolitical dynamics of the Internet in China*. Routledge.
Yu, J. and Zhang, Y. (2021). Chinese firms' move to the forefront in digital technologies. In X. Fu, B. McKern, & J. Chen (Eds.), *The Oxford handbook of China innovation*. Oxford University Press.
Zhang, Y. and Wu, T. (2021). Will Baidu's 'all in AI' strategy bring it back to the high-speed growth train? *Journal of Applied Business and Economics*, 23(4), 156–166.
关于Apollo-百度Apollo|Baidu阿波罗. (n.d.). Apollo. (2024). Apollo, about us. Available at: https://www.apollo.auto/aboutus, last accessed: 9 April 2024.

https://doi.org/10.1142/9789819807611_0009

Chapter 9

Sustainable Supply Chain Management as the Innovation Intermediary: Analysis on Frugal Innovation in Small and Medium-Sized Manufacturing Enterprises in China

Nan Wang[*,‡] **and Baolian Chen**[†,§]

[*]*Beijing Technology and Business University, Fucheng Road, Haidian District, Beijing, China*

[†]*Beijing Jiaotong University, Beixiaguan Road, Haidian District, Beijing, China*

[‡]*wangnan5819356@163.com*
[§]*chenbaolian1998@163.com*

Abstract

Based on the sustainable supply chain management perspective, this chapter conducts a qualitative exploration of 6 enterprises and an empirical test of 295 manufacturing SMEs to analyze the main influencing factors of frugal innovation in manufacturing SMEs. Conclusions are drawn as follows: in the internal management of sustainable supply chain, internal environmental management and internal social responsibility management promote enterprise frugal innovation. In external management of sustainable supply chains, sustainable cooperation between firms and suppliers promotes frugal innovative behavior, monitoring and assessing supplier sustainable practice does not affect firms' own frugal innovative behavior; firm size only plays a positive moderating role in the influence of internal management of sustainable supply chains on frugal innovative behavior.

In the analysis, supply chain management is viewed as the innovation intermediary needed to promote coordination and cooperation. As the results imply, supply chain management can act as an innovation intermediary by coordinating and aligning efforts across the value chain, fostering a collaborative environment for frugal innovation to thrive.

Keywords: Frugal innovation, sustainable supply chain management, firm size, small and medium-sized manufacturing enterprises.

1. Introduction

Different from the traditional "big is good" and "extreme is beautiful" innovation models pursued by Western countries, China, as a rising emerging economy, urgently needs to explore a distinctive innovation model adapted to the needs of the current stage of development (Chen *et al.*, 2020). Although China's economic level continues to rise, there is still a contradiction between the people's growing need for a better life and unbalanced and insufficient development. As of the end of 2019, 600 million people in China still have a monthly income of less than 1,000 yuan, and social progress should not only take into account the overall development situation but also need to pay attention to whether the needs of the lowest 20% of the income group can be satisfied (Basu 2000). To meet the consumer demand for a better life of the majority of low-income groups at the bottom of the pyramid (BOP) is not only in line with the needs of the national development strategy but also contains a huge commercial potential, which can realize the double value of the economy and society.

As an emerging innovation paradigm, frugal innovation is an important form of innovation to solve the problem of unsatisfied consumer demand of BOP groups, which can provide products, services, processes, or business models to satisfy the core functions through innovation under resource constraints (Sarkar *et al.*, 2022). The research on frugal innovation is dominated by theoretical deduction and qualitative analysis (Sharmelly *et al.*, 2021), lacking quantitative research. The influencing factors of frugal innovation are mainly examined from the aspects of managers' cognition, attitude, and resource acquisition (Dabi *et al.*, 2022), ignoring the important perspective of supply chain management. Frugal innovation often faces resource constraints and needs to overcome the limitations of limited material resources, financial resources, and institutional conditions.

Supply chain management becomes the innovation intermediary by integrating upstream and downstream enterprises into the enterprise innovation value chain to promote coordination and cooperation and achieve resource optimization, thus realizing the provision of value-added services to the users with fewer resources, overcoming resource constraints, and providing potential possibilities for frugal innovation (Corsini *et al.*, 2021). Compared with traditional supply chain management, sustainable supply chain management requires balanced development of economic performance, environmental performance, and social performance, and its concept is more compatible with the triple bottom line of economy, society, and environment advocated by frugal innovation, so it is necessary to explore the influence of sustainable supply chain management on frugal innovation.

In the context of advocating the realization of commonwealth, this chapter explores the paradigm of frugal innovation to meet the needs of the low-income group for a better life and adopts a combination of qualitative and quantitative methods to analyze the influence mechanism of sustainable supply chain management on the frugal innovation.

Taking small and medium-sized manufacturing enterprises as the research object, this paper explores the influencing factors of frugal innovation from the perspective of sustainable supply chain management as an innovation intermediary and bridges the theoretical gap in the relationship between the two. The findings not only broaden the research boundaries of frugal innovation and enrich the literature research on frugal innovation but also provide reference and guidance for the practice of frugal innovation in SMEs in China.

2. Literature Review

2.1 *Frugal innovation*

Frugal innovation is an innovation paradigm for emerging markets and is a solution to the scarcity of resources, meaning that by reducing the use of resources and lowering the cost of production, it provides users with low-priced products that satisfy the core functions, and thus achieves the goal of using fewer resources for more value creation (Hossain *et al.*, 2016).

Frugal Innovation research focuses on formative motives, business models, and success factors. Scarcity and constraints of internal resources as well as external competitive environment and institutional imperfections form the basic motives of frugal innovation (Sarkar *et al.*, 2022; Shibin *et al.*, 2018; Khanal *et al.*, 2021). (Hossain *et al.*, 2020) found that entrepreneurs will take the initiative to carry out frugal innovation and bring frugal products or services to the market when there are problems of insufficient raw materials, lack of manpower, and limited capital investment in the production process. Meanwhile, scholars believe that the value proposition of frugal innovation is to provide consumers with affordable products to satisfy basic needs (Sarkar *et al.*, 2022); the value creation process of frugal innovation is to use plain thinking to reduce costs and create more value by increasing cooperation with governments, enterprises, and non-profit organizations, using low-cost raw materials or reusing resources (Sharmelly *et al.*, 2021); and ultimately, using various methods such as on-demand usage charges and rental usage to adapt to the needs of cash-strapped users to capture value (Hossain *et al.*, 2020). In addition, scholars have also found through case studies that cooperation with other enterprises will promote the development of frugal innovation, such as (Niroumand *et al.*, 2021) found that sharing resources, information, and knowledge with other enterprises not only facilitates the use of cheap raw materials in the local market and reduces production cost but also helps enterprises obtain the experience and professional knowledge related to frugal innovation, and then create frugal products or services.

Existing quantitative research on frugal innovation is very limited. (Lei *et al.*, 2021) argued that transformational leadership can encourage employees to pay attention to frugal innovation and put it into practice. The existing quantitative research on the influencing factors of frugal innovation has not paid attention to the important factor of supply chain management, so this chapter discusses the influence of sustainable supply chain management on the performance of frugal innovation from the perspective of sustainable supply chain management.

2.2 *Sustainable supply chain management*

Sustainable supply chain management refers to the enterprise adhering to the connotation of sustainable development, through the management of supply chain operations, information, and funds, as well as the coordination and cooperation with supplier enterprises, to maximize the integration and realization of the organization's social, environmental and economic goals, and improve the long-term performance of the enterprise and its supply chain organization. Existing research on sustainable supply chain management is dominated by theoretical deductions and case studies, mainly focusing on drivers and governance mechanisms.

Existing research on the economic consequences of sustainable supply chain management is very scarce, mainly examining the impact on innovation capability, sustainable competitive advantage, and firm performance.

(Reefke *et al*., 2018) found that sustainable supply chain management improves the sustainable competitive advantage of firms by strengthening the linkages between upstream and downstream partners, facilitating the exchange of technology and knowledge, enhancing firms' innovation capability, and capitalizing on the synergies of firms throughout the supply chain. These findings outline the need to consider supply chain management in its intermediary linking role.

(Kitsis *et al*., 2020) found that sustainable supply chain management improves firms' financial, environmental, and social performance. Both sustainable supply chain management and frugal innovation are characterized by thrift and resource constraints, and the triple bottom line of economic, environmental, and social performance they advocate fits well, so it is necessary to explore the role of the relationship between the two.

3. Exploratory Research

3.1 *Theoretical framework prefiguration*

Case studies need to integrate existing research theories and provide a guiding framework for empirical research. Sustainable supply chain management integrates the theories of sustainable development and supply chain management, and core enterprises focus on environmental protection and social responsibility in the production process of products by managing relevant resources in the supply chain and coordinating and cooperating with suppliers to maximize the integration of resources and achieve the organization's social, environmental, and economic goals.

Frugal innovation reduces the use of resources and production costs for enterprises and provides users with inexpensive products that fulfill core functions and perform well. Sustainable supply chain management can help enterprises integrate the concepts of remanufacturing, reuse, and recycling into product design, improve the level of product recycling, reduce the use of resources and pollutant emissions, and reduce production costs under the premise of guaranteeing product quality. In addition, sustainable supply chain management can promote synergy and cooperation between enterprises and suppliers, which is beneficial to the formation of a consistent concept of innovation and the sharing of knowledge, skills, and information, thus promoting frugal innovation. These roles are typical of innovation intermediary.

3.2 *Case selection*

This paper determines the following case selection criteria to ensure the screening of suitable research subjects: (1) the enterprise's supply chain management needs to follow the sustainable concept, and has practical experience in sustainable supply chain management; (2) the enterprise has engaged in frugal innovation, and its frugal innovation product or service sales account for more than 50% of total sales.

After screening, six enterprises in Jiangsu and Zhejiang were finally selected as the case study objects of this chapter, and the basic information is shown in Table 1.

3.3 *Data collection and analysis*

In this chapter, the triangulation method is used to collect and analyze data from the case companies to ensure the reliability and validity of the research findings. The data sources mainly include the following parts: (1) in-depth interviews with the top management of the case enterprises, with an average interview time of 2 hours. During the interviews, the managers were questioned according to the interview outline prepared in advance, and additional interviews were conducted. (2) Interviews with

Table 1. Basic information of case enterprises.

Corporations	Provinces	Size	Years	Industry
A	Jiangsu	<50	7	Communications equipment manufacturing
B	Jiangsu	500–999	16	Pharmaceuticals
C	Jiangsu	50–99	10	Furniture manufacturing
X	Zhejiang	100–500	12	Textile and apparel industry
Y	Zhejiang	100–500	25	Food manufacturing
Z	Zhejiang	500–999	11	Specialized equipment manufacturing

employees of six enterprises, with an average interview time of 15 minutes for a single employee. (3) Internal information provided by the enterprises on sustainable supply chain management and frugal innovation. (4) Downloading the annual reports of the enterprises for 2018–2020 as well as the CSR reports from the official websites of the enterprises. (5) Searching for news reports on enterprises' sustainable supply chain management and frugal innovation as well as texts and videos of interview speeches by enterprise leaders in recent years in various mainstream media.

After the data collection is completed, the information is first summarized and organized. According to the sustainable development theory, enterprises should focus on strengthening the awareness of environmental protection and social responsibility. In addition to strengthening their own internal management, enterprises should be responsible for the negative environmental and social impacts generated by their supplier members (Kitsis *et al.*, 2020). This study will discuss the impact of the internal and external management dimensions of sustainable supply chain on frugal innovation. The researchers coded the collected data, sorted the sentences with certain meaningful representations, eliminated the variables that were less than 1% of the total number of entries in the category, and then coded sustainable supply chain internal management and sustainable supply chain external management again to summarize the main variables in these two categories. Table 2 lists typical evidence entries from the case firms on sustainable supply chain management and its mechanism of action on frugal innovation.

Table 2. Sustainable supply chain management categories and typical entries.

Typical evidence	Entry	Define	Category
A : The application of modularity in the supply chain, the integration of components, the incorporation of new technologies and the continuous updating of old components significantly reduces product costs by streamlining processes. B : Enterprises allocate special funds for environmental protection every year and evaluate the environmental, economic and social benefits generated by environmental protection inputs. Z : Enterprises strengthen the selection of raw materials and energy in the manufacturing process, avoiding the use of toxic and harmful materials.	35	A range of behaviors implemented within enterprises to promote green development.	Internal environmental management
C : It builds a systematic and three-dimensional employee protection system, establishes a modern training base, and creates a platform for employees to realize their own values. X : Pre-employment training is provided to new employees, and new employees are required to take a written safety education test before starting work to reduce accidents. Y : Businesses are choosing to embrace migrant workers by developing easy-to-make products that provide jobs for more people who lack knowledge and specialized skills.	26	Internal corporate social responsibilities undertaken by enterprises to promote sustainable development.	Internal social responsibility management

Table 2. (*Continued*)

Typical evidence	Entry	Define	Category
B : Enterprises and suppliers jointly utilize process improvement, the introduction of new materials, new technologies, and other ways to reduce costs. C : Enterprises establish partnerships with suppliers to simplify relevant procedures between the two parties, reduce transaction costs, speed up the response time of sustainable supply chains, and ensure product quality and productivity. X : Enterprises build supply chain partnerships with many strong companies to acquire new innovative knowledge and skills, while mobilizing suppliers to actively participate in market research and product design.	24	Companies and suppliers work together on the basis of mutual trust to achieve common environmental, social, and economic goals.	Sustainable cooperation with suppliers
A : Mutual oversight between firms and suppliers allows purchased materials to go directly to the firm's manufacturing department, speeding up the response time of sustainable supply chains, and ultimately fostering frugal innovation. Y : Enterprises require suppliers to sign a supplier's commitment to ensure that the quality of the products provided by the supplier is up to standard. Z : Enterprises to set up a reporting telephone and reporting website, all personnel can anonymously report suppliers of corporate misconduct.	30	The company monitors and evaluates the sustainable supply behavior of suppliers with whom it does business.	Monitoring and evaluation of supplier sustainable practice

(*Continued*)

Table 2. (*Continued*)

Typical evidence	Entry	Define	Category
B : Companies choose simple packaging designs to reduce waste and pollution, lower production costs and improve frugal innovation. C : Provide a platform for employees to utilize their creativity to facilitate exchanges and discussions among employees, and draw new ideas for frugal innovation from their discussions. Z : Companies are choosing raw materials that can be recycled twice in the manufacturing process as well as clean energy sources to increase the recycling rate of frugal products.	32		Sustainable supply chain internal management and frugal innovation
A : Corporate monitoring of supplier sustainability behavior enables suppliers to provide sustainable raw materials and reduces production costs, improves the sustainable use of products, and drives frugal innovation. X : Companies partner with strong companies and involve strong suppliers in product development to reduce development costs. Y : Companies require suppliers to sign a supplier commitment, which helps to ensure product quality and improve product durability.	23		Sustainable supply chain external management and frugal innovation

By summarizing the above codes and analyzing the theory, firms implementing frugal innovation aim to achieve cost advantage, they need to adopt a variety of ways to develop products and services that are affordable to consumers. Utilizing factors such as process design capabilities, supply chain talent, infrastructure quality, corporate environmental awareness, and knowledge and technology in sustainable supply chain management to improve the efficiency of raw material or energy use, overcoming resource and cost constraints, and facilitating the realization of firms' frugal innovation (Shibin *et al.*, 2018).

Based on the sustainable development theory, sustainable supply chain management requires enterprises to pay attention to environmental protection and social responsibility issues both inside and outside the supply chain and harmonize environmental and social benefits while pursuing their economic interests. For one, the internal management of enterprise sustainable supply chain requires to reduce the resource utilization rate, improve the product recycling rate, and the ability to practice of social responsibility, which can not only reduce the production cost of the product but also improve the employees' environmental awareness and collaborative innovation ability, so as to promote the frugal innovation (Shibin *et al.*, 2018). For another, carrying out sustainable cooperation with suppliers or monitoring and evaluating supplier behaviors, promoting knowledge and resource sharing between both parties, reducing potential unreasonable behaviors of suppliers (Seles *et al.*, 2016), and ultimately the enterprise obtains the advantage of resources and partners necessary for frugal innovation.

4. Hypothesis

Through the collection and analysis of the above data, the role of sustainable supply chain management on frugal innovation is explored considering its broader role as innovation intermediary. In order to ensure the validity of the model, this section uses hypothetical reasoning to theoretically deduce the proposed model and put forward formal research hypotheses.

4.1 *Sustainable supply chain internal management and frugal innovation*

Unlike other innovation behaviors, frugal innovation should have both environmental and economic benefits. By applying eco-design capabilities, firms are able to minimize pollutant emissions or resource consumption, improve product recyclability and remanufacturing, and satisfy customer demand for environmentally sound products (Seles *et al.*, 2016). In addition, when business managers develop environmental awareness, companies are able to understand the benefits of environmentally friendly initiatives on organizational performance (Shibin *et al.*, 2018), which pushes them to improve technological innovation and to develop new products that satisfy customers' requirements and are environmentally beneficial (Demirel *et al.*, 2019). Therefore, by utilizing the environmental management approach within sustainable supply chain, enterprises can reduce pollution emissions to protect the environment, reduce production costs by reducing the use of resources (Shibin *et al.*, 2018), and satisfy the environmental and economic benefits of frugal innovation.

CSR management within the enterprise through such means as employee training programs to form an open and creative work environment provides employees with valuable and self-fulfilling development opportunities, which not only brings new ideas for frugal innovation to the enterprise, but also may prompt employees to optimize business processes, improve organizational performance, and reduce operating costs, thus promoting frugal innovation (Shibin *et al.*, 2018). Meanwhile, internal CSR management helps to cultivate employee motivation and has a positive impact on employee value creation (Wang *et al.*, 2022), encouraging employees to actively seek new methods or technologies in order to change the existing processes and implement new production processes, which will help the enterprise to quickly launch products that meet the needs of BOP customers and are good value for money.

H1a: Enterprise environmental management positively affects frugal innovation.

H1b: Enterprise Social responsibility management positively affects frugal innovation.

4.2 *Sustainable supply chain external management and frugal innovation*

Research has shown that collaboration is an effective means of promoting R&D and innovation. By establishing sustainable partnerships with suppliers, firms are able to strengthen their ties with suppliers and encourage them to participate in their innovation activities in order to achieve value creation, thus creating a wider and deeper network of innovation relationships. The subjects in the innovation network can share technology, knowledge, and innovation ideas, reduce the development investment of both sides, minimize the cost of innovation, and thus bring low-priced products to customers, effectively promoting frugal innovation (Shibin *et al.*, 2018). In addition, as a result of reverse engineering existing products in the market, frugal innovation relies on the acquisition and utilization of external knowledge. Sustainable cooperation with suppliers facilitates the inflow of new external knowledge into the enterprise, expands the knowledge base of the enterprise, compensates for the lack of internal knowledge, and promotes frugal innovation.

Behaviors such as impaired product quality, delayed shipments, and social irresponsibility of suppliers can jeopardize the corporate image to a certain extent (Shevchnko *et al.*, 2020). Monitoring and assessing suppliers enterprises can reduce the information asymmetry between the two sides, help enterprises to confirm whether the behavior of suppliers meets their requirements, identify and eliminate the shortcomings of suppliers in sustainable development in a timely manner, ensure that the interests of suppliers and enterprises are consistent (Shevchnko *et al.*, 2020), and make the raw materials provided by the suppliers to meet the enterprise's requirements of frugal innovation. In addition, by monitoring and evaluating supplier sustainable practices, enterprises can help suppliers reduce material and organizational resource use in the production process, achieve higher production efficiency and lower waste emissions (Zeschky *et al.*, 2011), and provide a guarantee for enterprises to carry out frugal innovation.

H2a: Sustainable cooperation between firms and suppliers positively affects frugal innovation.

H2b: Monitoring and evaluating supplier sustainable practice positively affects frugal innovation.

4.3 *The moderating role of firm size*

Firm size reflects the scale of a firm's activities as well as differences in resource endowments, flexibility, and skills. Compared to small-sized firms, medium-sized firms have more access to knowledge and capital to acquire expertise and experience, and promote effective innovation by utilizing restructuring capabilities that enable firms to create new scientific and technological knowledge. Meanwhile, medium-sized firms are more likely to have a structured new product development process that helps firms perfectly capture product development opportunities, effectively identify market needs, and avoid unnecessary trial-and-error processes (Deng *et al.*, 2021). Therefore, frugal innovation will be better when SMEs have a larger size.

H3: In SMEs, firm size positively affects frugal innovation.

Size differences in SMEs affect the role of sustainable supply chain management on frugal innovation. In internal supply chain management, the executive team of medium-sized enterprises has a higher perception of the environmental pressure given by stakeholders and is more likely to clarify environmental goals and proactively adopt environmental practices in the innovation, fulfill social responsibility, and invest more resources in improving the efficiency of resource utilization as well as in preventing environmental damage (Vanpoucke *et al.*, 2014), which promotes the enterprise to develop frugal products with high resource utilization and reusable recycling. In addition, medium-sized enterprises have a more complete organizational structure, provide more incentives and promotion channels for employees, and improve employee satisfaction, loyalty, and enthusiasm for frugal innovation, so that employees voluntarily participate in corporate innovation activities and carry out frugal innovations.

H4a: In SMEs, firm size positively moderates the relationship between internal environment management and frugal innovation

H4b: In SMEs, firm size positively moderates the relationship between internal CSR management and frugal innovation.

In the external management of sustainable supply chains, medium-sized firms are more attractive to potential partners than small firms, and these firms are more capable of integrating partners into sustainable development activities and increasing cooperation and exchange of sustainable behaviors among firms. Larger firms also have higher absorptive capacity and are more adept at sharing sustainable resources and information, increasing the heterogeneity of the firm's resources (Wu *et al.*, 2017), and enriching the knowledge needed for firms to innovate in a parsimonious manner. In addition, the bigger enterprise will put more resources into supply chain management and put pressure on suppliers to adopt sustainable development behaviors through unannounced visits to suppliers, so as to ensure that the enterprise carries out frugal innovation smoothly.

H4c: In SMEs, firm size positively moderates the relationship between sustainable cooperation between firms and suppliers and frugal innovation.

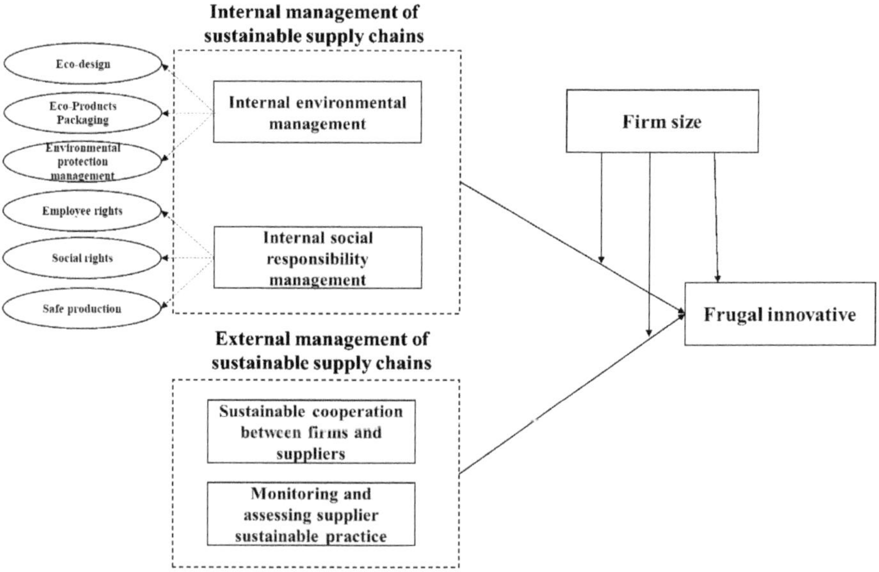

Figure 1. Research Model.

H4d: In SMEs, firm size positively moderates the relationship between monitoring and evaluation supplier sustainable practice and frugal innovation (Figure 1).

5. Empirical Tests

5.1 *Data collection*

In order to test the research hypotheses, this paper conducts data collection in Jiangsu and Zhejiang provinces. The reasons for selecting manufacturing SMEs in Jiangsu and Zhejiang to distribute the questionnaires are as follows: first, manufacturing enterprises are the important main body of frugal innovation, and most of the sustainable supply chain management practices are also carried out in the manufacturing industry. Secondly, the frugal innovation method with limited resources and lower cost investment is more suitable for SMEs' practical needs. Finally, Jiangsu and Zhejiang provinces are one of the regions with the largest manufacturing SMEs in China and have formed industrial agglomerations. The products produced in these regions are the typical representatives of China's frugal innovation.

Table 3. Descriptive statistical analysis ($N = 295$).

Characteristic	Categories	Sample	Percentage
Positions	Grassroots workers	54	18.3
	Middle manager	116	39.3
	Senior management	125	42.4
Years of employment in the enterprise	1–3	33	11.2
	3–5	57	19.3
	5–8	83	28.1
	>8	122	41.4
Years of business operation	1–5	26	8.8
	6–10	89	30.2
	11–15	82	27.8
	>15	98	33.2
	Others	70	23.7
Number of employees	<100	39	13.2
	100–400	68	23.1
	401–700	80	27.1
	701–999	108	36.6

Data collection was from October 2021 to December 2021, 400 questionnaires were distributed, and 357 questionnaires were recovered, with a recovery rate of 89.25%, excluding invalid questionnaires with problems such as no answer and too uniform answers, 295 valid questionnaires were screened out, with a validity rate of 82.63%. The sample characteristics of the questionnaire are shown in Table 3.

5.2 *Variable measurement*

In this study, the measurement items of each variable were adapted from the English literature. After the pre-survey, the questionnaires were revised to ensure that the language, structure, and logic of the questionnaires were reasonable. Internal environmental management (IE) was adapted from the scale developed by (Zhu *et al.*, 2005), which contains three dimensions: eco-design (ED), eco-packaging (EP), and environmental protection management (EPM). Internal social responsibility management (IS) was adapted from the scale developed by (Carter *et al.*, 2002), which is divided into three dimensions: employee rights and interests (ER), social welfare (SW), and safe production (SP). Sustainable cooperation between firms and suppliers (SC) was adapted from the scale developed by (Flynn *et al.*, 2010), with five items; Monitoring and assessing supplier sustainable practice (MAS) adapted from the scale developed by (Carter *et al.*, 2002), with five items. Frugal Innovation (FI) was adapted from the scale developed by (Rossetto *et al.*, 2017), with six items, which are represented in Table 4. Year (YE) and size (SI) were used as control variables for the study.

Table 4. Variable measurement and indicator results.

Variables	Items	Factor loading	CR	AVE
ED Cronbach's $\alpha = 0.831$	Extent to which companies design their products to reduce the use of raw materials and energy	0.718	0.834	0.505
	Extent to which companies design products using recyclable raw materials	0.703		
	Extent of product design by firms to reduce emissions in the production process	0.718		
	Extent to which firms use reusable recycled or reused product designs	0.709		
	Extent to which enterprises have good waste recycling systems in place	0.689		
EP Cronbach's $\alpha = 0.807$	Extent to which companies recycle product packaging materials	0.699	0.817	0.531
	Extent to which enterprises use low-consumption product packaging materials	0.808		
	Extent to which companies minimize the use of product packaging materials	0.787		
	Degree of compliance of product packaging materials used by enterprises with environmental standards	0.603		

(Continued)

Table 4. (*Continued*)

Variables	Items	Factor loading	CR	AVE
EPM Cronbach's $\alpha = 0.836$	Level of senior-level support for the implementation of corporate environmental management	0.701	0.838	0.564
	Extent of cross-functional collaboration among departments within the enterprise to protect the environment	0.743		
	Extent to which enterprises have set up environmental protection and environmental monitoring organizations to protect the environment	0.784		
	Extent to which enterprises use policies and regulations to promote environmental protection measures	0.772		
ER Cronbach's $\alpha = 0.890$	Extent to which firms provide good working conditions for their employees	0.792	0.891	0.621
	Extent to which firms provide good living conditions for their employees	0.813		
	Extent to which companies provide reasonable career planning for their employees	0.786		
	Extent to which enterprises regularly provide vocational training and education for their employees	0.752		
	Extent to which companies emphasize the reasonable needs of their employees	0.793		
SW Cronbach's $\alpha = 0.859$	Degree of corporate social responsibility	0.731	0.860	0.606
	Extent of corporate contributions to the BOP masses	0.799		
	Extent to which businesses provide jobs for the BOP masses	0.785		
	Extent to which firms support BOP mass quality education and skills training	0.797		

Table 4. (*Continued*)

Variables	Items	Factor loading	CR	AVE
SP Cronbach's $\alpha = 0.867$	Extent to which companies offer security products to their customers	0.739	0.867	0.688
	Extent to which enterprises use safe production facilities to produce their products	0.932		
	Degree of safety norms for the daily operations of the employees of the enterprise	0.806		
SC Cronbach's $\alpha = 0.880$	Extent to which enterprises share sustainable decision-making with key suppliers	0.798	0.881	0.597
	Extent to which companies share sustainability information with key suppliers	0.791		
	Extent to which companies engage in sustainable product development with key suppliers	0.748		
	Extent to which enterprises work with key suppliers to forecast demand for sustainable products	0.777		
	Extent to which enterprises have sustainable strategic cooperation with key suppliers	0.743		
MAS Cronbach's $\alpha = 0.874$	Extent to which companies require environmental management from suppliers	0.809	0.874	0.583
	Extent to which companies require suppliers to ensure employee rights and benefits	0.841		
	Extent to which firms require suppliers to produce products in a safe manner	0.688		
	Extent to which companies require suppliers to care about social welfare	0.739		
	Extent of monitoring and evaluation of suppliers' environmental and social responsibility by enterprises	0.731		

(*Continued*)

Table 4. (*Continued*)

Variables	Items	Factor loading	CR	AVE
FI Cronbach's $\alpha = 0.901$	We specialize in products or services that offer core features rather than add-ons	0.697	0.901	0.604
	We regularly look for new solutions to improve the durability of our products or services	0.786		
	We provide high quality and low-price products or services through new solutions	0.803		
	We significantly reduce the price of our products or services	0.778		
	We always focus on the environmental sustainability of our operations	0.845		
	We always provide our customers with solutions that meet the needs of society and the environment	0.748		

5.3 *Reliability test*

This study tested the reliability and validity of the variables. As can be seen in Table 4, the Cronbach's α coefficients of the variables involved in this study exceeded the criterion of the critical value of 0.7. The AVE values of the variables were all greater than 0.5 and the CR values were all greater than 0.8, and the scales had high internal consistency. Meanwhile, the factor loadings are all greater than 0.6, and the constructs have good convergent validity. From the data results in Table 5, the arithmetic square roots on the diagonal are all greater than the standardized correlation coefficients in the lower left corner. The above results indicate that the scale adapted in this paper has good convergent validity and discriminant validity, and the scale has good structural validity. The fit coefficients of the model were $X2/df = 2.306 < 3$, $RMSEA = 0.052 < 0.06$, $CFI = 0.927$, $NFI = 0.878$, and $TFI = 0.917$, indicating that the measurement model in this paper has a good fit. In addition, the fit of the one-way model was not good and there was a significant difference between it and the measurement model, indicating that there was no serious common method bias in this study.

Table 5. Descriptive statistics and correlation coefficients.

	1	2	3	4	5	6	7	8	9
1. ED	**0.711**								
2. EP	0.566**	**0.729**							
3. EPM	0.314**	0.462**	**0.751**						
4. ER	0.502**	0.525**	0.599**	**0.788**					
5. SW	0.489**	0.542**	0.386**	0.581**	**0.778**				
6. SP	0.531**	0.272**	0.438**	0.535**	0.465**	**0.829**			
7. SC	0.524**	0.580**	0.500**	0.480**	0.510**	0.485**	**0.772**		
8. MAS	0.498**	0.584**	0.326**	0.510**	0.491**	0.500**	0.573**	**0.764**	
9. FI	0.534**	0.475**	0.398**	0.569**	0.376**	0.297**	0.344**	0.555**	**0.780**
MEAN	4.802	5.014	5.257	5.021	5.204	5.162	4.707	4.791	5.082
SD	1.351	1.362	1.304	1.307	1.242	1.361	1.248	6.041	1.173

Note: ***$p < 0.001$; **$p < 0.01$; *$p < 0.05$.

Table 6. Structural equation modeling path coefficients and C.R. values.

Hypothesis	Coefficients	C.R.	P-values	Findings
H1a	0.341***	4.780	$p < 0.001$	Supported
H1b	0.302**	2.774	$p < 0.01$	Supported
H2a	0.127*	1.976	$p < 0.05$	Supported
H2b	−0.039	−0.334	$p > 0.05$	Unsupported

Note: ***$p < 0.001$; **$p < 0.01$; *$p < 0.05$.

5.4 *Hypothesis testing*

5.4.1 *Main effects test*

In this chapter, AMOS22.0 data analysis software was used to conduct the main effects test, the model path coefficients and hypothesis testing are shown in Table 6.

The results show that both internal environmental management (H1a: $\lambda = 0.341, p < 0.001$) and internal social responsibility management (H1b: $\lambda = 0.302, p < 0.01$) have significant positive effect on frugal innovation. In the external management of sustainable supply chain, sustainable cooperation between enterprises and suppliers positively affects frugal innovation (H2a: $\lambda = 0.127, p < 0.05$), while monitoring and evaluation of supplier sustainable practice are not significant on frugal innovation (H2b: $\lambda = -0.039, p > 0.05$), H1a, H1b, and H2a are verified. The reason why monitoring and evaluation of supplier sustainable practice is not significant for frugal innovation may be that the enterprise's supervision and evaluation of suppliers will increase the enterprise's cost inputs, although this will help establish a long-lasting strategic partnership between the enterprise and the supplier to ensure the effective supply of environmentally friendly materials and enhance the enterprise's commitment to environmental protection, more inputs can not reduce the cost of the enterprise's frugal product development costs, and in some cases it also In some cases, it may also jeopardize the relationship of trust between suppliers and enterprises.

5.4.2 *Moderating effects test*

This paper uses stratified regression analysis to test the moderating effect, and the results are shown in Table 7. Model 1 shows that the firm size has a significant positive effect on frugal innovation, and H3 is supported. This suggests that the larger the firm size, the more resources and capabilities the company will have for frugal innovation, which will improve the efficiency of frugal innovation.

In Model 3, internal environmental management ($b = 0.246, p < 0.001$) and internal social responsibility management ($b = 0.209$, $p < 0.001$) positively affect frugal innovation, and the cross-multiplier terms of internal environmental management and firm size ($b = 0.083$, $p < 0.05$) and internal social responsibility management and firm size ($b = 0.105$, $p < 0.01$) are significant, which shows that firm size has a significant positive moderating effect on sustainable supply chain internal management and frugal innovation, as shown in Figure 2, while firm size has no significant moderating effect on sustainable supply chain external management and frugal innovation. The data results support H4a and H4b and do not support H4c and H4d. Firm size does not have a significant moderating effect in the relationship between sustainable supply chain external management and frugal innovation, probably because larger enterprises have greater voice and dominance in supplier selection, raw material bargaining, external knowledge absorption, and access to human, material, and financial resources, and the implementation of supplier monitoring and evaluation behaviors in the short term tends to erode the

Table 7. Moderating effects test.

	Model 1	Model 2	Model 3
YE	0.018	–0.008	–0.012
	(1.505)	(–0.624)	(–0.151)
SI	0.385***	0.279***	0.235***
	(6.313)	(5.812)	(5.243)
IE		0.305***	0.246***
		(6.059)	(5.237)
IS		0.267***	0.209***
		(5.521)	(4.571)
SC		0.191*	0.147
		(2.021)	(1.668)
MAS		–0.027	0.097
		(–1.031)	(0.825)
SI* IE			0.083*
			(2.103)
SI* IS			0.105**
			(2.841)
SI* SC			0.056
			(0.982)
SI* MAS			–0.023
			(–0.139)
R^2	0.173	0.438	0.516
Adjusted R^2	0.168	0.432	0.509
F	19.603***	45.625***	58.381***

Note: ***$p < 0.001$; **$p < 0.01$; *$p < 0.05$.

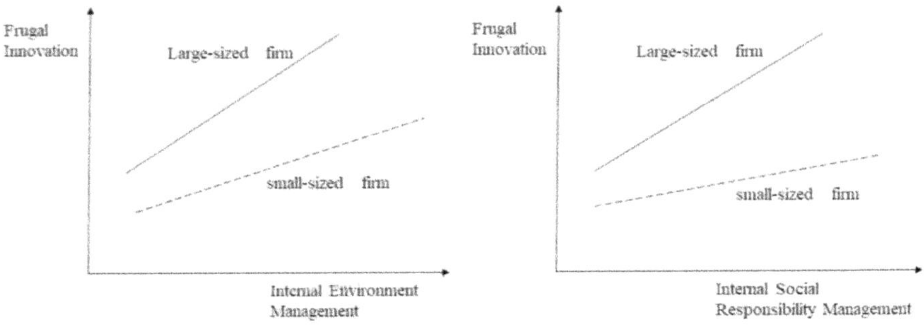

Figure 2. Diagram of conditioning effect.

level of financial performance of the supplier enterprises, and the acquisition of non-financial performances such as the ability to innovate products is transformed into financial performance over a longer period of time, which may not be conducive in the short term for firms to increase frugal innovation.

6. Conclusion

The findings of this study show the role that supply chain management can have within the innovation intermediary literature.

In particular: First, both internal environmental management and internal social responsibility management have a positive impact on frugal innovation. Strengthening internal environmental management can promote enterprises to use as few resources as possible to realize the dual advantages of price and environmental protection for their products. In addition, the establishment of corporate social responsibility awareness can help protect the rights and interests of employees, and respond positively to frugal innovation behavior, so that BOP can get learning and work opportunities, reduce the income gap, and help realize common prosperity.

Second, sustainable cooperation between enterprises and suppliers can stimulate the exchange of knowledge and technology and promote frugal innovation. However, monitoring and evaluation of supplier sustainable practice does not impact frugal innovation, probably because enterprise supervision and evaluation of suppliers' sustainable development behavior needs to invest more resources and costs, so it is not conducive to the improvement of enterprise's economic performance level in the short term. Third, firm size positively moderates the effect on the impact of sustainable supply chain internal management and frugal innovation. In SMEs, medium-sized firms are more capable of coordinating resources and focusing on balancing economic, social, and environmental performance when carrying out frugal innovation.

The theoretical contributions of this study: First, explore the influencing factors of frugal innovation from the perspective of sustainable supply chain management. The research framework reflects the causal relationship between the variables of "sustainable supply chain management and frugal innovation and explores the moderating role of company size in it, so as to expand the research perspective and application context of frugal innovation. Second, the combination of qualitative and quantitative research is utilized to explore the influencing factors of plain innovation, to make up for the shortcomings of the past research on plain innovation, which is dominated by qualitative analysis and case studies and insufficient quantitative research, and to enhance the rigor and standardization of the argumentation results. Third, it confirms the role of sustainable supply chain management in promoting frugal innovation in the Chinese context and expands and extends the research on frugal innovation in small and medium-sized manufacturing enterprises in China.

The practical contributions of this study: First, Enterprises should actively implement internal environmental management and incorporate internal environmental management and internal social responsibility management into the enterprise's competitive strategy, to minimize the consumption of resources to achieve the lowest level of cost and realize frugal innovation. Second, to cope with the changes in the market environment of plain innovation, enterprises should hold regular discussions with suppliers, establish a long-term and stable cooperative relationship, and invite suppliers to participate in frugal innovation to reduce the cost of innovation, enhance the ability of product design, and improve the efficiency of frugal innovation.

Third, enterprises should focus on coordinating sustainable supply chain management at the overall level, expanding the scale of the company, making full use of both internal and external resources of the enterprise, not only strengthening internal environmental and social responsibility management but also paying attention to the horizontal integration with suppliers in the target market, efficiently matching and dynamically optimizing external and internal resources, and realizing the sharing of information and the complementarity of resources in the innovation activities to launch the frugal innovation products.

Due to data limitations, this chapter has certain limitations, and subsequent research can be further supplemented and explored. First, the empirical research sample is only selected from the manufacturing industry in the region of China.

It can be extended to the enterprise data of other regions and industries to further verify the conclusions of this study. Second, there are many factors affecting frugal innovation. We can continue to explore the influencing factors of frugal innovation, consider more moderating variables and other situational factors, and construct a more complete mechanism model. These types of analysis can provide more experience and suggestions for enterprises to carry out frugal innovation exploiting the role of supply chain management as innovation intermediary.

References

Basu, K. (2000). The intriguing relation between adult minimum wage and child labour. *The Economic Journal*, 110(462), 50–61.

Carter, C. R. and Jennings, M. M. (2002). Logistics social responsibility: An integrative framework. *Journal of Business Logistics*, 23(1), 145–180.

Chen, J., Burgelman, R. A., Li, J. X., *et al.* (2020). Leading for constructive innovation: Preliminary evidence from China. *Journal of Engineering and Technology Management*, 57, 101588.

Corsini, L., Dammicco, V., and Moultrie, J. (2021). Frugal innovation in a crisis: The digital fabrication maker response to COVID-19. *R&D Management*, 51(2), 195–210.

Dabi, M., Obradovi, T., Vlai, B., *et al.* (2022). Frugal innovations: A multidisciplinary review & agenda for future research. *Journal of Business Research*, 142, 914–929.

Demirel, P. and Kesidou, E. (2019). Sustainability-oriented capabilities for eco-innovation: Meeting the regulatory, technology, and market demands. *Business Strategy and the Environment*, 28(5), 847–857.

Deng, C., Yang, J., Su, Z., *et al.* (2021). The double-edged sword impact of effectuation on new product creativity: The moderating role of competitive intensity and firm size. *Journal of Business Research*, 137, 1–12.

Flynn, B. B., Huo, B., and Zhao, X. (2010). The impact of supply chain integration on performance: A contingency and configuration approach. *Journal of Operations Management*, 28(1), 58–71.

Hossain, M. (2020). Frugal innovation and sustainable business models. *Technology in Society*, 64, 101508.

Hossain, M., Simula, H., and Halme, M. (2016). Can frugal go global? Diffusion patterns of frugal innovations. *Technology in Society*, 46, 132–139.

Khanal, P. B., Aubert, B. A., Bernard, J., *et al.* (2021). Frugal innovation and digital effectuation for development: The case of Lucia. *Information Technology for Development*, 2021(1), 1–30.

Kitsis, A. M. and Chen, I. J. (2020). Do motives matter? Examining the relationships between motives, SSCM practices and TBL performance. *Supply Chain Management: An International Journal*, 25(3), 325–341.

Lei, H., Gui, L. N., and Le, P. B. (2021). Linking transformational leadership and frugal innovation: The mediating role of tacit and explicit knowledge sharing. *Journal of Knowledge Management*, 25(7), 1832–1852.

Niroumand, M., Shahin, A., Naghsh, A., *et al.* (2021). Frugal innovation enablers, critical success factors and barriers: A systematic review. *Creativity and Innovation Management*, 30(2), 348–367.

Reefke, H. and Sundarem, D. (2018). Sustainable supply chain management: Decision models for transformation and maturity. *Decision Support Systems*, 113, 56–72.

Rossetto, D. E., Borini, F. M., Bernardes, R. C., *et al.* (2017). A new scale for measuring frugal innovation: The first stage of development of a measurement tool. In *VI International Symposium on Project Management, Innovation, and Sustainability* (pp. 1–16). SINGEP, Sao Paulo.

Sarkar, S. and Mateus, S. (2022). Value creation using minimal resources inimum wage and child labour. al innovati *Technological Forecasting and Social Change*, 179, 121612.

Seles, B. M. R. P., Jabbour, A. B. L. D. S., and Jabbour, C. J. C. (2016). The green bullwhip effect, the diffusion of green supply chain practices, and institutional pressures: Evidence from the automotive sector. *International Journal of Production Economics*, 182, 342–355.

Sharmelly, R. and Ray, P. K. (2021). Managing resource-constrained innovation in emerging markets: Perspectives from a business model. *Technology in Society*, 65, 101538.

Shevchnko, A., Pagell, M., Levesque, M., *et al.* (2020). Preventing supplier non-conformance: Extending the agency theory perspective. *International Journal of Operations & Production Management*, 40(3), 315–340.

Shibin, K. T., Dubey, R., Gunasekaran, A., *et al.* (2018). Frugal innovation for supply chain sustainability in SMEs: Multi-method research design. *Production Planning and Control*, 29(11), 908–927.

Vanpoucke, E., Vereecke, A., and Wetzels, M. (2014). Developing supplier integration capabilities for sustainable competitive advantage: A dynamic capabilities approach. *Journal of Operations Management*, 32(7–8), 446–461.

Wang, C., Qureshi, I., Guo, F., *et al.* (2022). Corporate social responsibility and disruptive innovation: The moderating effects of environmental turbulence. *Journal of Business Research*, 139, 1435–1450.

Wu, L., Liu, H., and Zhang, J. (2017). Bricolage effects on new-product development speed and creativity: The moderating role of technological turbulence. *Journal of Business Research*, 70, 127–135.

Zeschky, M., Widenmayer, B., and Gassmann, O. (2011). Frugal innovation in emerging markets. *Research Technology Management*, 54(4), 38–45.

Zhu, Q., Sarkis, J., and Geng, Y. (2005). Green supply chain management in China: Pressures, practices and performance. *International Journal of Operations & Production Management*, 25(5–6), 449–468.

https://doi.org/10.1142/9789819807611_0010

Chapter 10

The Engagement Ecosystem as an Innovation Broker: A Case from China

Chuanjuan Wu[*,†,§], Lei Cui[*,†,¶], and Guofeng Shen[‡,‖]

[†]*Doctor of Business Administration Department, Emlyon Business School Shanghai, People's Republic of China*

[‡]*School of Biomedical Engineering, Shanghai Jiao Tong University, Shanghai, People's Republic of China*

[§]*chuanjuan.wu@edu.executive.em-lyon.com*
[¶]*lei.cui@edu.executive.em-lyon.com*
[‖]*shenguofeng@sjtu.edu.cn*

Abstract

The purpose of this chapter is to develop a discussion regarding the concept of "engagement ecosystem" as an innovation broker via a single case study, based on the entrepreneurial experience of a knowledge-based Chinese medical firm. Precisely, this chapter attempts to understand how the engagement ecosystem has become China's "Innovation Broker" from technology development to prototype development levering on collaborations with upstream and downstream partners to carry out market promotion and new product development. The findings show

---

[*]These authors contributed to the work equally and should be regarded as co-first authors and corresponding authors.

that within the engagement ecosystem, the interaction between government, capital, and industry provides necessary conditions for innovation, especially for high-tech startups. This case study also brings a managerial implication on interdisciplinary talent cultivation and development.

Keywords: Engagement ecosystem, knowledge-based enterprise, triple helix of governments -capital-industries, value co-creation, co-experience, academic marketing.

1. Introduction

In today's dynamic business landscape, characterized by rapid technological advancements and evolving consumer expectations, the concept of engagement ecosystems has emerged as a possible framework for understanding interactions among diverse stakeholders (Jacobides *et al.*, 2018). Even if the concept of "Engagement Ecosystem" has been around for some time, there is little empirical research on its entire process in the literature (Maslowska *et al.*, 2016). This chapter aims to address this gap by exploring the brokerage role of an engagement ecosystem built around a knowledge-based Chinese medical enterprise with a focus on the new product development process of Magnetic Resonance–Guided High-Intensity Focused Ultrasound (MRgHIFU). Through a case study approach, the chapter uncoveres key insights into the mechanisms underlying engagement ecosystem formation and evolution. Incisively, the findings reveal the central role of knowledge-based firms in driving innovation and collaboration within engagement ecosystems. Moreover, the study highlights the importance of interdisciplinary collaboration and the strategic alignment of stakeholders in fostering the growth of these ecosystems.

The chapter is structured as follows. First, it stresses the theoretical background of grounding the discussion. The following section explores the emergence of the engagement ecosystem through a single case study. Finally, the chapter highlights the implications and suggestions for further studies.

2. An Overview of the Engagement Ecosystem

"An ecosystem is a set of actors with varying degrees of multilateral, nongeneric complementarities that are not fully hierarchically controlled." (Jacobides *et al.*, 2018). Engagement ecosystem is "a configuration of individual, mutually dependent engagement platforms that represent specific interactivity-facilitative loci." (Breidbach *et al.*, 2014). The objects of the engagement ecosystem include the brands and their actions, all stakeholders, their behaviors, and their experiences (Maslowska *et al.*, 2016). All the engaged companies orchestrate innovation on complements in the context with a coherent set of strategic moves (Gawer and Cusumano, 2014).

In the engagement ecosystem, there are a series of actors along the up- and down-stream of the industrial chain. How the players interact with one another shapes the dynamic capabilities of the engagement ecosystem.

As a focal firm, the knowledge-based firm orchestrates the interaction between actors in the engagement ecosystem defining a mutually beneficial strategy. The knowledge-based view (KBV) of the firm, as a late extension of the Resource-Based View (RBV), draws on organization theory as well as resource-based theory (Kaplan *et al.*, 2001). Kaplan *et al.* argued that a strategic knowledge-based theory has five important elements, comprising the existence of the firm, and the effects of knowledge on the firm's behavior, structure, boundaries, and performance. Kogut and Zander (1992) proposed that the organization exists to create, transform, and transfer knowledge into competitive advantage. The task of production of goods and services through the transformation of inputs into outputs by creating, storing, acquiring, and deploying knowledge is the main organizational activity (Grant, 1996). The nature of the most critical resources of the knowledge-based view (KBV) of the firm is intangible and dynamic, and the idiosyncratic intangible assets are the basis of the mechanism for the economic rent creation in the KBV of the firm (Curado and Bontis, 2006).

There is not a dominant actor in the engagement ecosystem, instead, all the players are interdependent and co-create with one another. Value co-creation is always subordinate to the firm's strategy and the firm's customer value proposition, and value co-creation mechanisms, such as co-promotion, co-design, or co-development, can offer additional customer resources to support the firm's delivery of the customer value proposition. In other words, the customer's role is refined from only a provider of money to an important resource provider, through customer insight and customer creativity for instance (Saarijärvi, 2012; Ordanini and Pasini, 2008). High-quality interactions enable customers to co-create with the firm thus unlocking new sources of competitive advantage

(Prahalad and Ramaswamy, 2004b; Wikström, 1996). Therefore, the firm creates opportunities to foster interactions with its customers during the process of their value-generating and hence becomes a value co-creator (Grönroos, 2008). Especially in the case of knowledge-intensive products and services, the suppliers contribute based on their accumulated specialization and professional integrity, whereas the customers and buyers of complex offerings share information on their needs and integrate their applicable resources. Thus, they can jointly enhance collaborative problem-solving (Aarikka-Stenroos and Jaakkola, 2012), and benefit from a win-win approach (Ramaswamy and Ozcan, 2014, 2018). A firm cannot create anything of value independently of the beneficiary (Vargo and Akaka, 2009), without the engagement of individuals (Prahalad and Ramaswamy, 2004a). Incorporating customer opinions, customer interaction, and customer participation can improve new product development (NPD) performance (Hsu, 2017), "it is the experience that is co-created, with value as a derived outcome" (Minkiewicz *et al.*, 2014).

Co-experience is used to exposit the experiences that people create, elaborate, and evaluate together with others, and products may be involved as the object, subject, or means of these interactions (Battarbee and Koskinen, 2005). Hence, co-experience is relevant to the relationship between the players in the engagement ecosystem and may modulate its development. Taking advantage of a product, its functionality and usability need to pave the road for pleasure. A product entails functionality and usability, and pleasure depends on it. The user values are perceived depending on the context of use, such as touch, taste, or sensual, as physio-pleasure; compliance to user's cognitive and emotional reactions as psycho-pleasure; and socio-pleasure (Jetter and Gerken, 2007). Therefore, co-experience, which is user experience in interaction, includes needs experience, technology experience, and brand experience (Zarour and Alharbi, 2017).

However, there are some important factors that impair the research information from academia to practice, such as attributes of the information itself and the characteristics of academics and practitioners (Grundvåg Ottesen and Grønhaug, 2004). How can an engagement ecosystem function as an innovation broker? What could be the advantages for a knowledge-based firm to overcome these challenges? Will the interaction between the knowledge-based firm and other players in the engagement ecosystem positively impact the development of the engagement ecosystem? Empirical research is desperately needed to contribute to this field.

3. Shaping of the Engagement Ecosystem: A Case from China

In an engagement ecosystem, firms jointly create a value proposition. For a value proposition to come true, the ecosystem's players interact with one another (Adner and Kapoor, 2016). The partners need a focal firm, an orchestrator, to align them toward the joint value proposition. How the orchestrator designs the alignment structure is at the very heart of the engagement ecosystem. Start-up as an orchestrator can bring in the needed flexibility and agility of new product development, which is beneficial for the development of the joint value proposition (Lingens *et al.*, 2021).

The following sections elaborate on the emergence of the engagement ecosystem and the interaction of the participants in the ecosystem and discuss how the engagement ecosystem becomes an innovation intermediary, through the historical development of the startup company from China and the development of its product technology roadmap.

3.1 *The technology roadmaps*

The application of imaging technology in modern medical treatment is no longer limited to general operations such as reading images, for instance, non-invasive uterine-preserving treatment instead of hysterectomy greatly benefits women with symptomatic uterine leiomyomas (fibroids) (Pron, 2015). The regional differences caused by the different technology roadmaps among countries lead to different enterprise development strategies. Thanks to strong capital support, different companies parallelly led different technology roadmaps in Europe and North America, such as X-ray medical imaging diagnosis technology, ultrasound medical diagnosis technology, nuclear medical imaging diagnosis technology, and magnetic resonance imaging diagnosis technology. In the emerging market of China, these technologies are gradually conquered in stages by concentrating advantageous resources. Ultrasound medical diagnosis technology started earlier, and magnetic resonance imaging diagnosis technology takes a longer time.

Just as electric vehicles are successfully developed only after lithium-ion battery technology is matured, the development of medical imaging diagnosis technology is also influenced by the development of related technologies. To develop Magnetic Resonance-Guided High-Intensity Focused Ultrasound (MRgHIFU) technology, the master of magnetic resonance imaging diagnosis technology is not avoided. As a result, China also takes a longer time to develop the MRgHIFU technology.

In the 1980s, many people in China suffered from stone disease (e.g., ureter stones and kidney stones) due to water quality issues but could not afford to benefit from the exciting revolution of kidney stone treatment (Malinaric *et al.*, 2023). Traditional Chinese medicine treatment was ineffective, and surgical treatment was unaffordable for most patients due to the high cost of the imported equipment. In this situation, a university professor led a biomedical engineering research team spending 20 months on research and development, successfully created China's first extracorporeal shock wave lithotripsy equipment with the same functionality and useability as the imported equipment but only 1/30 or less of the selling price. The professor was later elected a Member of the Chinese Academy of Engineering for her outstanding contributions. The equipment she developed is vastly used in hospitals nowadays. This is a typical innovation (Scuotto *et al.*, 2022) example, combining product-level innovations and core dynamic capabilities. The first stage of the MRgHIFU technology development adopts the same approach.

Incremental innovation is to enhance existing knowledge and improve existing products (Sheng and Chien, 2016). The MRgHIFU equipment was first developed by an Israeli company. Due to a lack of cognition of the Chinese market and low attention to local demand, this company's products have not performed well as expected since entering the Chinese market in 2014. Based on a large amount of extensive market research and in-depth interactions with relevant hospitals and experts, the local branded products not only have the same functionality and usability but are much better at meeting local needs and are applicable for more diseases, but at a much lower selling price. This has attracted more partners from upstream and downstream of the industrial chain to participate. At the same time, it has attracted more capital injection. Stimulated by this, the Israeli company proactively approached a local pharmaceutical (group) company for an equity joint venture in order to better explore the Chinese market. This is a good example of co-experience in some way.

In addition to interacting with hospitals and experts, there is also an exploration of upstream and downstream enterprises in the industrial chain to jointly solve disease problems. Then, more unmet market demands were discovered. Ideas of disruptive innovation, namely new-to-the-world products and/or new-to-the-world business models

(Markides, 2006), are inspired by each other along the industrial chain and then productization and industrialization through joint development and/or equity joint venture (EJV). Thus, forge the embryonic form of the engagement ecosystem.

3.2 *The development of the knowledge-based firm*

This research aims to interpret how the engagement ecosystem is shaped as an innovation broker through a single case of the development of a knowledge-based firm from the medical industry in China. In order to protect the company's identity, it is identified as Company S. Semi-structured interviews are adopted to collect data. Participants include the Founder, CEO, CTO, COO, HR Director, some early joined employees, and some recently joined employees.

Secondary data are collected through various channels, such as accessing archival interviews, keynote speeches, and other archival resources in Chinese and English, including but not limited to press releases, analyst reports, industry reports, blogs, and material from the selected company's website, relative social media, and other websites. Gioia method (Gioia *et al.*, 2013) is used for data interpretation and analysis.

The following citation illustrates the motivation of the founder to create the start-up:

> "I have been working in the biomedical engineering field for 30 years, focusing on Magnetic Resonance Imaging-Phased High-Intensity Focused Ultrasound (MRI-PHIFU). Before that, my postdoctoral supervisor, a Member of Chinese Academy of Engineering, had been researching for 10 years. Cumulatively, hundreds of masters, doctors and postdoctors supervised by us have graduated. These talents are important resources for the development of advanced technology medical equipment. Many of them have joined foreign companies or even immigrated overseas to pursue their career development. Someone needs to do something to change this situation. Otherwise, foreign medical technology will become increasingly advanced, while China will become increasingly backward. China will then heavily rely on imported advanced medical equipment to fulfill domestic medical needs. This is something that my supervisor and I don't want to see. Strong support from the government and the university that I'm working at enabled us to realize our entrepreneurial dreams, this is also very important."

When the employees were asked why they chose to join Company S, the most frequently heard answers are as follows:

> "During the interview, I was greatly inspired by the personal charisma of the founder and the CEO."

> "Working in a knowledge-based atmosphere, I feel comfortable. I don't need to worry about how to build good relationships with others, I just concentrate on how to drive my best potential and contribute as much as possible to bring the product to the market as sooner as we can."

> "This enterprise focuses on the development of advanced technology medical equipment, integrating research and development, manufacturing, and operation. This is a truly high-tech innovative enterprise."

When the interviewees were asked what characteristics made them stay and grow with the company, the respondents answered very enthusiastically. The following citations are some of the answers; more details are summarized in Figure 1:

> "I think my work is valuable. I love to be recognized by leaders. I'm comfortable with the interaction with colleagues. My regret is not being able to join this company earlier."

> "In the early stages, it was a team of less than 50 people, majorly research and development personnel, mainly self-management. We voluntarily worked overtime with a common goal of developing the product as sooner as possible. Currently, the company provides training to cultivate versatile talents, and encourages employees to take on more tasks to increase income. I am willing to support the company in reducing costs and increasing efficiency through this approach, because it's good for my career development."

> "I enjoy very much the atmosphere where research and development are the main focus, everyone actively discusses with each other and collaboratively solves problems. I'm happy to see that the number of employees has increased to four times than 2 years ago, when we encounter problems, we will quickly form a working group to jointly solve the key technical problems. I love this."

> "Since rotated from research and development to management role, I have trained some people successfully, I think we're ready to support more product lines. I feel very happy. Honestly, compared to being a manager, I love research and development better. I enjoy tackling unresolved technical challenges from predecessors, and every time I have tackled a technical challenge, I feel a great sense of accomplishment."

> "At this knowledge-based firm, leaders with academic backgrounds are quite nice. Many of my colleagues are masters or doctors. I am inspired to work harder to improve my professional knowledge and comprehensive qualities. I am preparing for a certification exam. Before joining company S, I thought about getting a certification as well but never took any action."

Based on the product characteristics of MRgHIFU, the development of Company S' product requires a highly effective cross-border integrative interdisciplinary collaboration team of acoustic algorithm, mechanical technique, electrical technology, imaging technology, and software technique.

During the interview, the Founder, CEO, COO, CTO, and HR Director introduced in detail how the cross-border integrative interdisciplinary collaboration team is developed. Leading a team of masters, doctors, and postdoctors continually research for decades, the Founder, who is also a professor of a School of Biomedical Engineering, together with his postdoctoral supervisor, had solved most of the technical problems and obtained various patents and other forms of intellectual properties. The biggest obstacle to the development of complicated advanced medical equipment demands plenty of interactive practices together with MRI equipment in the context of hospitals. In this situation, the startup company S was established. Meanwhile, a Research and Development Center and an Engineering Doctor Recruitment Center were jointly founded by the university and Company S. Moreover, as the first and the sole pioneer, Company S undertakes part of the function of the National Engineering Research Center for high-tech equipment and technology integrated with MRI diagnosis and treatment.

The interdisciplinary working team formed by companies through recruitment usually takes a longer time to form a highly trusted and tacit work collaboration relationship. In Company S, most of the team members are educated and developed through the joint Research and

Development Center that was supervised by the Founder and Professor, the rest are attracted by the personality charm of the Founder and the company's high-tech products. The team cohesion and tacit understanding are significantly higher than other companies. The corporate culture of the knowledge-based firm of Company S is more relaxed, friendly, and conducive to creativity and innovation. As mentioned by the vast majority of the respondents,

> "The spiritual inspiration of the Member of Chinese Academy of Engineering and the daily influence of scholar leaders have become the genes of Company S."

The market development team of a company that adopts the academic marketing approach often faces challenges in that the research information is impaired while translating from academia to practice. This is a significant advantage for the knowledge-based high-achieving team of Company S, as they do not involve translation. During the interaction between Company S and the hospital, the academic marketing approach fully demonstrated its unique advantages. The research team of Company S had in-depth dialogue with relevant experts, inspired each other, and generated more innovative ideas, including disruptive innovation. Consequently, while maximizing the functionality and usability of the medical device, the doctors actively and voluntarily promote this new technology, which speeds up and widens the consumer acceptance of the new technology. Benefited from the technical, product, and service support provided by Company S, the doctors publish their academic research results with the clinical experiment data, further expanding the promotion of the new technology and fascinating the attention, support, and co-creation of the upstream and downstream enterprises as well as capital and government. As a result, Company S has established production bases in multiple locations. Furthermore, a local brand MRI manufacturer, whose core technical team including a student of the Member of Chinese Academy of Engineering, proactively approached Company S for the partnership of MRI and PHIFU device, and mutually profited from market development. Besides, a global drug maker (microbubble maker) who encounters a problem with the verification of its medications for neurological disorders of the brain also approached Company S for cooperation (i.e. enabling blood-brain barrier (BBB) permeability with the medical device provided by Company S). Once this clinical research and experiment is completed, Company S will further expand its service scope to be a Contract Research Organization (CRO).

Different from a hierarchical organization chart in big companies, the architecture of Company S is designed to be flexible and agile. An interdisciplinary collaborative shared platform of acoustic algorithm, mechanical technique, electrical technology, imaging technology, and software technique, grounds a basis to support multiple product portfolios for different application fields, such as tumor treatment, neurological diseases, blood-brain barrier (BBB) permeability, arteria renalis sympathetic nerve non-invasive thermal ablation, ultrasound medical aesthetics, thrombolysis, lithotripsy, and atherosclerosis. Once a developed technology is ready for productization, an Integrated Product Development (IPD) Manager is named and a cross-border integrative interdisciplinary collaboration team of acoustic algorithm, mechanical technique, electrical technology, imaging technology, and software technique is formed by the IPD Manager per actual demand, including supportive functions such as supply chain, production, and other administrative roles. In this way, everyone matters, and everyone has opportunities to strengthen his/her professional profile while developing multiple skills, "*let the cause inspire talents, let talents accomplish the cause.*" As summarized by the Founder and the CEO, Company S

> "attaches importance to, cares for, makes rational use of and develops together with the talents; aimes to build a whole industrial chain with the 'MRgPHIFU' technology innovation platform as the core, covering high-end medical industrial manufacturing, commercial sales and after-sales service; and to build a diversified business ecosystem, combining the 'MRgHIFU' training centre, 'MRgPHIFU' non-invasive diagnosis and treatment hospitals and 'MRgPHIFU' diagnosis and treatment centres in major hospitals."

Magnetic Resonance–Guided High-Intensity Focused Ultrasound (MRgHIFU) Treatment is a complicated technology which not only requires the integration of Magnetic Resonance and High-Intensity Focused Ultrasound but also needs the coordination of doctors and patients. In order to delve deeper into the characteristics of the key actors involved in the engagement ecosystem, the authors also interviewed a representative of the engaged hospitals. The following citation from the interview describes the interactions between multi-players:

> "The value proposition of non-invasive, green, and precise MRgPHIFU technology, from invasive to minimally invasive to non-invasive, is the trend. Rather than the traditional therapies such as chemotherapy and radiation therapy may cause chemical damage, this greener and safer treatment represents a higher pursuit. Among numerous subcategories of technology, MRgPHIFU provides an optimal solution for the transformation of various aspects such as doctor use, patient experience, and the medical system. The doctors leverages their expertise, provide academic insights, and collaborates with Company S to promote the application of products and technology, applying the MRgPHIFU technology to a wider user base and maximizing social benefits."

> "Hospitals and enterprises aim for scientific research, clinical trials, and commercial operations in the short, medium, and long term. Projects are jointly developed in the form of research, jointly applied for and undertaken by national and provincial level projects. During this period, a series of academic achievements will be generated, including intellectual property rights, papers, product prototypes, etc. There will be a sharing mechanism for these academic achievements, and corresponding allocation mechanisms will be agreed upon."

> "The hospitals and the enterprises, with different perspectives and expertise and represent the providers of demand and technology or product solutions, can easily reach a very precise consensus, with unified values and visions, shared interests, and complementary skills. Enterprises can help doctors achieve their ideas, and doctors can also help enterprises capture market demands and user pain points. Therefore, they play an irreplaceable role in the value co-creation process."

> "The MRgPHIFU is a technological revolution, it needs to be promoted through the transformation of commercial scenarios. It is necessary to jointly build an MRgPHIFU non-invasive diagnosis and treatment center, in a multidisciplinary model, with the participation of departments such as radiology, neurosurgery, gynecology, orthopedics, etc., to truly achieve integration and comprehensively promote all products and application fields generated by the new technology."

"The government will guide the application of high-precision and cutting-edge innovative medical technologies to the market and users to realize their value. Both the government and capital strongly support science and technology innovation projects with high technological content, scarcity, and uniqueness, which represent new productive forces. This is undoubtedly a very important resource for the entire industry chain."

Adopting the Gioia methodology, a series of keywords are extracted from the interview materials as first-order concepts and then grouped into five second-order themes, comprising beliefs and behaviors, impact and influence, the core of the company's ideology and practice, technology roadmap, and market. The first three themes are finally aggregated into the dimension of corporate culture; the latter two themes are aggregated into the dimension of product. The empirical data interpretation and analysis results are presented in Figure 1.

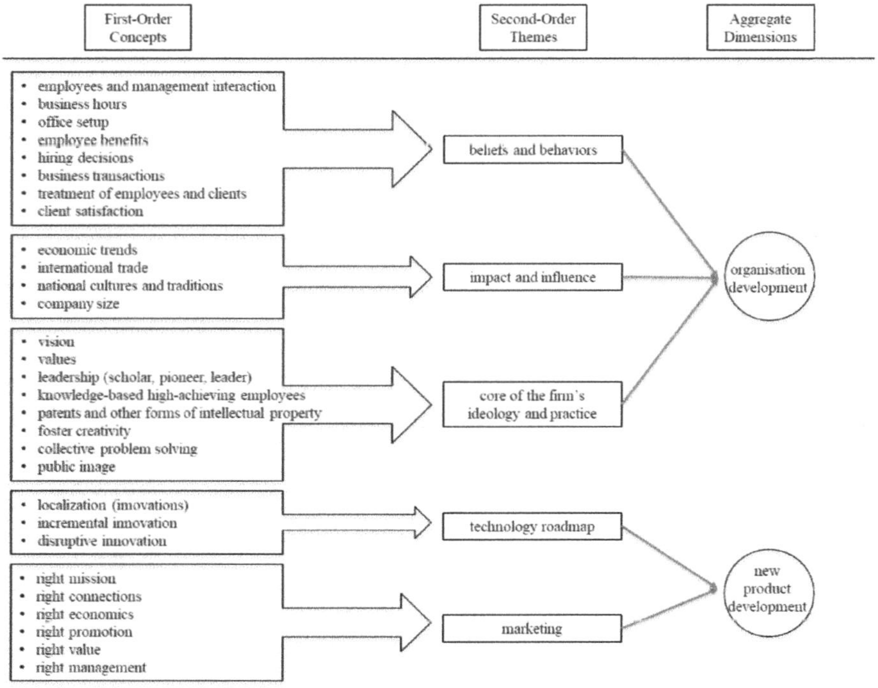

Figure 1. Empirical data interpretation and analysis.

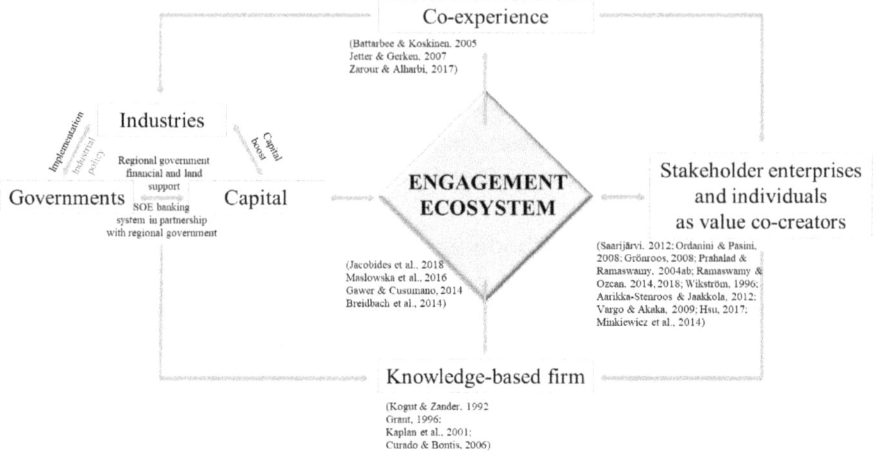

Figure 2. Shaping of the engagement ecosystem.

In the case of the knowledge-based firm Company S, the shaping process of the engagement ecosystem is presented in Figure 2.

The Triple Helix (Compagnucci *et al.*, 2020) of governments, capital, and industries, is a fundamental factor and an important building block of the engagement ecosystem. Long-term strategic vision and strong support by the central government, including but not limited to strategy and plan, pilot program, fiscal incentive, regulation, and standard, steers and encourages capital flow and industrial development trends. With state-owned enterprise (SOE) banking system in partnership with the regional government, the financial and land support by the regional government empowers enterprises to steadily develop, which is a strong motivation to boost industrialisation. With the mutual support of the government and capital, enterprises can focus on creating and acquiring new knowledge and achieving technological transformation. Knowledge-based enterprises have unique advantages in this regard. The co-creation of upstream and downstream enterprises and individuals along the industrial chain, including the interaction between competing enterprises, helps to optimize technology transformation and productization. The engagement ecosystem consists of government, capital, industry, the firm, and other stakeholders along the industrial chain. The enabled (by digital technology), informed, networked, empowered, and active consumers increasingly co-create value with the firm. The interaction between the firm and the proactive consumers becomes a locus of value creation and value extraction. Value shifts to experiences, and the market becomes a forum for conversation and interaction between consumers, communities, and firms. The co-experience feedback to not only stakeholder enterprises but also the Triple Helix of government, industry and capital. While the firms acquire dynamic capabilities, the industry will sublimate, and the engagement ecosystem will sustainably develop.

4. Discussion and Conclusion

This chapter contributes to the discussion on the engagement ecosystem through the case of a knowledge-based firm. The development of cutting-edge technology entails the effective collaboration of interdisciplinary groups. The more advanced the technology, the more cross-border integrative interdisciplinary collaboration is needed for productization and industrialization. Through, its role as an innovation broker, an engagement ecosystem enables the firm to consistently engage with stakeholders, gain insights, and drive outcomes that align with the firm's goal. The political, economic, legal, and organizational factors shape the operating environment and the type of partnership model, formalities of the model arrangement, and available resources to implement the engagement. The foundational factors center on the relationship dynamics and interactions between the actors involved in an engagement ecosystem, their level of trust in one another, their mutual understanding of each other's roles, motivations, and capacities, and their willingness to expend time and effort engaging with one another. The operational factors include the rationale or overall goal for participating in an engagement ecosystem, as well as the knowledge and skills of the partners related both to the technical area of focus and the capacities to effectively manage the activities of the engagement, and the communication and accountability mechanisms that support day-to-day operations.

The team development approach of Company S demonstrates leadership as a process of social influence, which maximizes the efforts of others, toward the achievement of a goal, and helps others realize their potential toward a greater purpose. The more excellent and diversified the stakeholders, enterprises, and individuals participating in the engagement ecosystem, the greater its development potential and sustainability. The case study reveals that team strength cannot be divorced from team collaboration. Team spirit and cohesion should be maintained in daily work, such as harmonious coexistence, interdependence, respect for personality, mutual tolerance, solidarity, and common responsibility. The same with an engagement ecosystem. To maintain an engagement ecosystem as a robust and thriving innovation broker, it must be responsive to the needs of the market, informed and informing at the ecosystem-wide level, empowered to make timely and appropriate decisions, valued by the firms, community, region, and state, initiate a shift in culture and values, strengthen meaningful and equitable stakeholder engagement, and practice authentic community relations and advocacy.

This chapter puts forward interesting insights that may be useful for future scholars who are interested in developing this emerging research field. Future research might address such potential topics as interdisciplinary research of human-robot collaboration and interaction, for instance, artificial intelligence generative content (AIGC), artificial general intelligence (AGI), and relative data assets exploration.

References

Aarikka-Stenroos, L. and Jaakkola, E. (2012). Value co-creation in knowledge intensive business services: A dyadic perspective on the joint problem solving process. *Industrial Marketing Management*, 41(1), 15–26.

Adner, R. and Kapoor, R. (2016). Innovation ecosystems and the pace of substitution: Re-examining technology S-curves. *Strategic Management Journal*, 37(4), 625–648.

Battarbee, K. and Koskinen, I. (2005). Co-experience: User experience as interaction. *CoDesign*, 1(1), 5–18.

Breidbach, C., Brodie, R., and Hollebeek, L. (2014). Beyond virtuality: From engagement platforms to engagement ecosystems. *Managing Service Quality*, 24(6), 592–611.

Compagnucci, L., Lepore, D., and Spigarelli, F. (2020). Exploring the foreign exposure of Chinese science parks in a triple helix model. *Forum for Social Economics*, 50(3), 1–25.

Curado, C. and Bontis, N. (2006). The knowledge-based view of the firm and its theoretical precursor. *International Journal of Learning and Intellectual Capital*, 3(4), 367–381.

Gawer, A. and Cusumano, M. A. (2014). Industry platforms and ecosystem innovation. *Journal of Product Innovation Management*, 31(3), 417–433.

Gioia, D. A., Corley, K. G., and Hamilton, A. L. (2013). Seeking qualitative rigor in inductive research: Notes on the Gioia methodology. *Organizational Research Methods*, 16(1), 15–31.

Grant, R. M. (1996). Toward a knowledge-based theory of the firm. *Strategic Management Journal*, 17(Winter Special Issue), 109–122.

Grönroos, C. (2008). Service logic revisited: Who creates value? And who co-creates? *European Business Review*, 20(4), 298–314.

Grundvåg Ottesen, G. and Grønhaug, K. (2004). Barriers to practical use of academic marketing knowledge. *Marketing Intelligence & Planning*, 22(5), 520–530.

Hsu, Y. (2017). Cocreation experiences: A strategic approach to product innovation and design. *International Journal of Organizational Innovation*, 10(2), 106–126.

Jacobides, M. G., Cennamo, C., and Gawer, A. (2018). Towards a theory of ecosystems. *Strategic Management Journal*, 39(8), 2255–2276.

Jetter, H. and Gerken, J. (2007). A simplified model of user experience for practical application. *2nd International Open Workshop on COST294-MAUSE*, 106–111.

Kaplan, S., Schenkel, A., von Krogh, G., and Weber, C. (2001). Knowledge-based theories of the firm in strategic management: A review and extension. *Academy of Management Review*, 617, 1–47.

Kogut, B. and Zander, U. (1992). Knowledge of the firm, combinative capabilities, and the replication of technology. *Organisation Science*, 3(3), 383–397.

Lingens, B., Miehé, L., and Gassmann, O. (2021). The ecosystem blueprint: How firms shape the design of an ecosystem according to the surrounding conditions. *Long Range Planning*, 54(2), 1–53.

Malinaric, R., Mantica, G., Martini, M., Balzarini, F., Mariano, F., Marchi, G., Tognoni, P., Panarello, D., Bottino, P., and Terrone, C. (2023). The lifetime history of the first Italian public extra-corporeal shock wave lithotripsy (ESWL) lithotripter as a mirror of the evolution of endourology over the last decade. *International Journal of Environmental Research and Public Health*, 20(5), 1–12.

Markides, C. (2006). Disruptive innovation: In need of better theory. *Journal of Product Innovation Management*, 23(1), 19–25.

Maslowska, E., Malthouse, E. C., and Collinger, T. (2016). The customer engagement ecosystem. *Journal of Marketing Management*, 32(5–6), 469–501.

Minkiewicz, J., Evans, J., and Bridson, K. (2014). How do consumers co-create their experiences? An exploration in the heritage sector. *Journal of Marketing Management*, 30(1–2), 30–59.

Ordanini, A. and Pasini, P. (2008). Service co-production and value co-creation: The case for a service-oriented architecture (SOA). *European Management Journal*, 26(5), 289–297.

Prahalad, C. K. and Ramaswamy, V. (2004a). Co-creating unique value with customers. *Strategy & Leadership*, 32(3), 4–9.

Prahalad, C. K. and Ramaswamy, V. (2004b). Co-creation experiences: The next practice in value creation. *Journal of Interactive Marketing*, 18(3), 5–14.

Pron, G. (2015). Magnetic resonance-guided high-intensity focused ultrasound (MRgHIFU) treatment of symptomatic uterine fibroids: An evidence-based analysis. *Ontario Health Technology Assessment Series*, 15(4), 1–86.

Ramaswamy, V. and Ozcan, K. (2014). *The co-creation paradigm*. Stanford University Press. Stanford, California.

Ramaswamy, V. and Ozcan, K. (2018). What is co-creation? An interactional creation framework and its implications for value creation. *Journal of Business Research*, 84, 196–205.

Saarijärvi, H. (2012). The mechanisms of value co-creation. *Journal of Strategic Marketing*, 20(5), 381–391.

Scuotto, V., Garcia-Perez, A., Kalisz, D. E., and Dhir, A. (2022). Responsible I(m)ovation in Asia Pacific regions. *Asia Pacific Journal of Management*, 1–26.

Sheng, M. L. and Chien, I. (2016). Rethinking organizational learning orientation on radical and incremental innovation in high-tech firms. *Journal of Business Research*, 69(6), 2302–2308.

Vargo, S. L. and Akaka, M. A. (2009). Service-dominant logic as a foundation for service science: Clarifications. *Service Science*, 1(1), 32–41.

Wikström, S. (1996). Value creation by company-consumer interaction. *Journal of Marketing Management*, 12(5), 359–374.

Zarour, M. and Alharbi, M. (2017). User experience framework that combines aspects, dimensions, and measurement methods. *Cogent Engineering*, 4(1), 1–25.

https://doi.org/10.1142/9789819807611_bmatter

Index

A

artificial intelligence, 3, 15, 60, 89, 146, 151–152, 206

B

blockchain, 3, 15
boundary-spanning, 68
building information modeling (BIM), 39, 60, 71
business ecosystems, 155
business models, 164, 166, 196

C

cloud computing, 27, 146–147, 152
corporate culture, 203
cyber-physical systems, 60

D

3D printing, 46, 60
deep learning, 156
digital innovation ecosystems, 136, 148

F

focal firm, 193, 195

G

general purpose technologies (GPT), 59
global innovation index (GII), 2
guanxi, 4, 64, 70

I

incubator, 6
industrial clustering, 31–32, 45
industrial ecosystems, 24, 27–28
industrial value chains, 32, 45, 47
Industry 4.0, 3, 38, 126
Industry 5.0, 3
industry-university collaboration, 5
information and communication technology (ICT), 155
innovation ecological chains, 24
innovation openness breadth, 143–144, 147
intellectual assets, 153
intellectual property, 5, 17–18, 20, 33, 35, 85, 87, 96, 159
interdisciplinary research, 206
inter-firm networking, 6
internet of things, 3, 15

J
joint venture, 196

K
knowledge ecosystems, 57
knowledge spillover, 36

M
megalopolis, 113

O
organizational learning, 139

P
proof-of-concept, 83

Q
quadruple helix model, 3, 57

R
responsibility management, 174, 179, 183–184, 186

S
science-technology intermediaries, 36
social responsibility, 168–169, 173–174, 176, 179, 183–184, 186
social responsibility management, 163, 187
Society 5.0, 55–56

T
technology licensing, 5, 136
technology readiness level (TRL), 85
technology sourcing, 60
top-down policy, 86
transaction costs, 36
transformational leadership, 166
triple bottom line, 165, 167
Triple Helix model, 3–4

U
university satellite institutes, 7

V
venture capital, 136, 155

www.ingramcontent.com/pod-product-compliance
Ingram Content Group UK Ltd.
Pitfield, Milton Keynes, MK11 3LW, UK
UKHW022108170926
8624IPUK00024B/203

9 789819 807604